GIRL TOWN

CAROLYN NOWAK

Top Shelf
PRODUCTIONS

Published by Top Shelf Productions, PO Box 1282, Marietta, GA 30061-1282 USA
Editor-in-Chief: Chris Staros

Top Shelf Productions is an imprint of IDW Publishing, a division of Idea and Design Works, LLC. Offices: 2765 Truxtun Road, San Diego, CA 92106. Top Shelf Productions®, the Top Shelf logo, Idea and Design Works®, and the IDW logo are registered trademarks of Idea and Design Works, LLC. All Rights Reserved. With the exception of small excerpts of artwork used for review purposes, none of the contents of this publication may be reprinted without the permission of IDW Publishing. IDW Publishing does not read or accept unsolicited submissions of ideas, stories, or artwork.

Edited by Leigh Walton
Color assistance by Lisa DuBois and Luke Healy
Designed by Gilberto Lazcano

"Girl Town" originally published (uncolored) in *Irene #6* (Irene Comics, 2015)
"Radishes" originally self-published (uncolored) in 2015
"Diana's Electric Tongue" originally published by ShortBox in 2016
"The Big Burning House" originally published in *Critical Chips 2* (ShortBox, 2017)
"Please Sleep Over" previously unreleased

Visit our online catalog at www.topshelfcomix.com.

Printed in Korea.

ISBN: 978-1-60309-438-2
22 21 20 19   2 3 4 5

For Sean and Lisa

CONTENTS

FOREWORD
by Carta Monir

In February 2014, I sent an email to a stranger. It read:

Hi Carolyn,

My name is [Carta] - I just moved to Ann Arbor about a year and a half ago. I make comics (although at a really slow rate currently) and one thing I've really missed since moving to Ann Arbor is having people to make comics at the same time as. I got a copy of Rungs from [the local comics shop], and your work looks really good - If you ever want to hang out and make/talk comics, I think it would be super fun.

Luckily for me, she responded. Even though we hit it off immediately, I couldn't possibly have known how deep or special our friendship would become, or that in just a few years I would call her my chosen sister.

Looking back through these comics, though, it makes a lot of sense. Carolyn Nowak's work is all about women who are looking for connection, validation, and fulfillment. Women who are painfully jealous, and full of more feelings than they know what to do with. Women whose friendships with other women are their lifeline. Women like… Carolyn and me, I guess.

Carolyn inspires me on so many levels. In both her art and her life, nobody works harder. Reading her work has changed my life forever. Turn this page, and let her change yours a little too.

Carta Monir is a cartoonist, writer, and podcaster. She lives in Ann Arbor.

GIRL TOWN

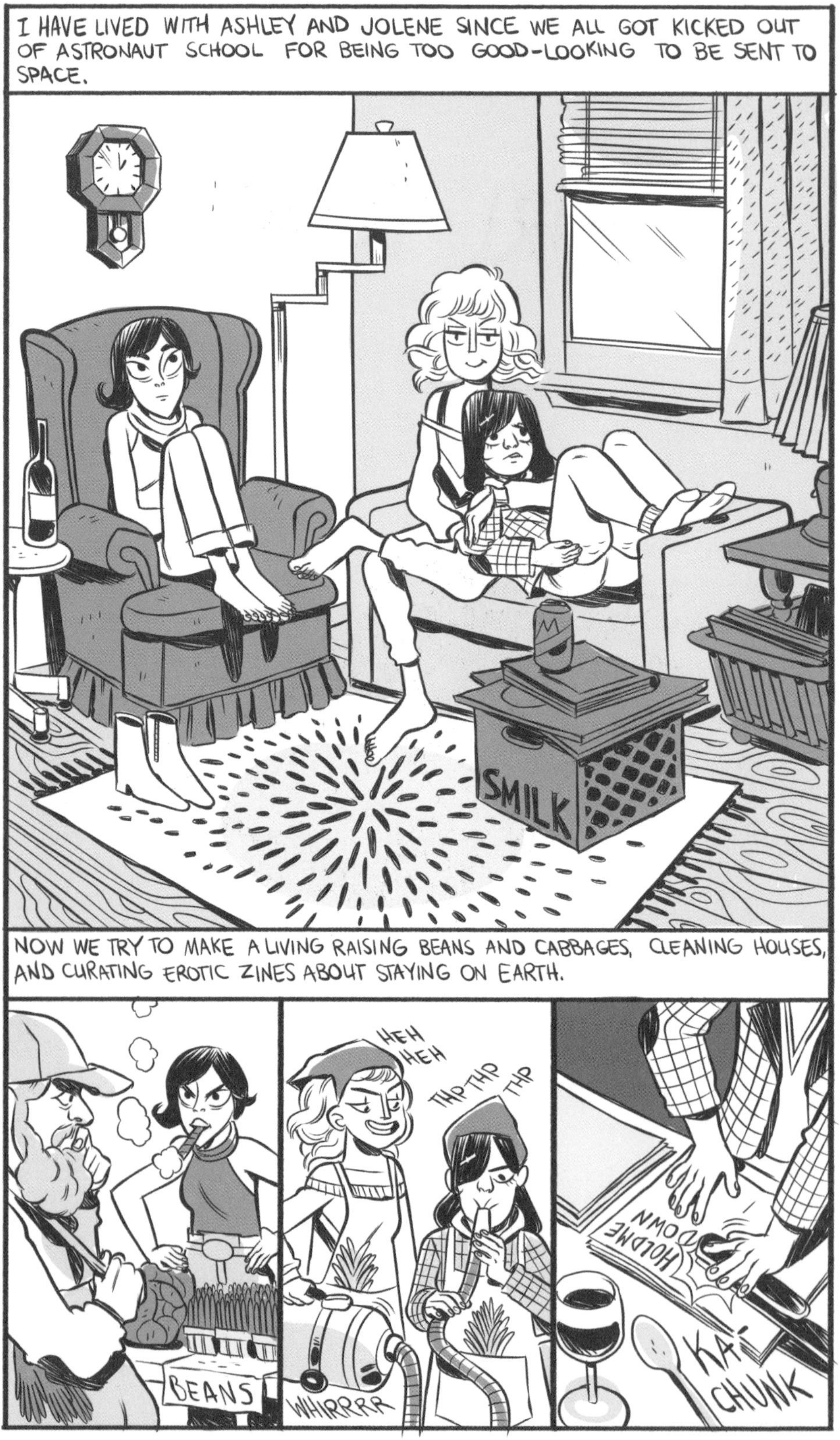
I HAVE LIVED WITH ASHLEY AND JOLENE SINCE WE ALL GOT KICKED OUT OF ASTRONAUT SCHOOL FOR BEING TOO GOOD-LOOKING TO BE SENT TO SPACE.
SMILK
NOW WE TRY TO MAKE A LIVING RAISING BEANS AND CABBAGES, CLEANING HOUSES, AND CURATING EROTIC ZINES ABOUT STAYING ON EARTH.
BEANS
HEH HEH
THP THP THP
WHIRRRR
HOLDME DOWN
KA-CHUNK

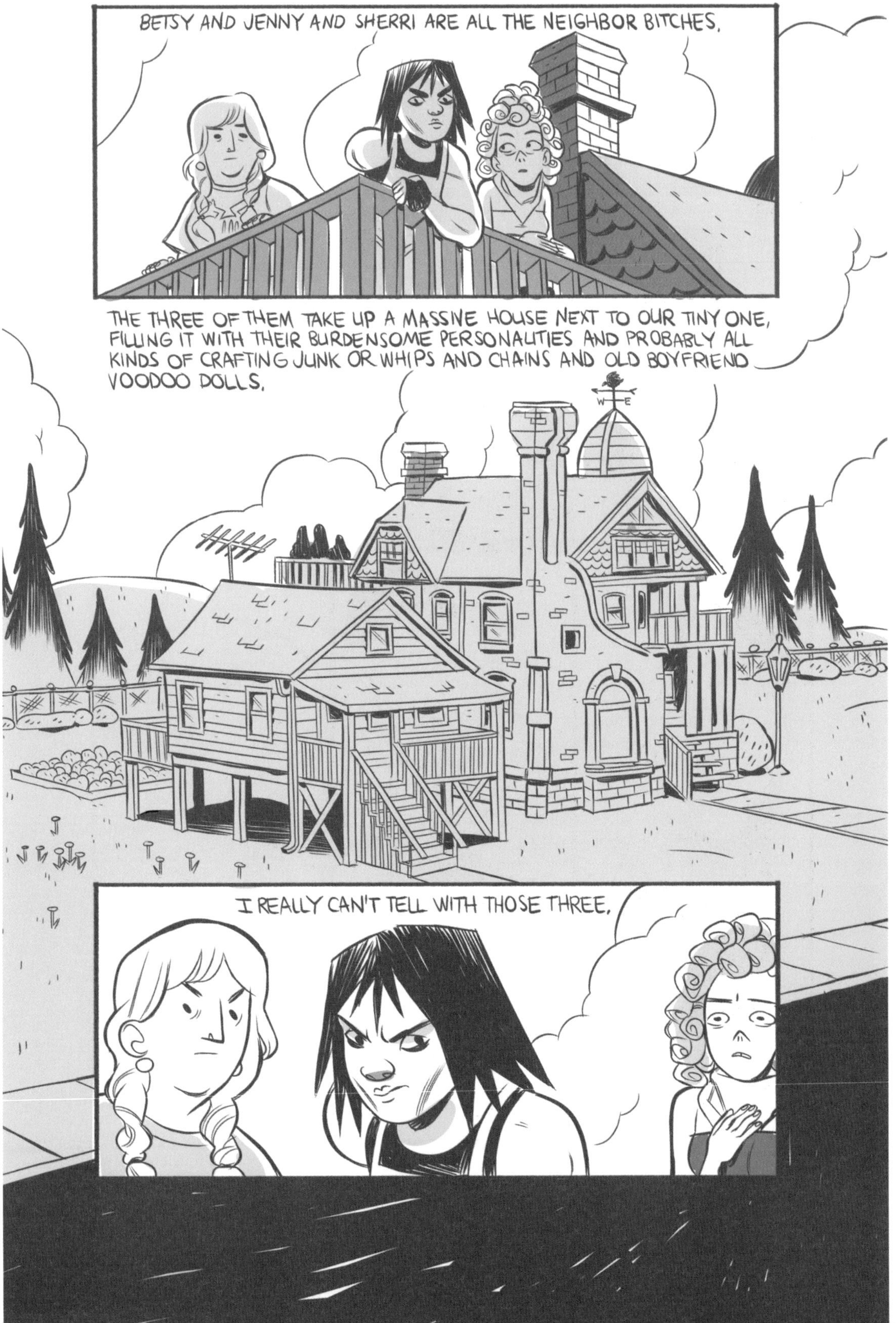
BETSY AND JENNY AND SHERRI ARE ALL THE NEIGHBOR BITCHES.
THE THREE OF THEM TAKE UP A MASSIVE HOUSE NEXT TO OUR TINY ONE, FILLING IT WITH THEIR BURDENSOME PERSONALITIES AND PROBABLY ALL KINDS OF CRAFTING JUNK OR WHIPS AND CHAINS AND OLD BOYFRIEND VOODOO DOLLS.
W E
I REALLY CAN'T TELL WITH THOSE THREE.

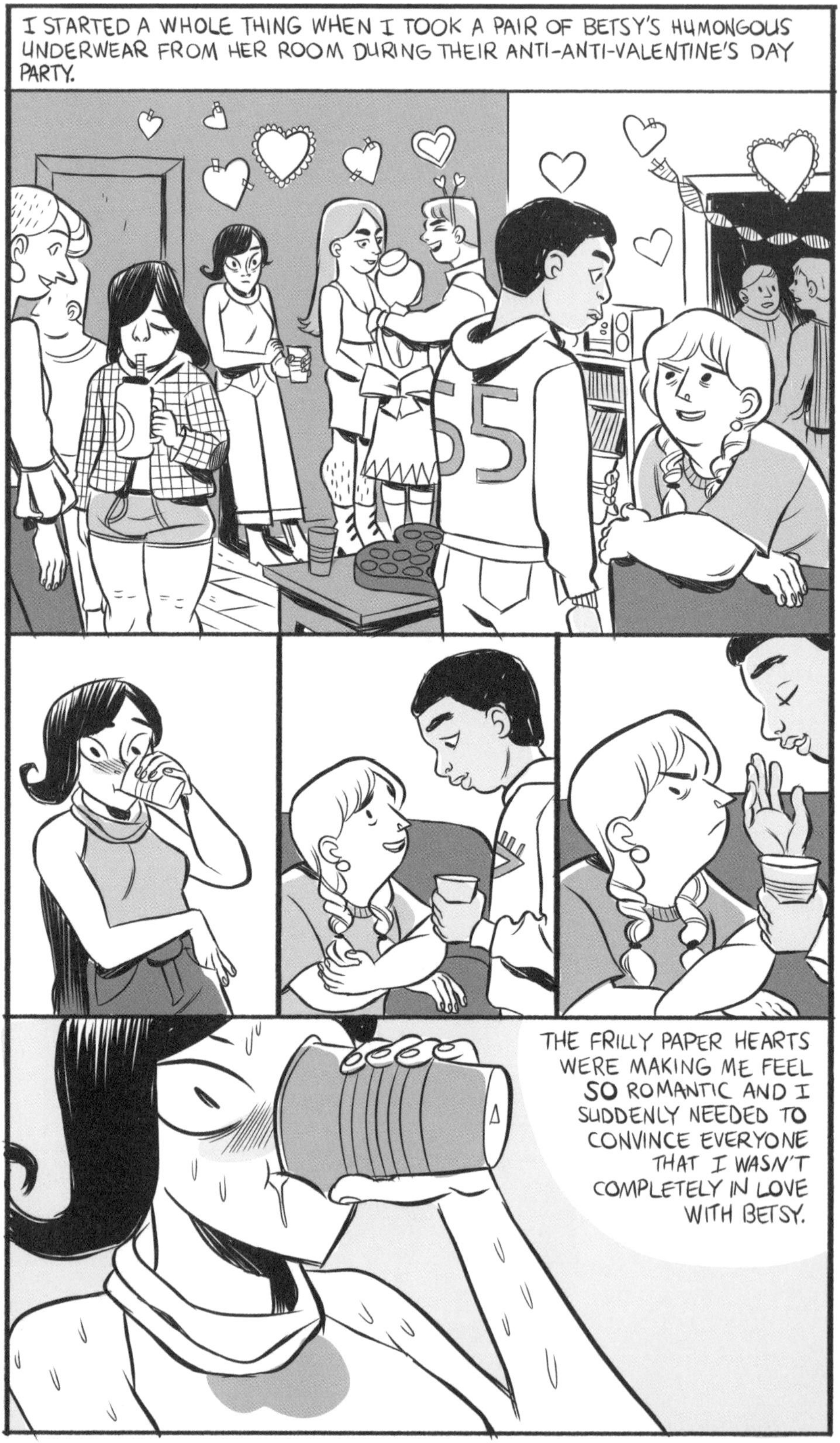
I STARTED A WHOLE THING WHEN I TOOK A PAIR OF BETSY'S HUMONGOUS UNDERWEAR FROM HER ROOM DURING THEIR ANTI-ANTI-VALENTINE'S DAY PARTY.
55
THE FRILLY PAPER HEARTS WERE MAKING ME FEEL SO ROMANTIC AND I SUDDENLY NEEDED TO CONVINCE EVERYONE THAT I WASN'T COMPLETELY IN LOVE WITH BETSY.

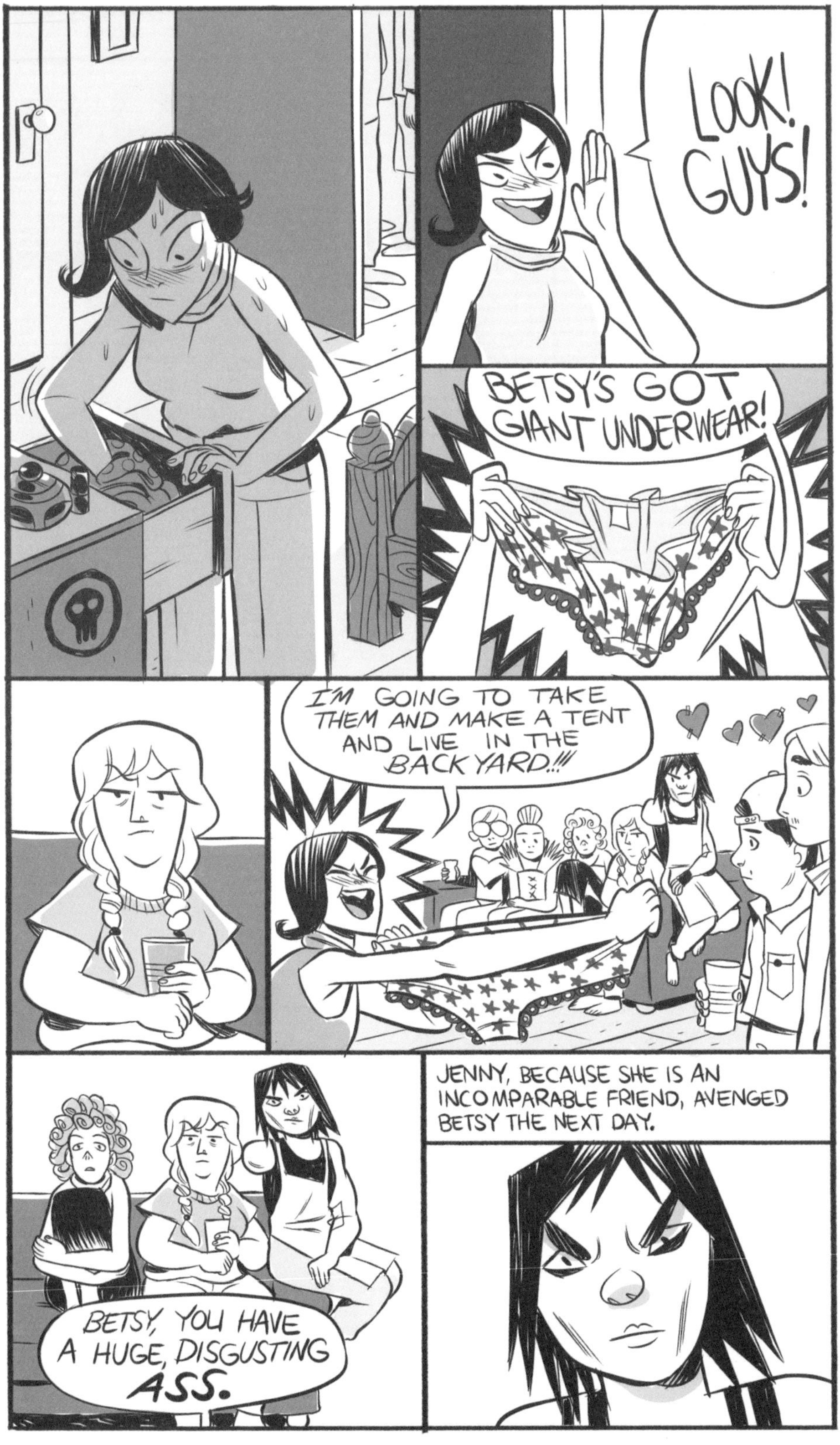
LOOK! GUYS!
BETSY'S GOT GIANT UNDERWEAR!
I'M GOING TO TAKE THEM AND MAKE A TENT AND LIVE IN THE BACKYARD!!!
BETSY, YOU HAVE A HUGE, DISGUSTING ASS.
JENNY, BECAUSE SHE IS AN INCOMPARABLE FRIEND, AVENGED BETSY THE NEXT DAY.

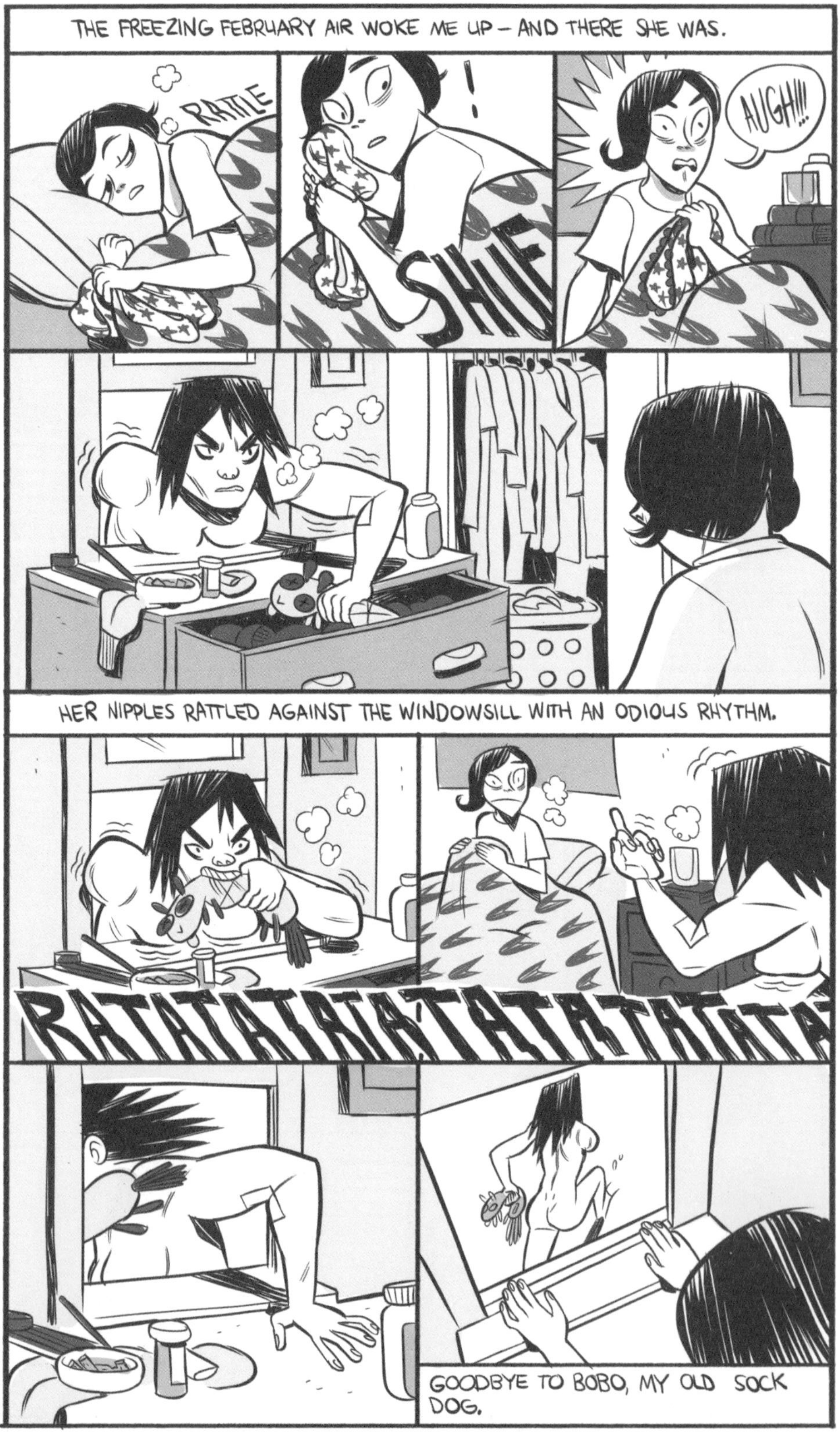
THE FREEZING FEBRUARY AIR WOKE ME UP — AND THERE SHE WAS.
RATTLE
!
SHIF
AUGH!!!
HER NIPPLES RATTLED AGAINST THE WINDOWSILL WITH AN ODIOUS RHYTHM.
RATATATATATATATATATATA
GOODBYE TO BOBO, MY OLD SOCK DOG.

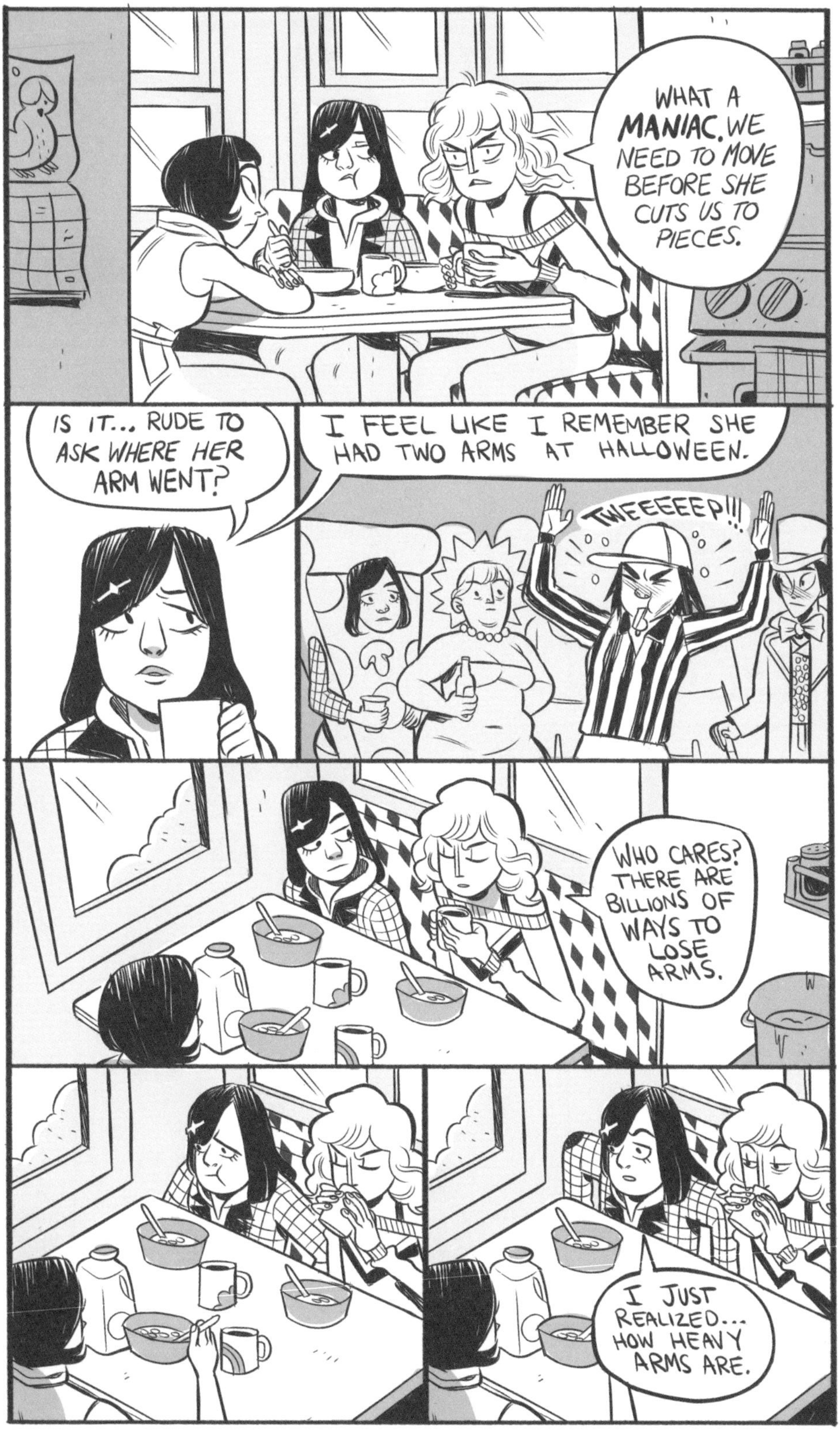
WHAT A MANIAC. WE NEED TO MOVE BEFORE SHE CUTS US TO PIECES.
IS IT... RUDE TO ASK WHERE HER ARM WENT?
I FEEL LIKE I REMEMBER SHE HAD TWO ARMS AT HALLOWEEN.
TWEEEEEP!!!
WHO CARES? THERE ARE BILLIONS OF WAYS TO LOSE ARMS.
I JUST REALIZED... HOW HEAVY ARMS ARE.

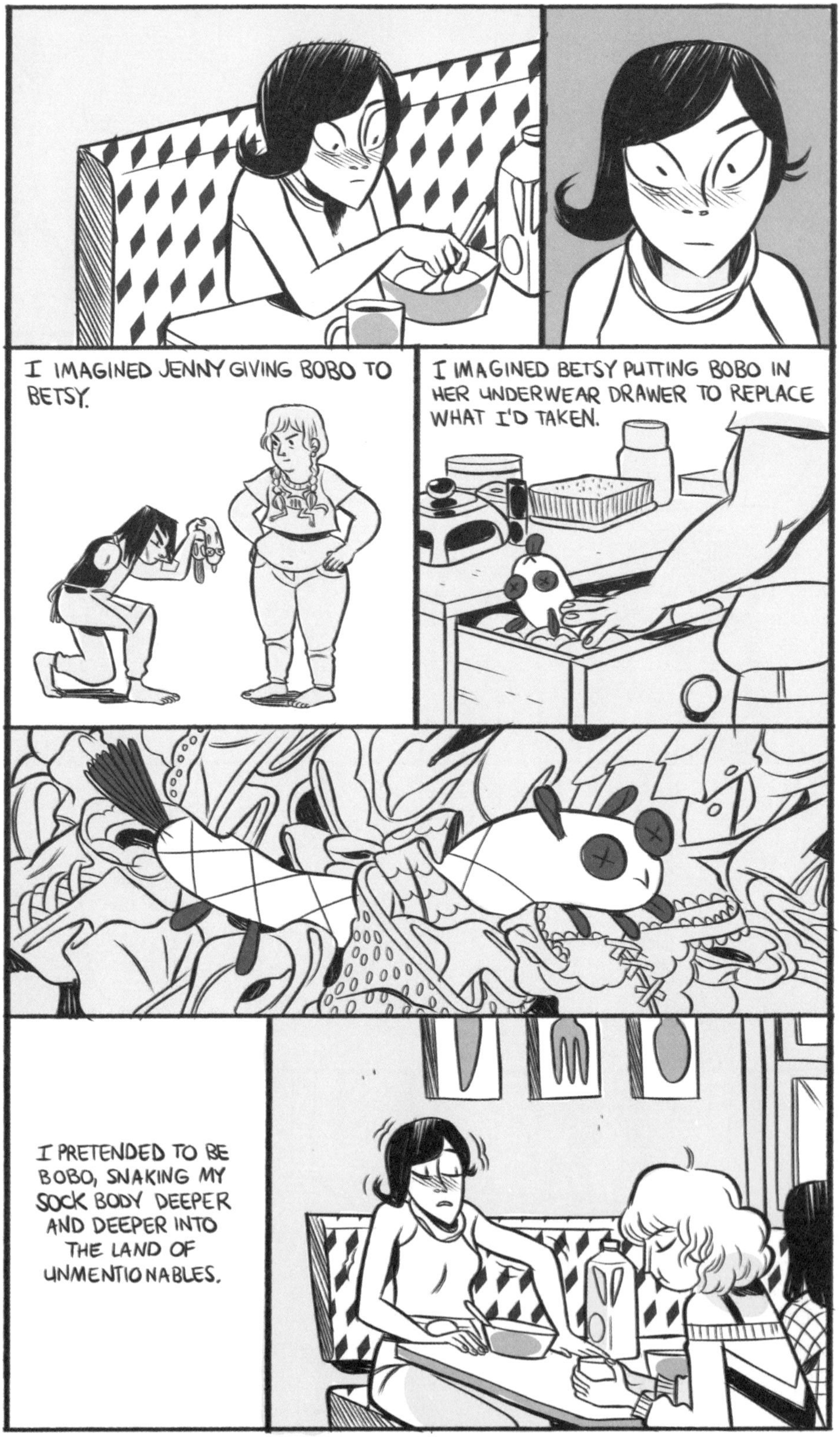
I IMAGINED JENNY GIVING BOBO TO BETSY.
I IMAGINED BETSY PUTTING BOBO IN HER UNDERWEAR DRAWER TO REPLACE WHAT I'D TAKEN.
I PRETENDED TO BE BOBO, SNAKING MY SOCK BODY DEEPER AND DEEPER INTO THE LAND OF UNMENTIONABLES.

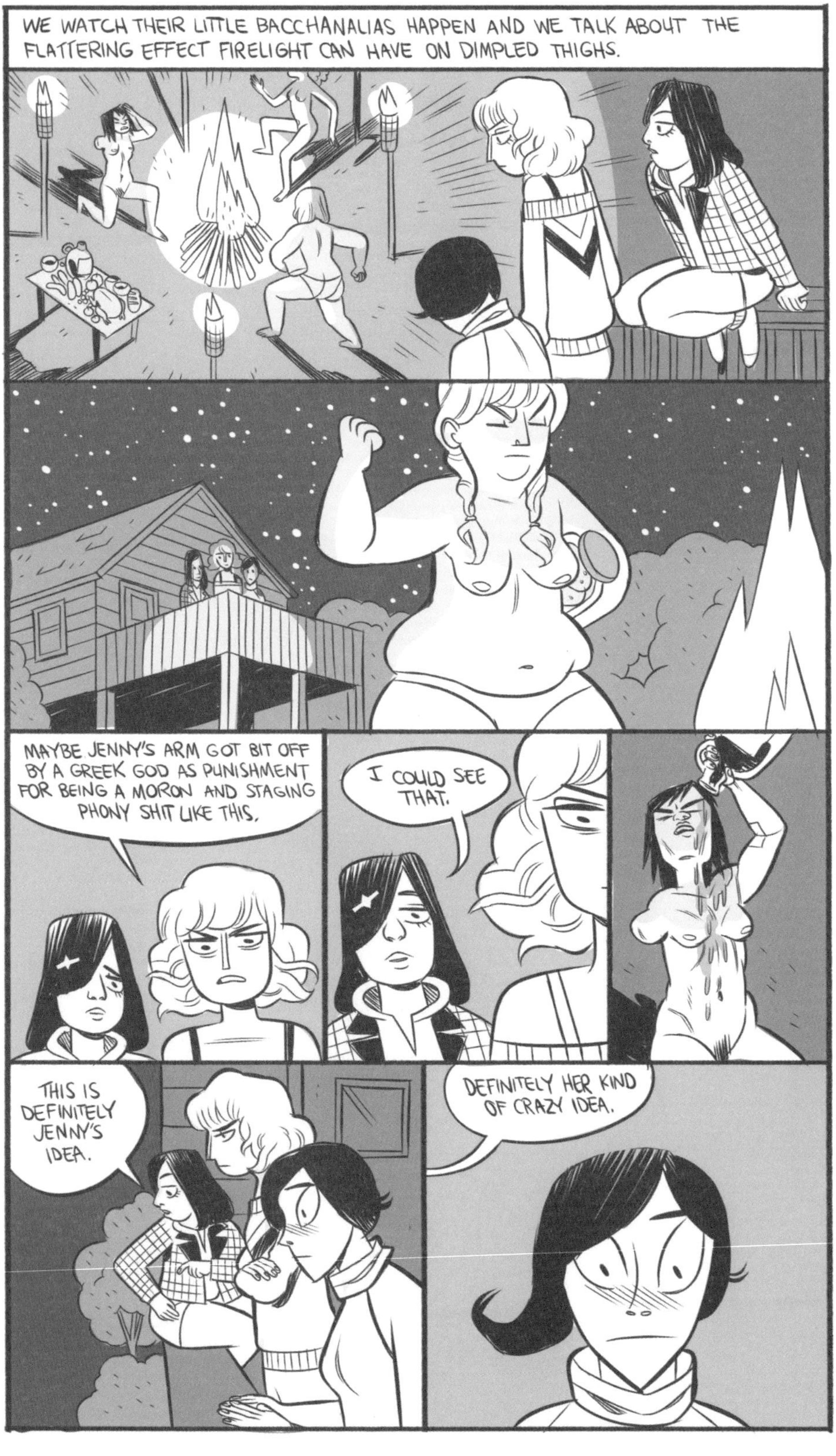
WE WATCH THEIR LITTLE BACCHANALIAS HAPPEN AND WE TALK ABOUT THE FLATTERING EFFECT FIRELIGHT CAN HAVE ON DIMPLED THIGHS.
MAYBE JENNY'S ARM GOT BIT OFF BY A GREEK GOD AS PUNISHMENT FOR BEING A MORON AND STAGING PHONY SHIT LIKE THIS.
I COULD SEE THAT.
THIS IS DEFINITELY JENNY'S IDEA.
DEFINITELY HER KIND OF CRAZY IDEA.

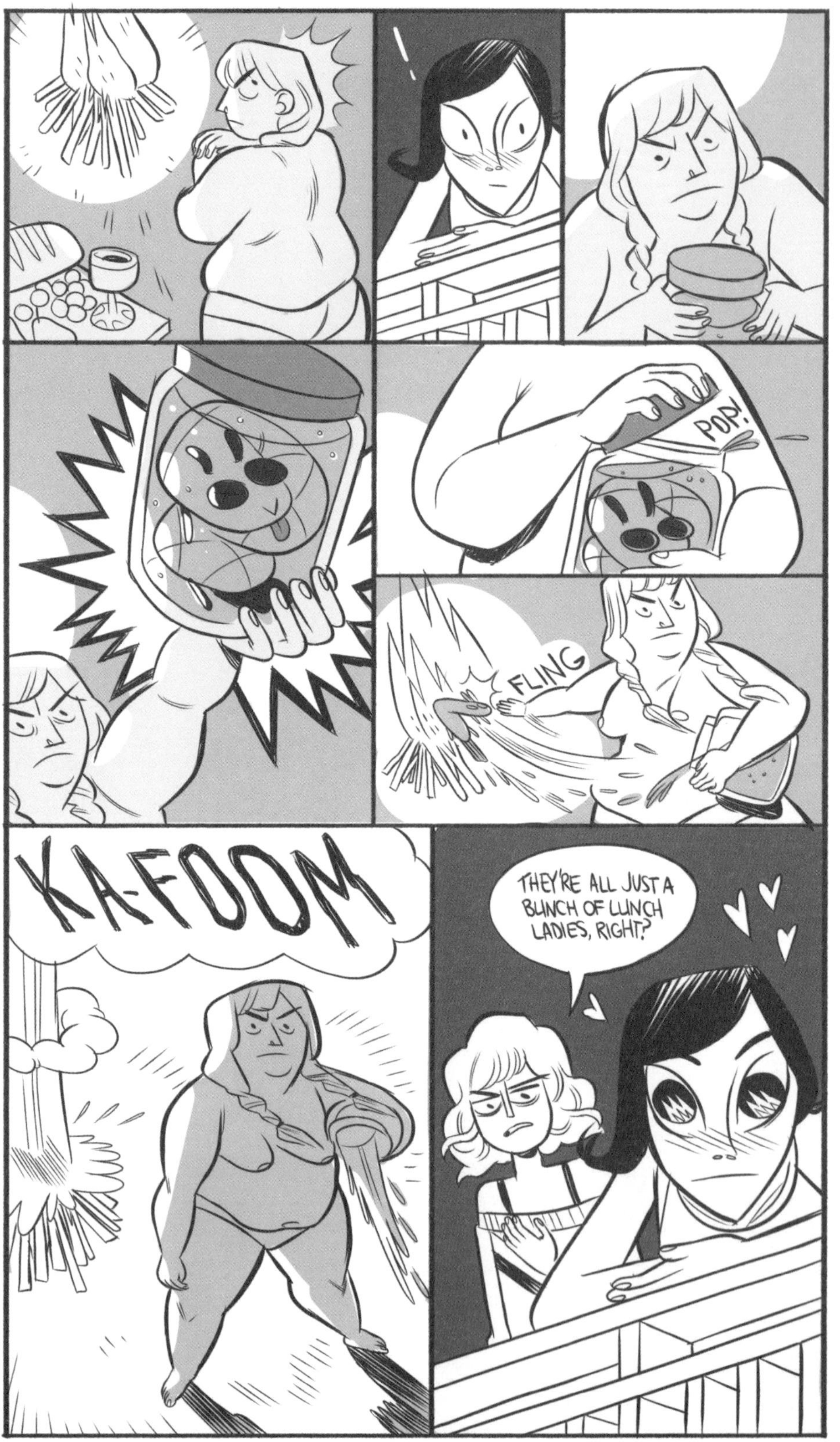

POP!
FLING
KA-FOOM
THEY'RE ALL JUST A BUNCH OF LUNCH LADIES, RIGHT?

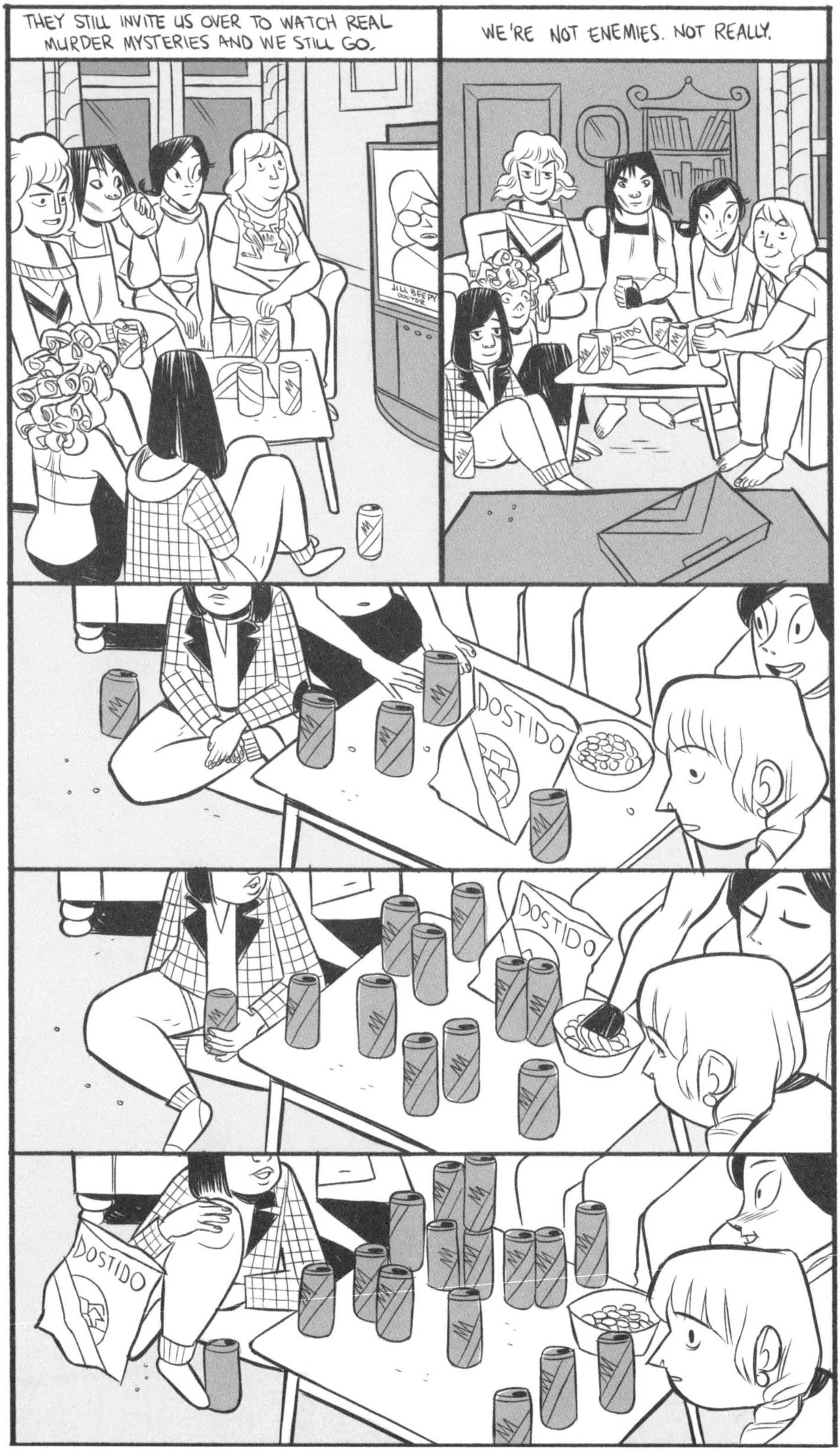
THEY STILL INVITE US OVER TO WATCH REAL MURDER MYSTERIES AND WE STILL GO,
WE'RE NOT ENEMIES. NOT REALLY.
JILL BEEPY
DOCTOR
DOSTIDO
DOSTIDO
DOSTIDO
DOSTIDO

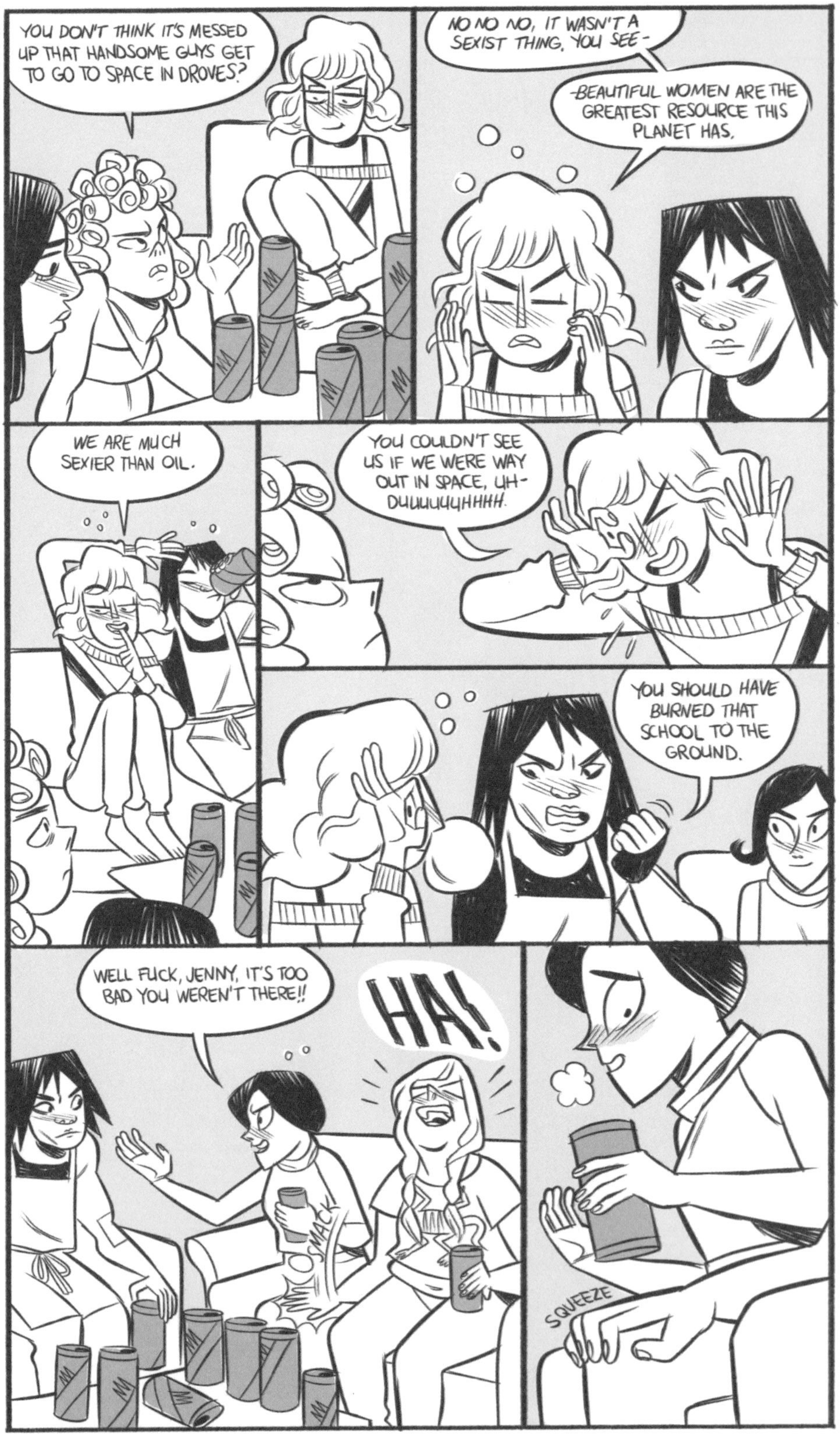
YOU DON'T THINK IT'S MESSED UP THAT HANDSOME GUYS GET TO GO TO SPACE IN DROVES?
NO NO NO, IT WASN'T A SEXIST THING, YOU SEE-
-BEAUTIFUL WOMEN ARE THE GREATEST RESOURCE THIS PLANET HAS.
WE ARE MUCH SEXIER THAN OIL.
YOU COULDN'T SEE US IF WE WERE WAY OUT IN SPACE, UH-DUUUUUUHHHH.
YOU SHOULD HAVE BURNED THAT SCHOOL TO THE GROUND.
WELL FUCK, JENNY, IT'S TOO BAD YOU WEREN'T THERE!!
HA!
SMACK
SQUEEZE

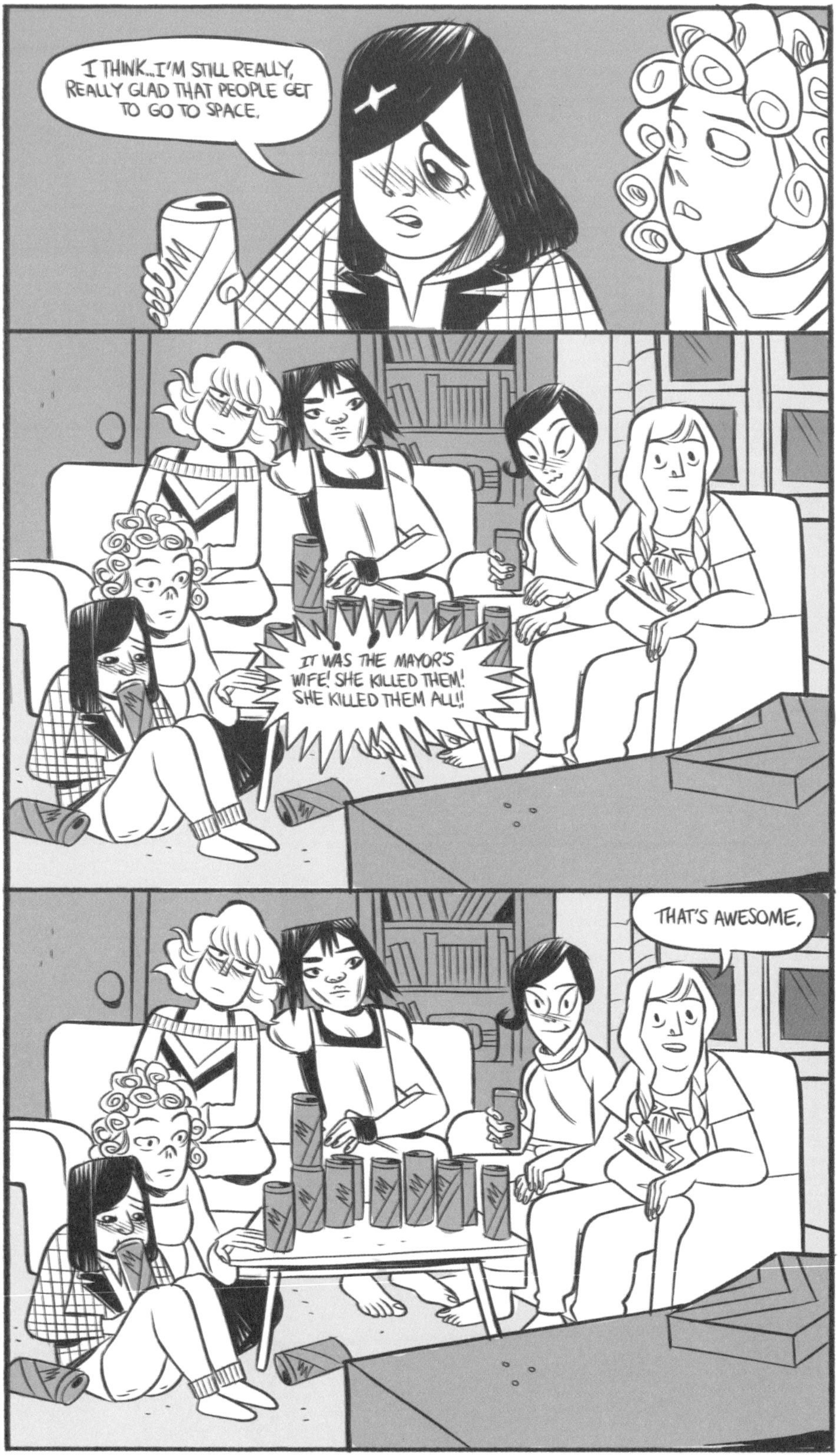
I THINK...I'M STILL REALLY, REALLY GLAD THAT PEOPLE GET TO GO TO SPACE.
IT WAS THE MAYOR'S WIFE! SHE KILLED THEM! SHE KILLED THEM ALL!!
THAT'S AWESOME.

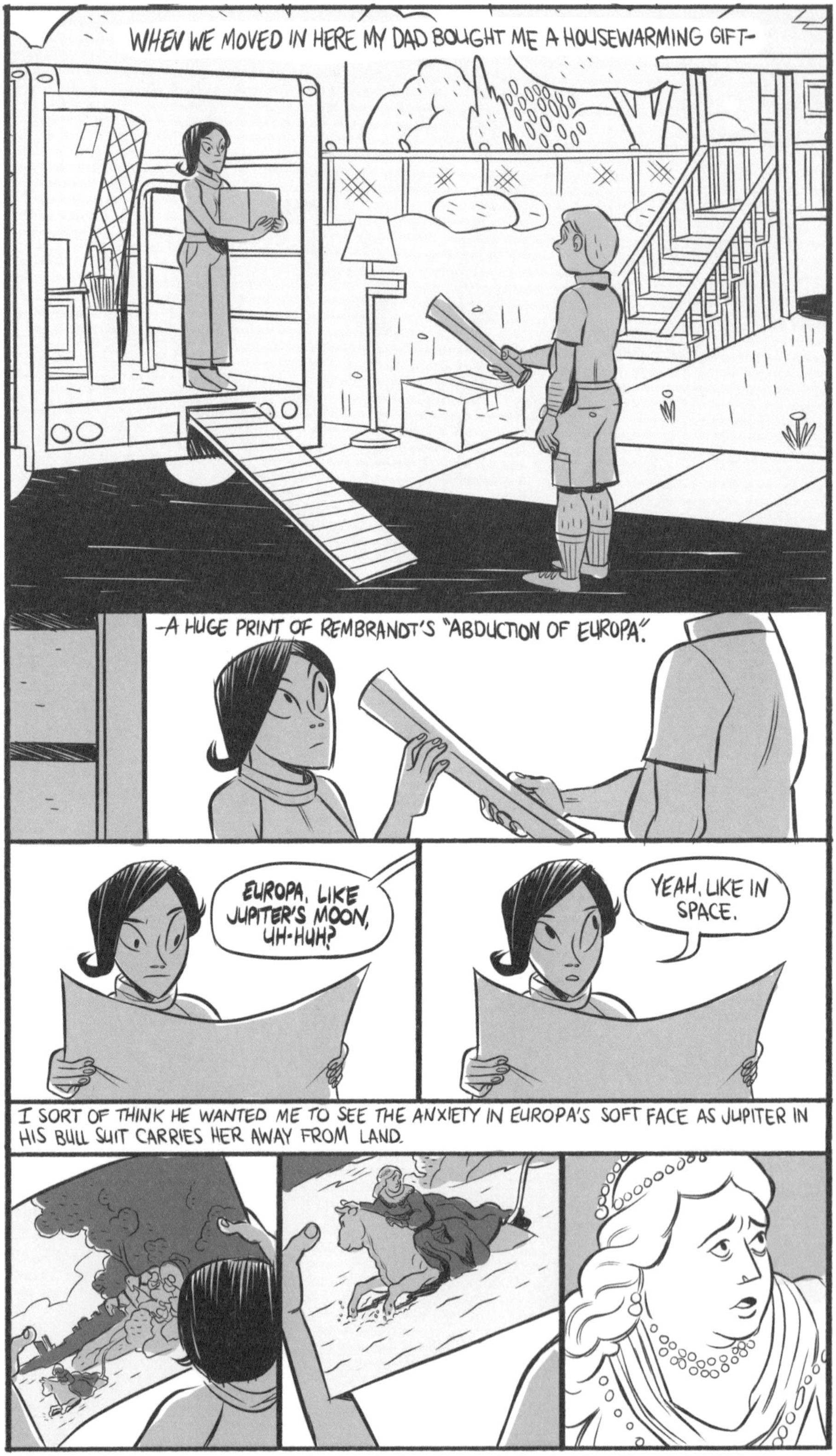
WHEN WE MOVED IN HERE MY DAD BOUGHT ME A HOUSEWARMING GIFT-
-A HUGE PRINT OF REMBRANDT'S "ABDUCTION OF EUROPA."
EUROPA, LIKE JUPITER'S MOON, UH-HUH?
YEAH, LIKE IN SPACE.
I SORT OF THINK HE WANTED ME TO SEE THE ANXIETY IN EUROPA'S SOFT FACE AS JUPITER IN HIS BULL SUIT CARRIES HER AWAY FROM LAND.

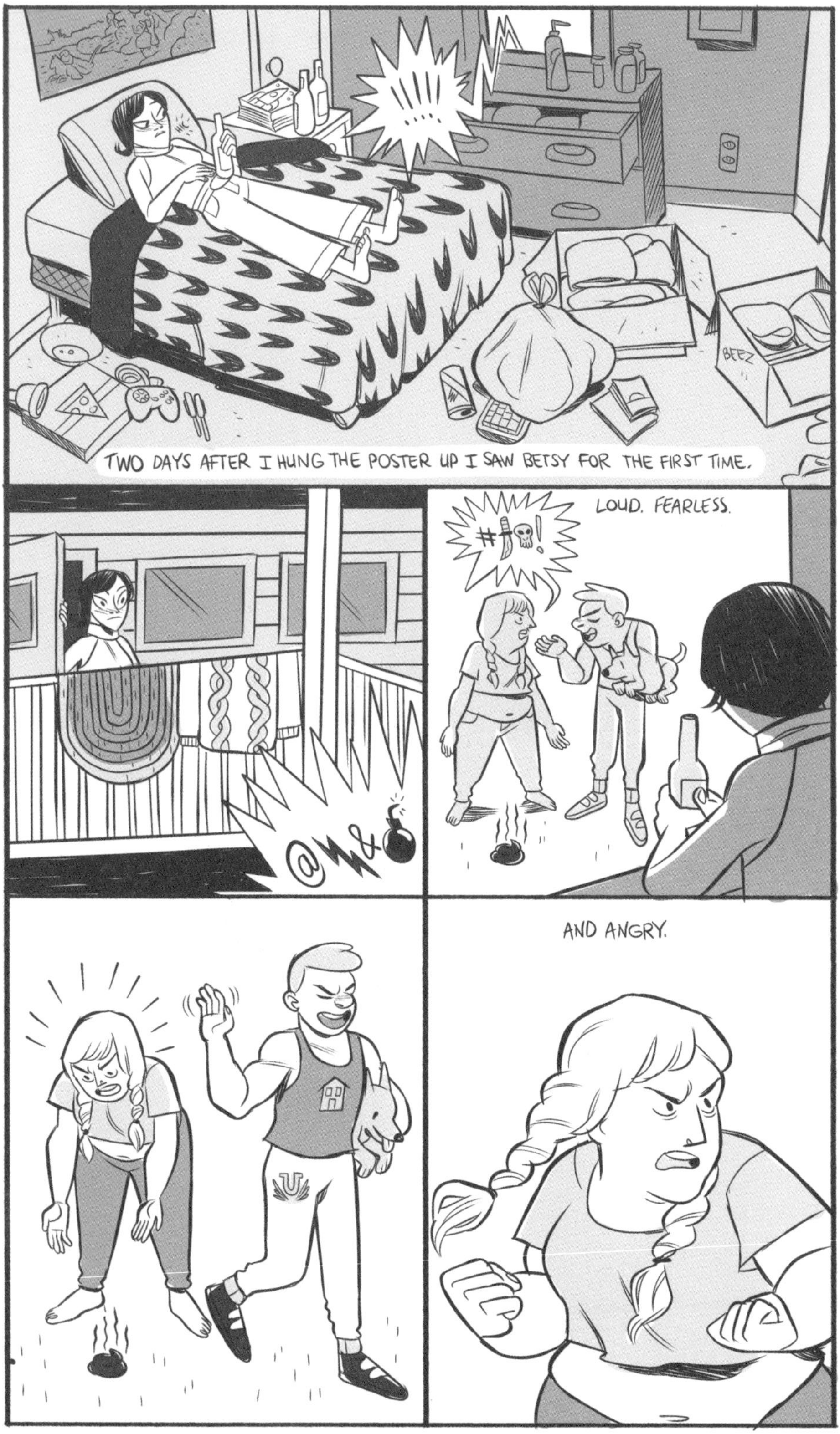

BEEZ
TWO DAYS AFTER I HUNG THE POSTER UP I SAW BETSY FOR THE FIRST TIME.
LOUD. FEARLESS.
AND ANGRY.

2015

RADISHES

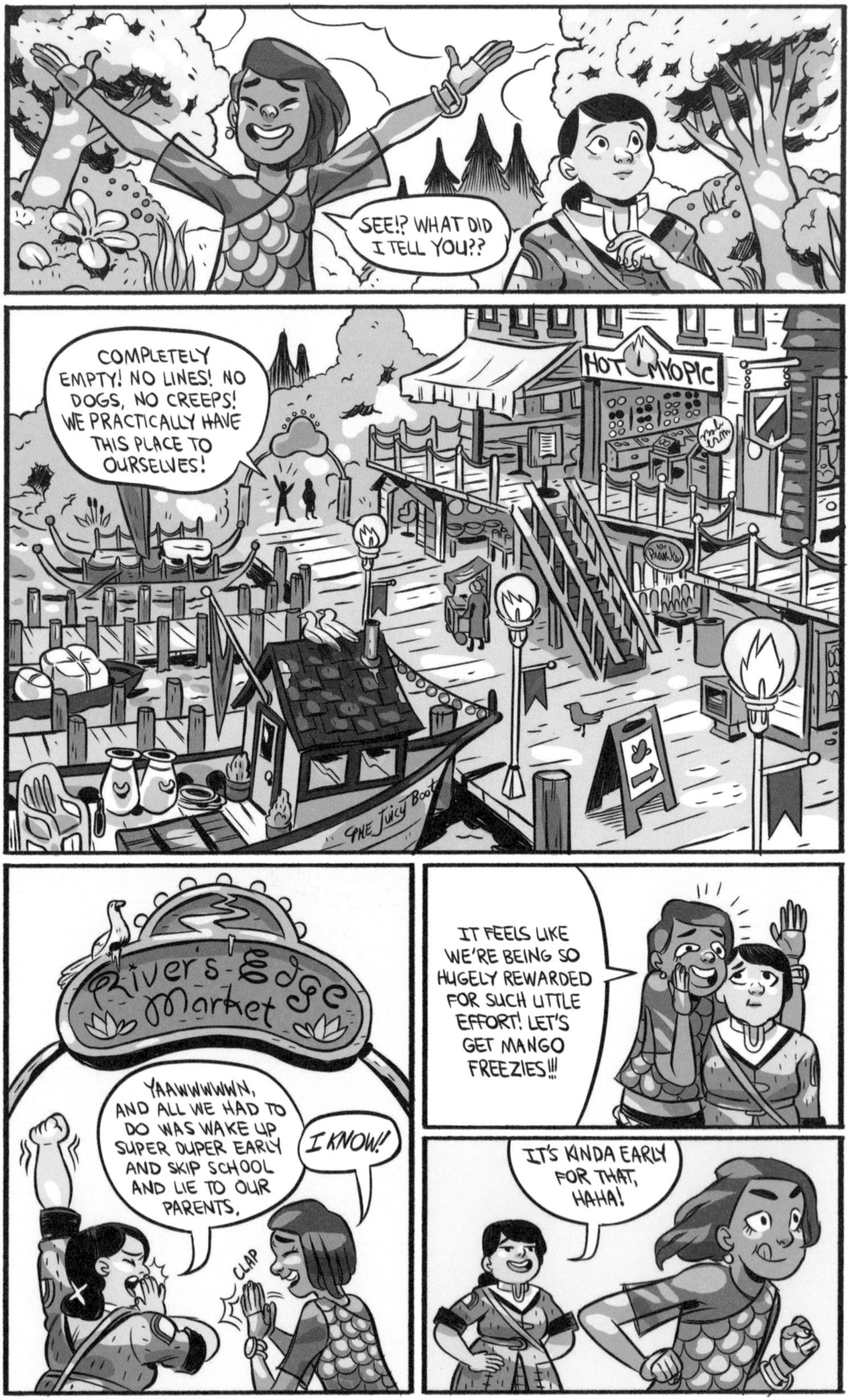
SEE!? WHAT DID I TELL YOU??
COMPLETELY EMPTY! NO LINES! NO DOGS, NO CREEPS! WE PRACTICALLY HAVE THIS PLACE TO OURSELVES!
HOT MYOPIC
THE Juicy Boot
River's Edge Market
YAAWWWWWN, AND ALL WE HAD TO DO WAS WAKE UP SUPER DUPER EARLY AND SKIP SCHOOL AND LIE TO OUR PARENTS.
I KNOW!
CLAP
IT FEELS LIKE WE'RE BEING SO HUGELY REWARDED FOR SUCH LITTLE EFFORT! LET'S GET MANGO FREEZIES!!!
IT'S KINDA EARLY FOR THAT, HAHA!

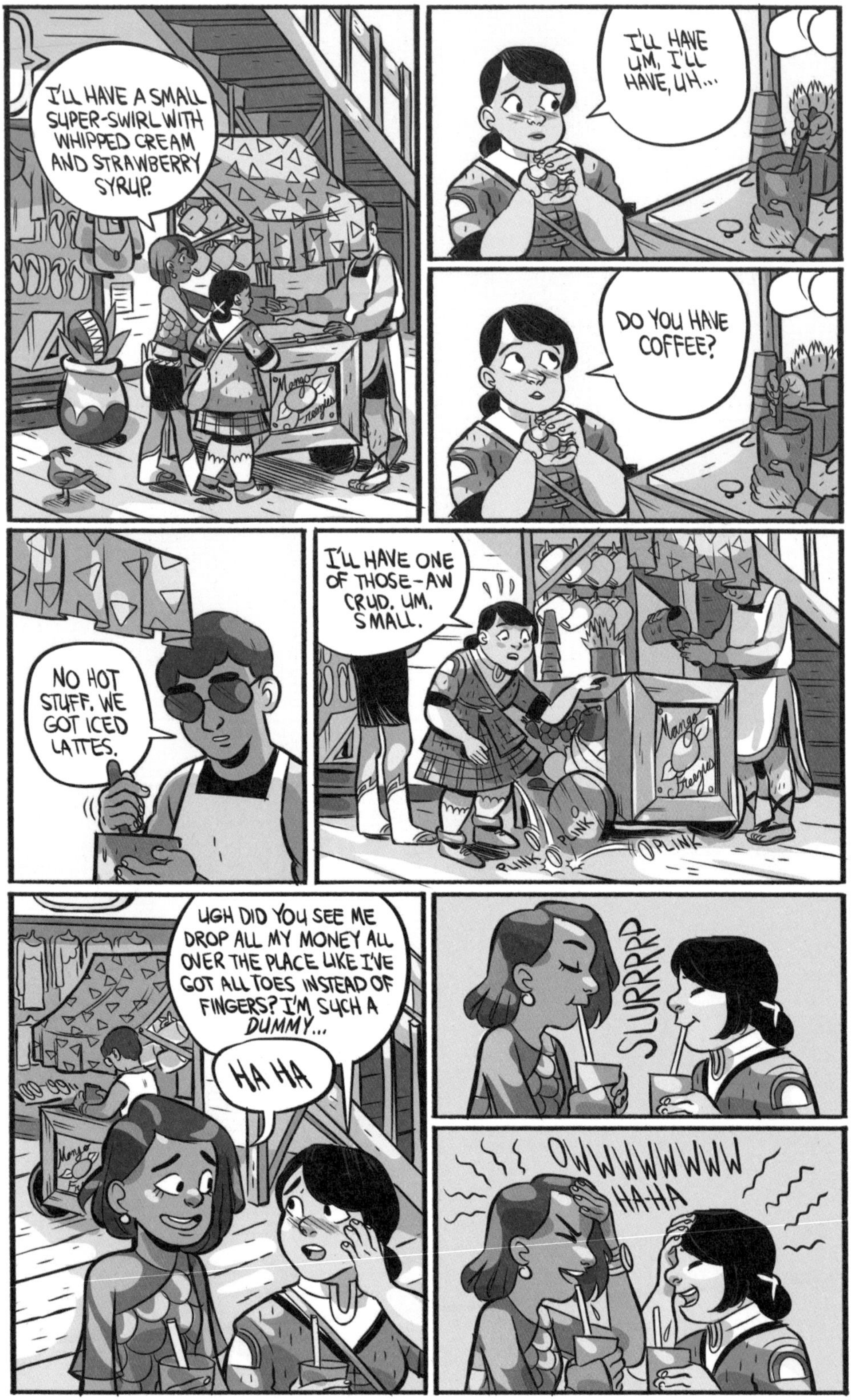
I'LL HAVE A SMALL SUPER-SWIRL WITH WHIPPED CREAM AND STRAWBERRY SYRUP.
I'LL HAVE UM, I'LL HAVE, UH...
DO YOU HAVE COFFEE?
NO HOT STUFF. WE GOT ICED LATTES.
I'LL HAVE ONE OF THOSE-AW CRUD. UM. SMALL.
Mango Freezies
PLINK PLINK PLINK
UGH DID YOU SEE ME DROP ALL MY MONEY ALL OVER THE PLACE LIKE I'VE GOT ALL TOES INSTEAD OF FINGERS? I'M SUCH A *DUMMY*...
HA HA
SLURRRRP
OWWWWWWWW
HA-HA

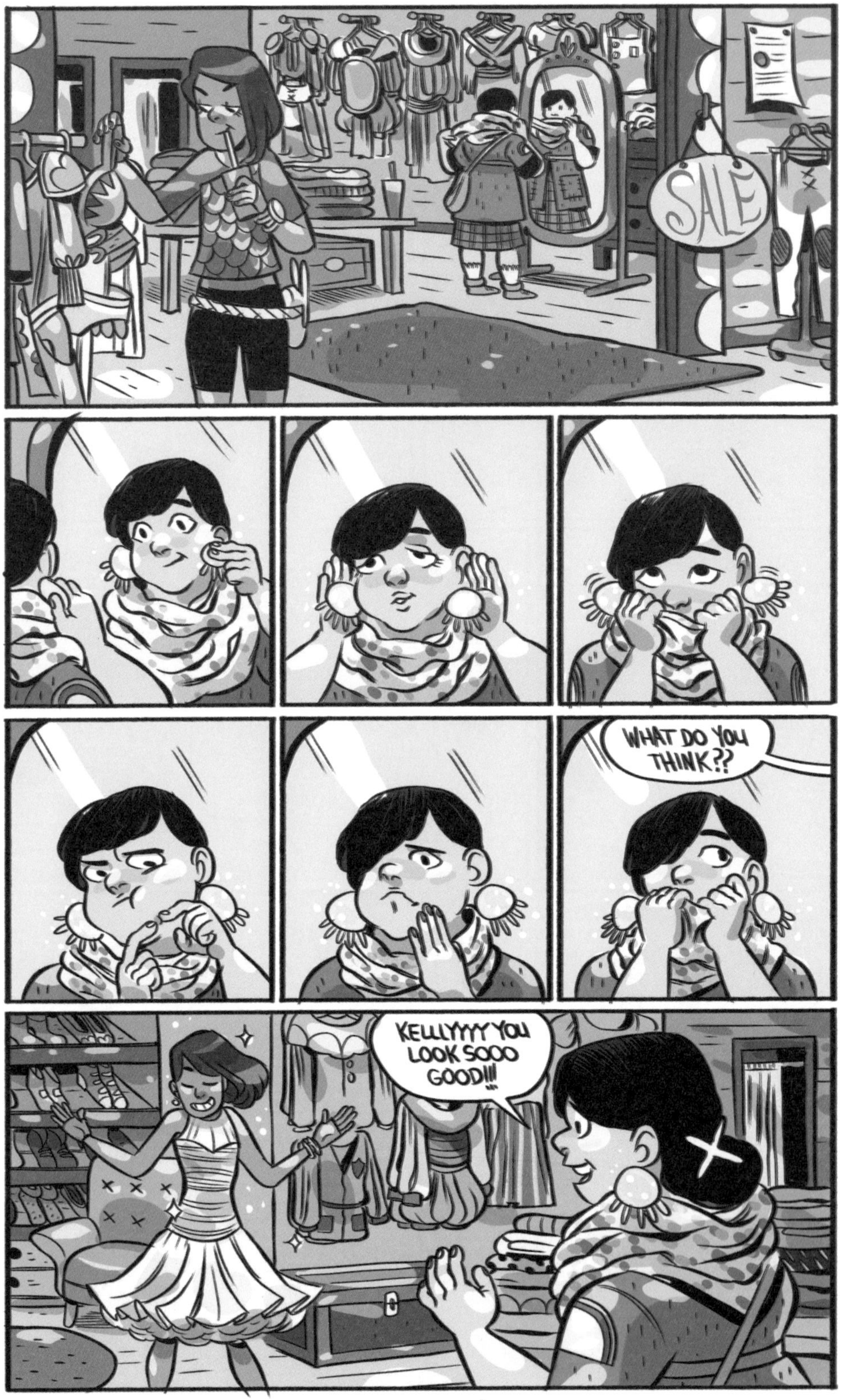
SALE
WHAT DO YOU THINK??
KELLLYYYY YOU LOOK SOOO GOOD!!!

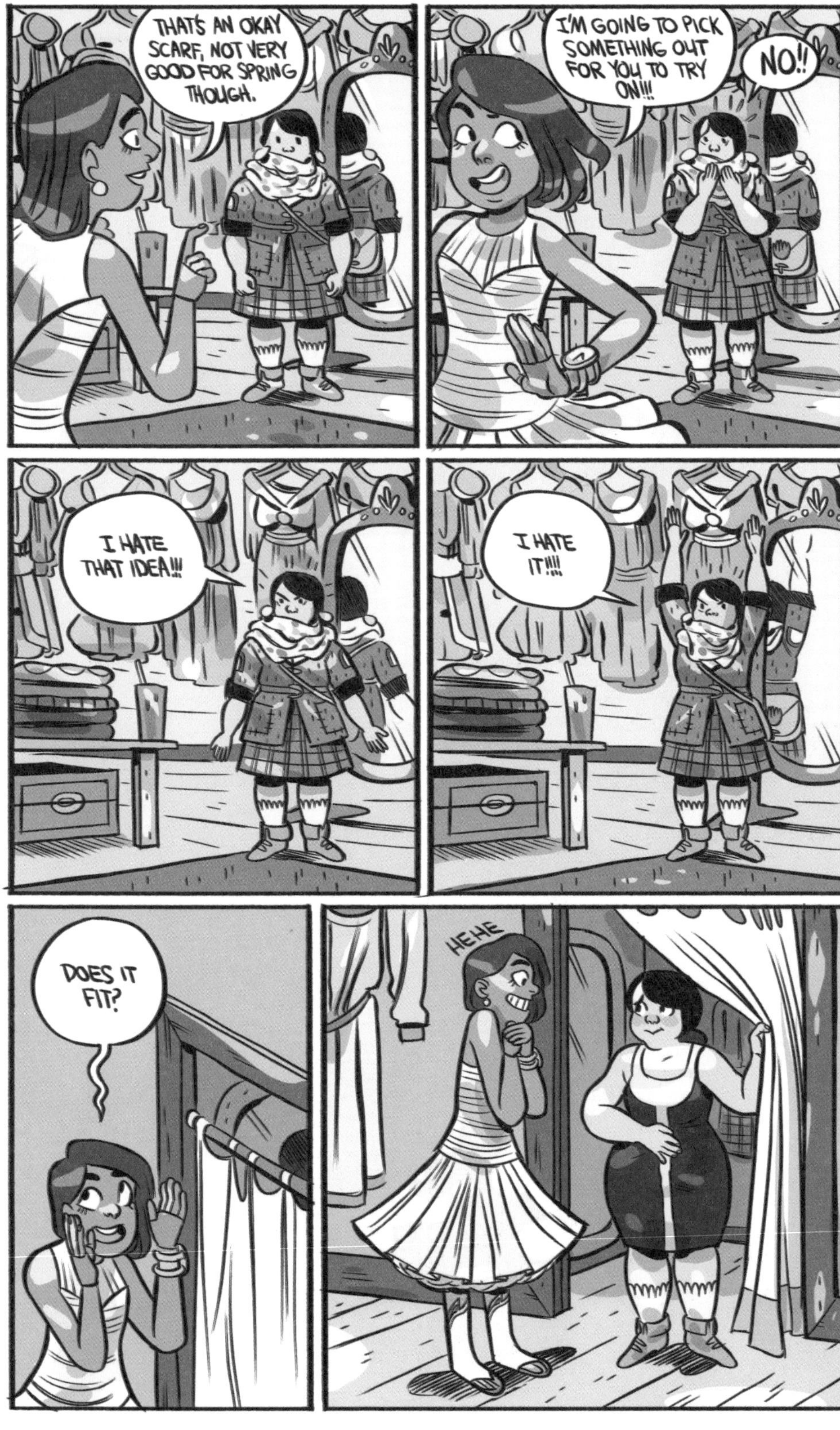
THAT'S AN OKAY SCARF, NOT VERY GOOD FOR SPRING THOUGH.
I'M GOING TO PICK SOMETHING OUT FOR YOU TO TRY ON!!!
NO!!
I HATE THAT IDEA!!!
I HATE IT!!!!
DOES IT FIT?
HEHE

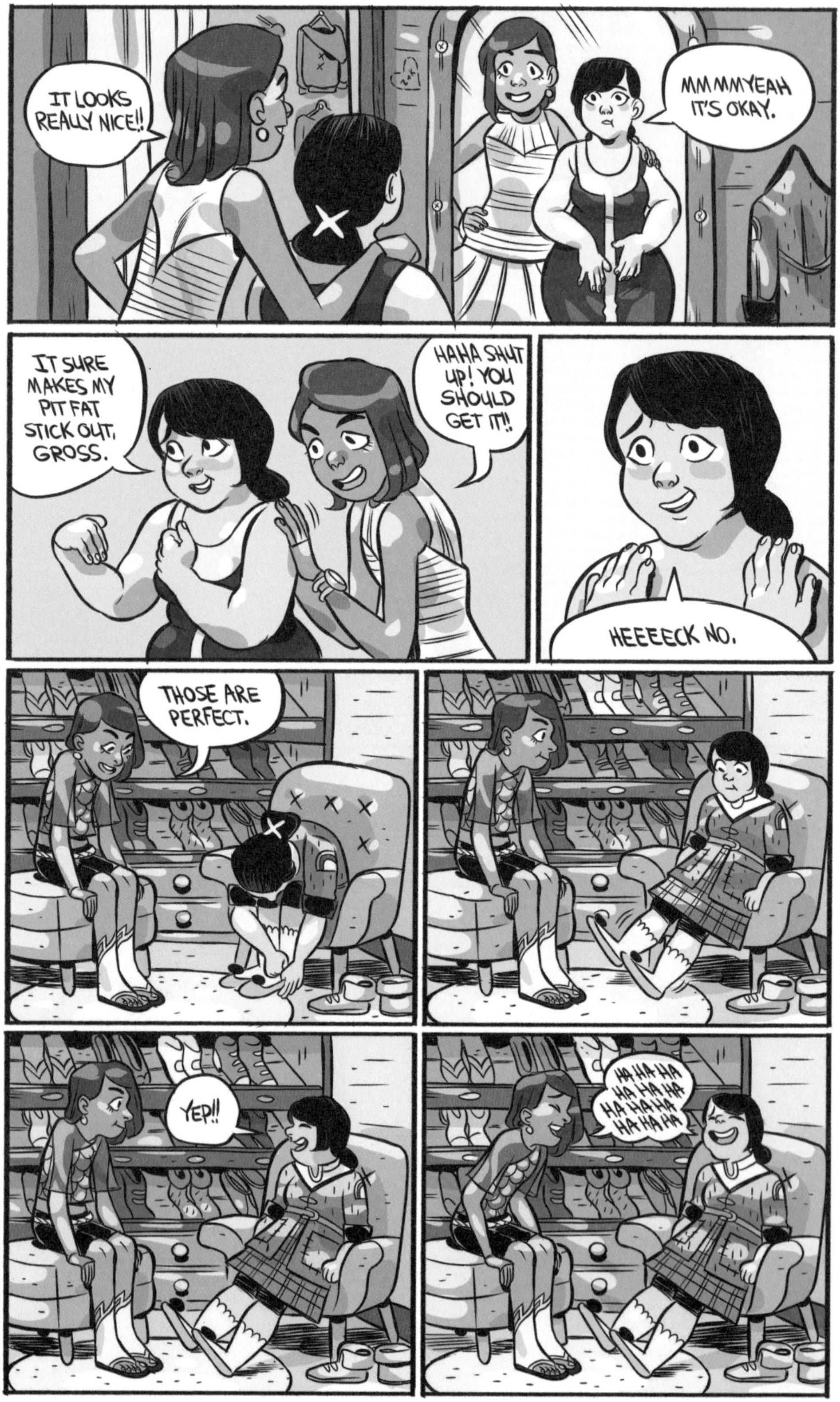
IT LOOKS REALLY NICE!!
MMMMYEAH IT'S OKAY.
IT SURE MAKES MY PIT FAT STICK OUT, GROSS.
HAHA SHUT UP! YOU SHOULD GET IT!!
HEEEECK NO.
THOSE ARE PERFECT.
YEP!!
HA HA HA HA HA HA HA HA HA HA HA HA

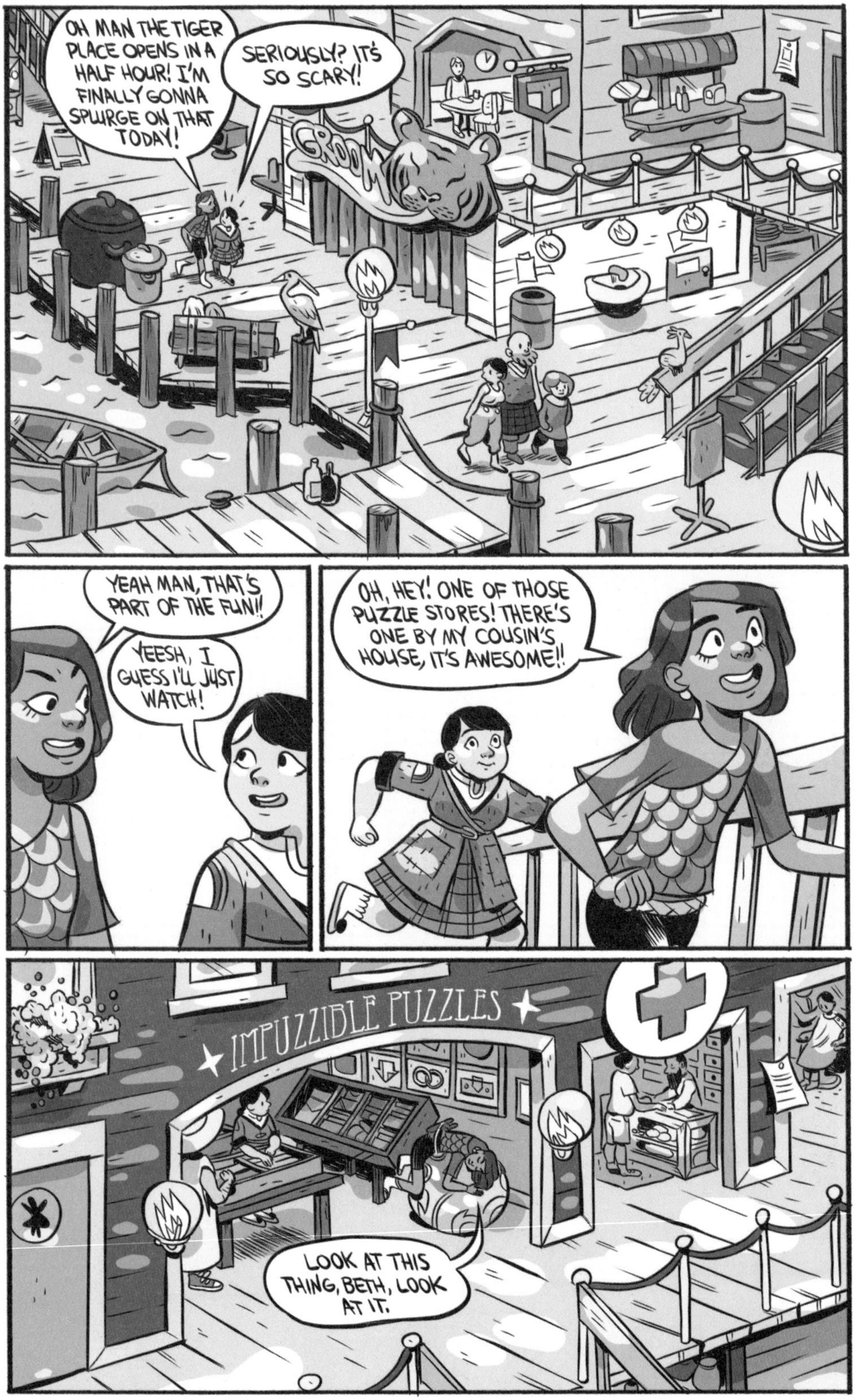
OH MAN THE TIGER PLACE OPENS IN A HALF HOUR! I'M FINALLY GONNA SPLURGE ON THAT TODAY!
SERIOUSLY? IT'S SO SCARY!
GROOM
YEAH MAN, THAT'S PART OF THE FUN!!
YEESH, I GUESS I'LL JUST WATCH!
OH, HEY! ONE OF THOSE PUZZLE STORES! THERE'S ONE BY MY COUSIN'S HOUSE, IT'S AWESOME!!
IMPUZZIBLE PUZZLES
LOOK AT THIS THING, BETH, LOOK AT IT.

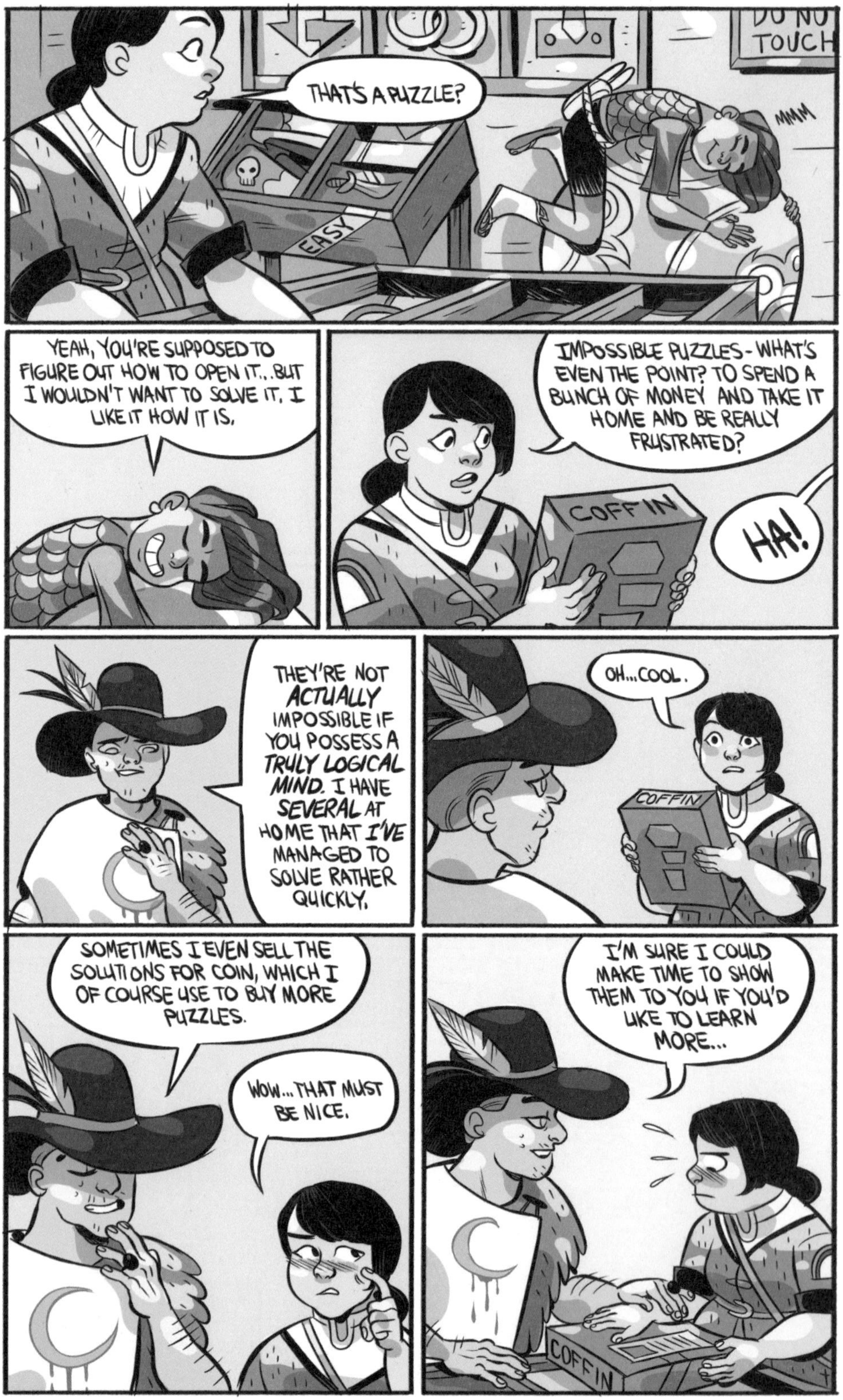
DO NOT TOUCH
THAT'S A PUZZLE?
EASY
MMM
YEAH, YOU'RE SUPPOSED TO FIGURE OUT HOW TO OPEN IT...BUT I WOULDN'T WANT TO SOLVE IT. I LIKE IT HOW IT IS.
IMPOSSIBLE PUZZLES - WHAT'S EVEN THE POINT? TO SPEND A BUNCH OF MONEY AND TAKE IT HOME AND BE REALLY FRUSTRATED?
COFFIN
HA!
THEY'RE NOT ACTUALLY IMPOSSIBLE IF YOU POSSESS A TRULY LOGICAL MIND. I HAVE SEVERAL AT HOME THAT I'VE MANAGED TO SOLVE RATHER QUICKLY.
OH...COOL.
COFFIN
SOMETIMES I EVEN SELL THE SOLUTIONS FOR COIN, WHICH I OF COURSE USE TO BUY MORE PUZZLES.
WOW...THAT MUST BE NICE.
I'M SURE I COULD MAKE TIME TO SHOW THEM TO YOU IF YOU'D LIKE TO LEARN MORE...
COFFIN

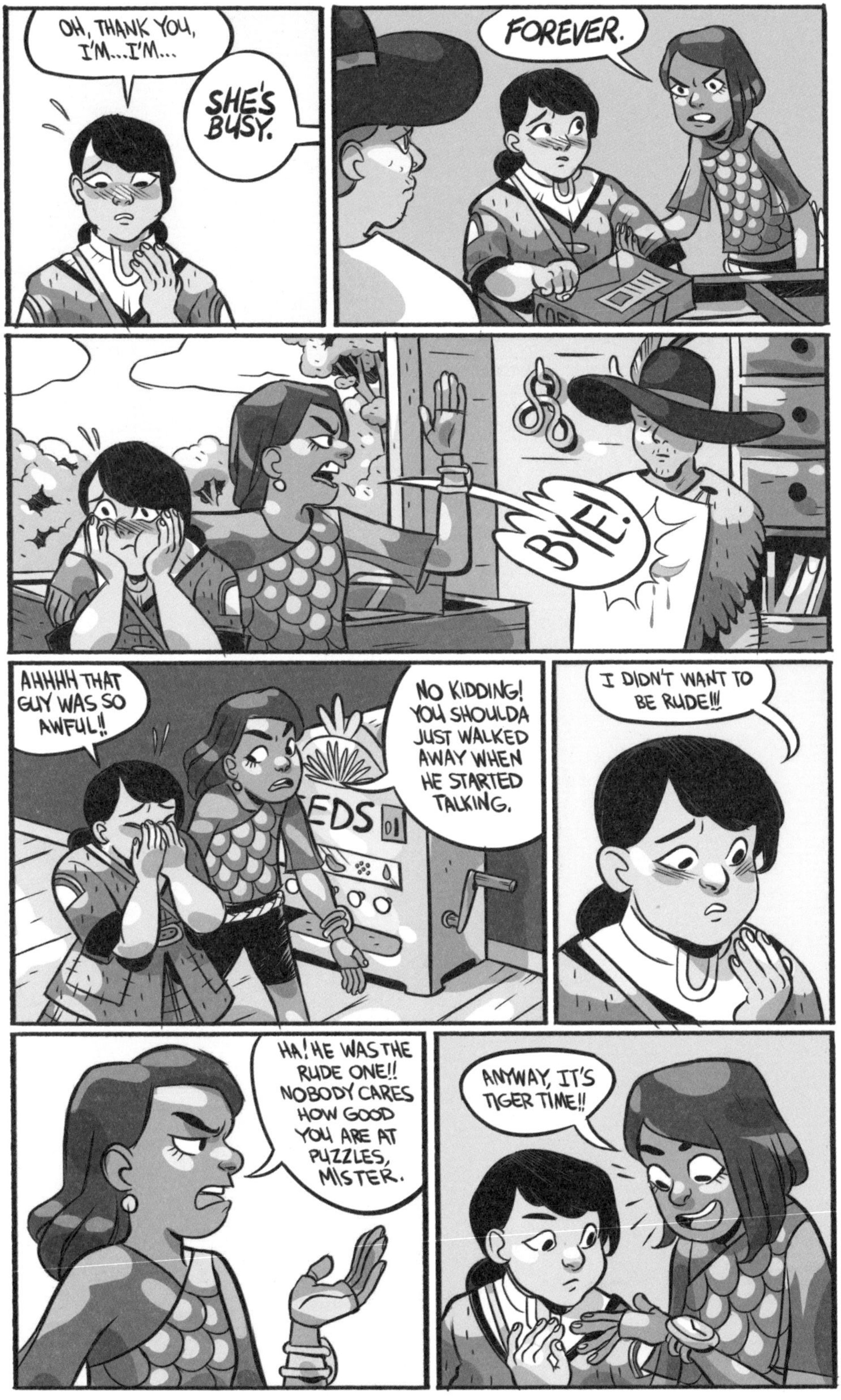
OH, THANK YOU, I'M...I'M...
SHE'S BUSY.
FOREVER.
BYE!
AHHHH THAT GUY WAS SO AWFUL!!
NO KIDDING! YOU SHOULDA JUST WALKED AWAY WHEN HE STARTED TALKING.
I DIDN'T WANT TO BE RUDE!!!
HA! HE WAS THE RUDE ONE!! NOBODY CARES HOW GOOD YOU ARE AT PUZZLES, MISTER.
ANYWAY, IT'S TIGER TIME!!

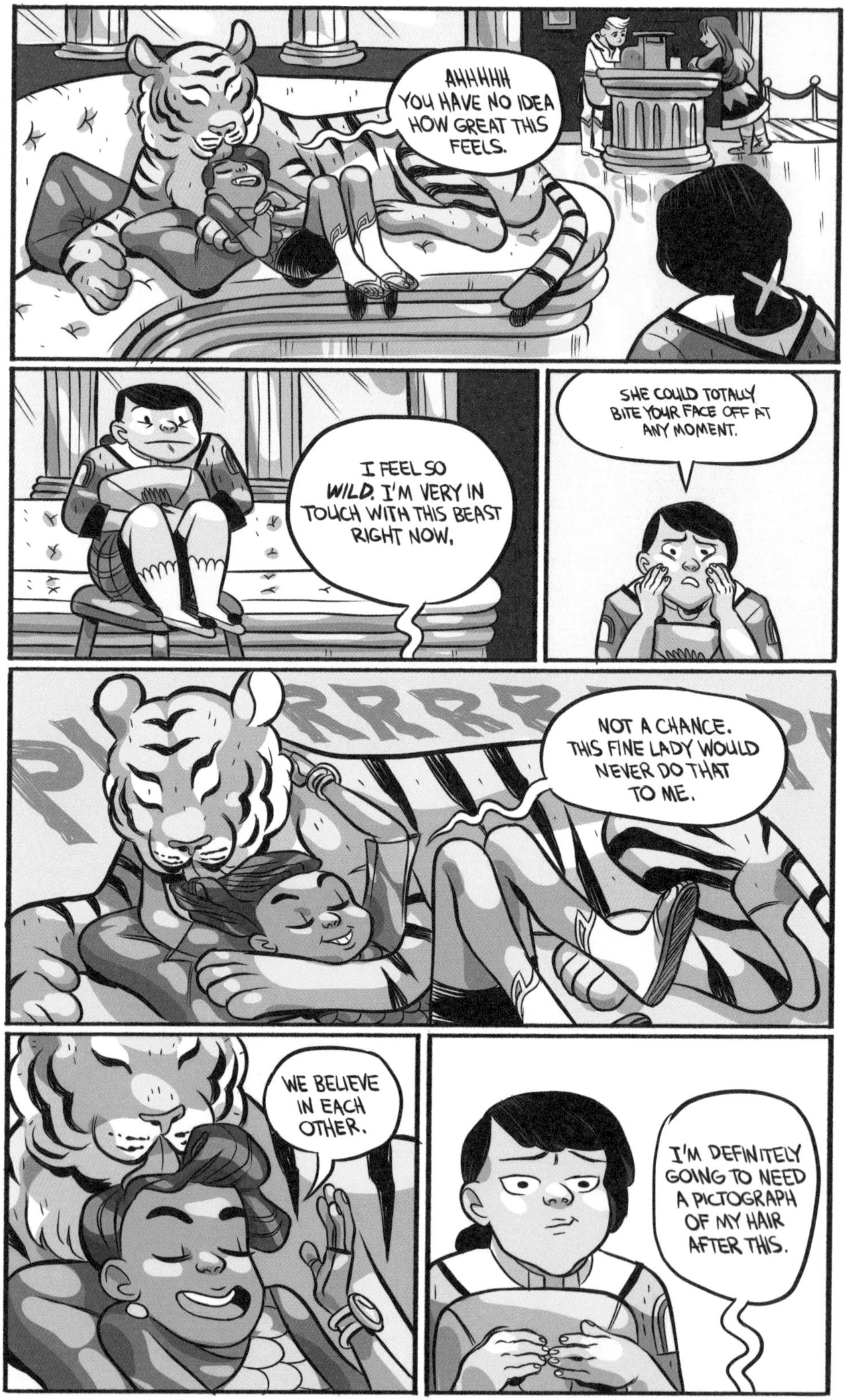
AHHHHH YOU HAVE NO IDEA HOW GREAT THIS FEELS.
I FEEL SO WILD. I'M VERY IN TOUCH WITH THIS BEAST RIGHT NOW.
SHE COULD TOTALLY BITE YOUR FACE OFF AT ANY MOMENT.
PRRRRRR
NOT A CHANCE. THIS FINE LADY WOULD NEVER DO THAT TO ME.
WE BELIEVE IN EACH OTHER.
I'M DEFINITELY GOING TO NEED A PICTOGRAPH OF MY HAIR AFTER THIS.

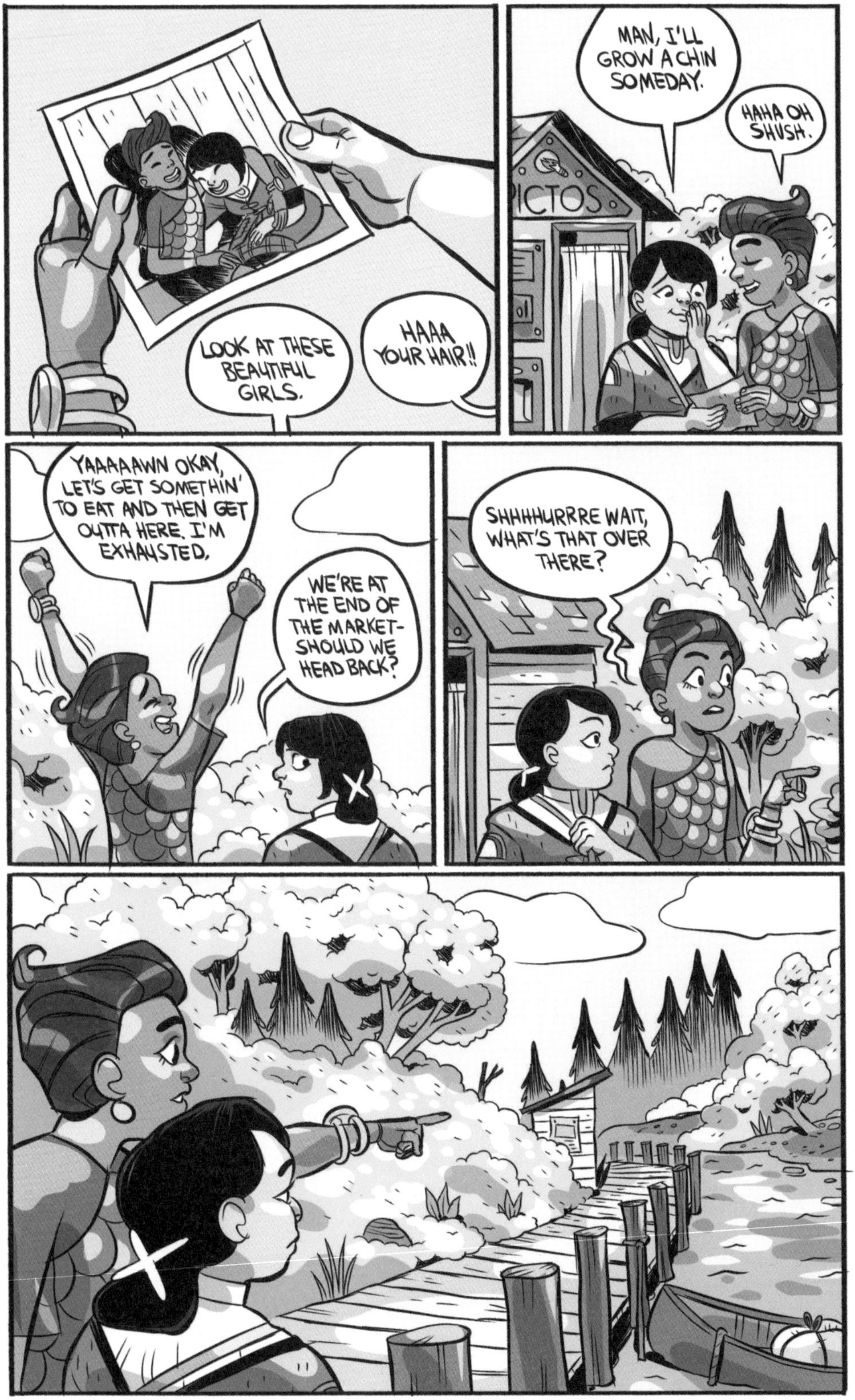
LOOK AT THESE BEAUTIFUL GIRLS.
HAAA YOUR HAIR!!
MAN, I'LL GROW A CHIN SOMEDAY.
HAHA OH SHUSH.
PICTOS
YAAAAAWN OKAY, LET'S GET SOMETHIN' TO EAT AND THEN GET OUTTA HERE. I'M EXHAUSTED.
WE'RE AT THE END OF THE MARKET- SHOULD WE HEAD BACK?
SHHHHURRRE WAIT, WHAT'S THAT OVER THERE?

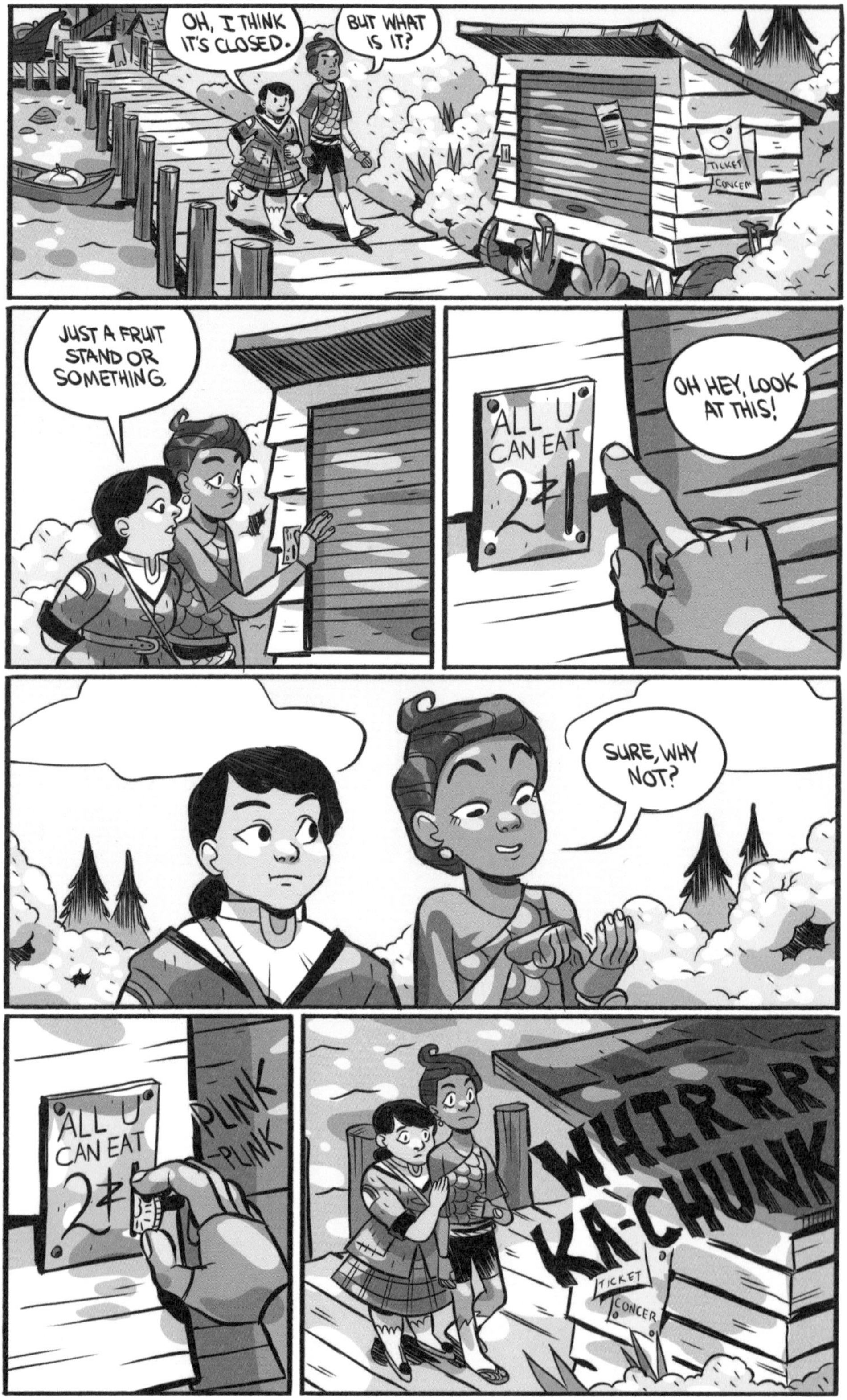
OH, I THINK IT'S CLOSED.
BUT WHAT IS IT?
TICKET
CONCEM
JUST A FRUIT STAND OR SOMETHING.
ALL U CAN EAT 2¢
OH HEY, LOOK AT THIS!
SURE, WHY NOT?
ALL U CAN EAT 2¢
PLINK
PLINK
WHIRRR
KA-CHUNK
TICKET
CONCER

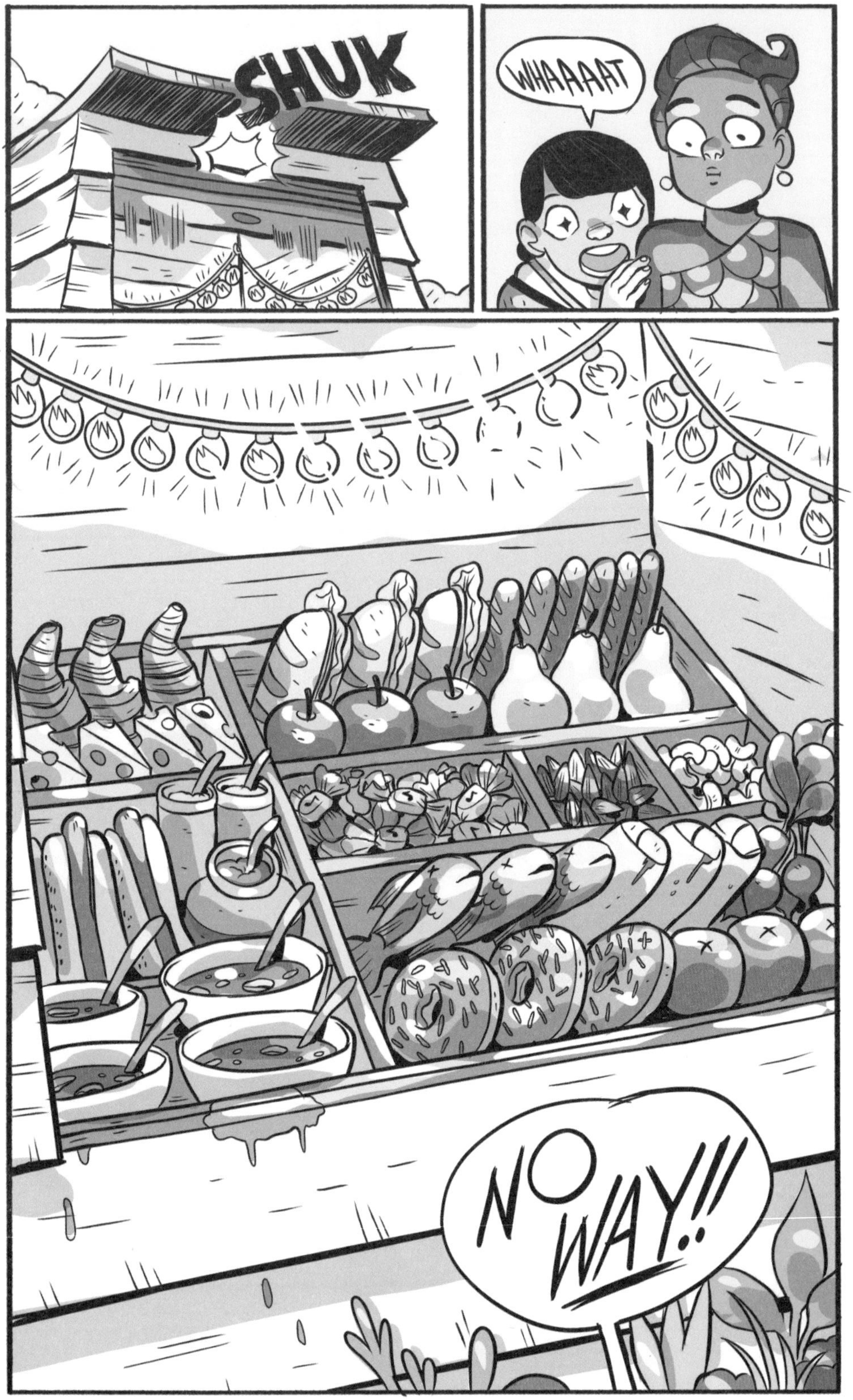
SHUK
WHAAAAT
NO WAY!!

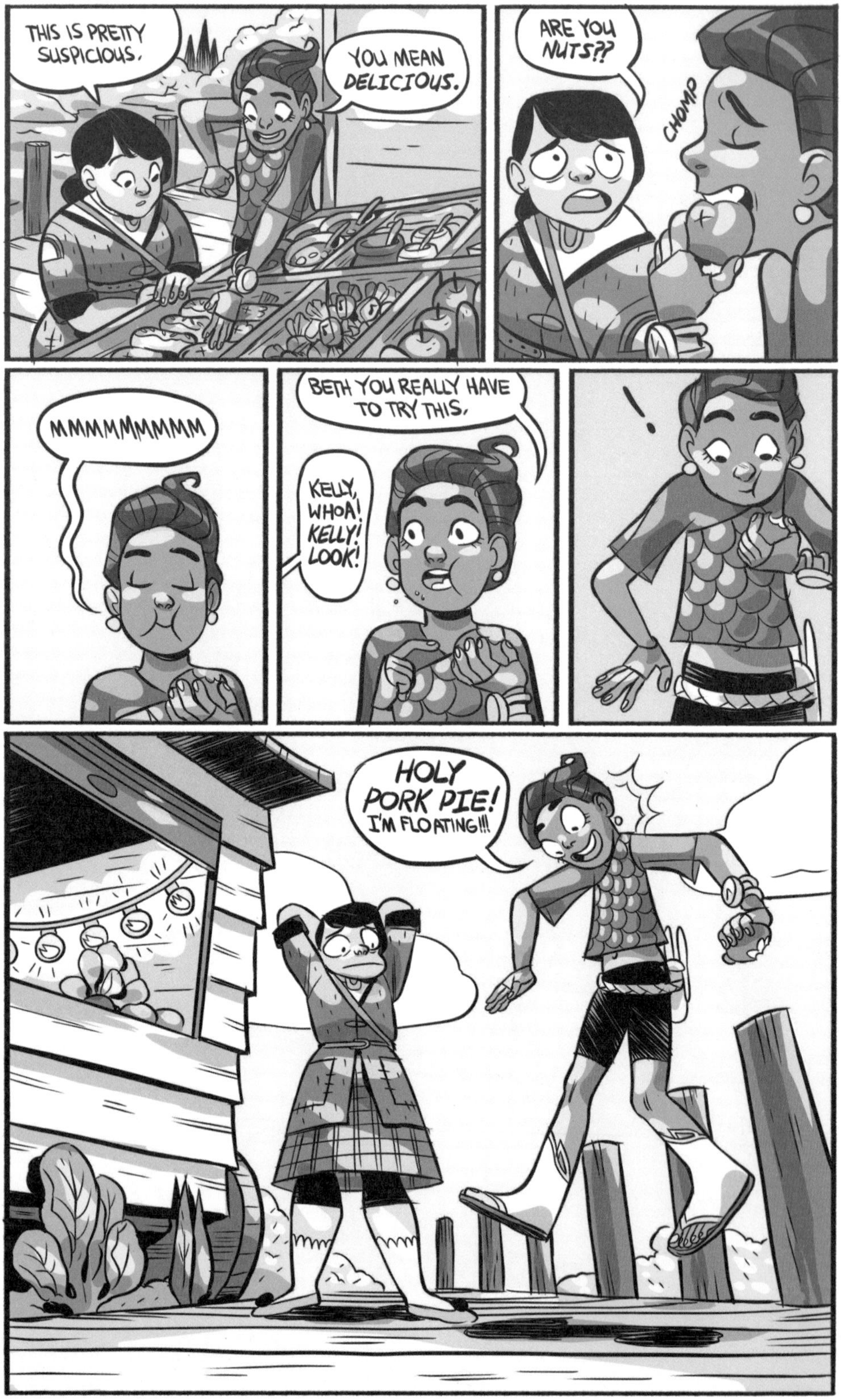
THIS IS PRETTY SUSPICIOUS.
YOU MEAN DELICIOUS.
ARE YOU NUTS??
CHOMP
MMMMMMMMM
BETH YOU REALLY HAVE TO TRY THIS.
KELLY, WHOA! KELLY! LOOK!
!
HOLY PORK PIE! I'M FLOATING!!!

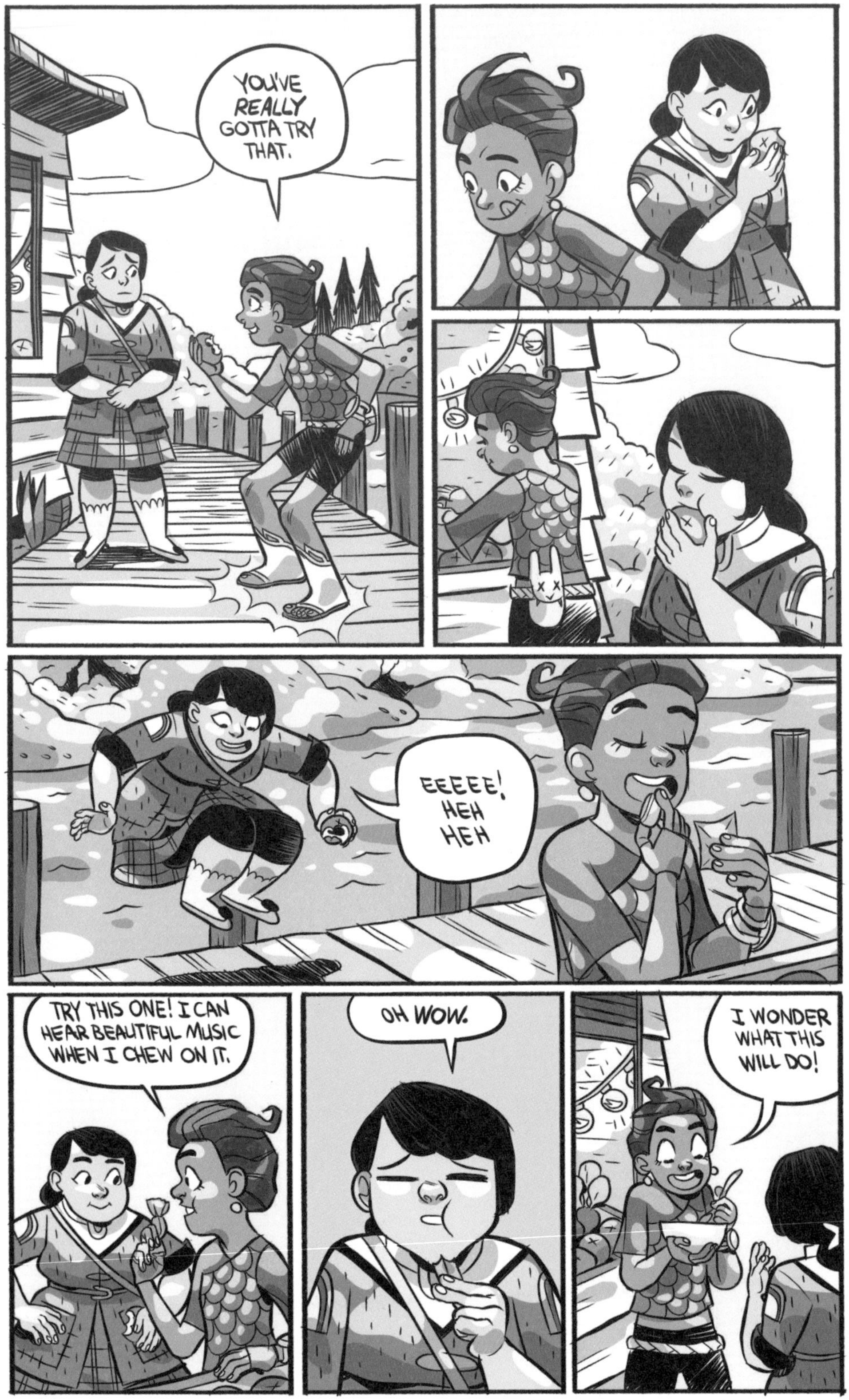
YOU'VE REALLY GOTTA TRY THAT.
EEEEE! HEH HEH
TRY THIS ONE! I CAN HEAR BEAUTIFUL MUSIC WHEN I CHEW ON IT.
OH WOW.
I WONDER WHAT THIS WILL DO!

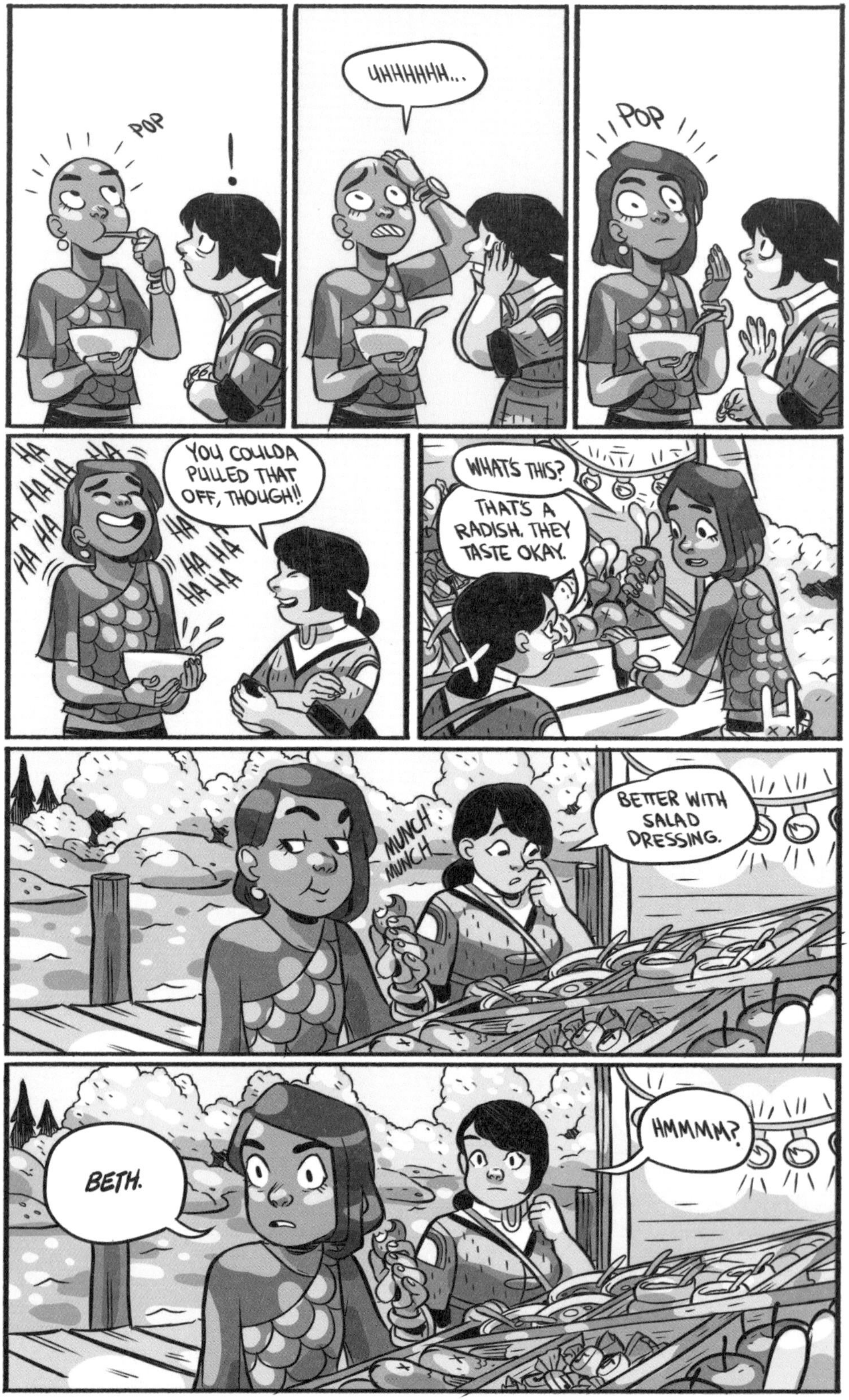
POP
!
UHHHHHH...
POP
HA HA HA HA HA HA HA HA HA HA HA HA HA
YOU COULDA PULLED THAT OFF, THOUGH!!
WHAT'S THIS?
THAT'S A RADISH. THEY TASTE OKAY.
MUNCH MUNCH
BETTER WITH SALAD DRESSING.
BETH.
HMMMM?

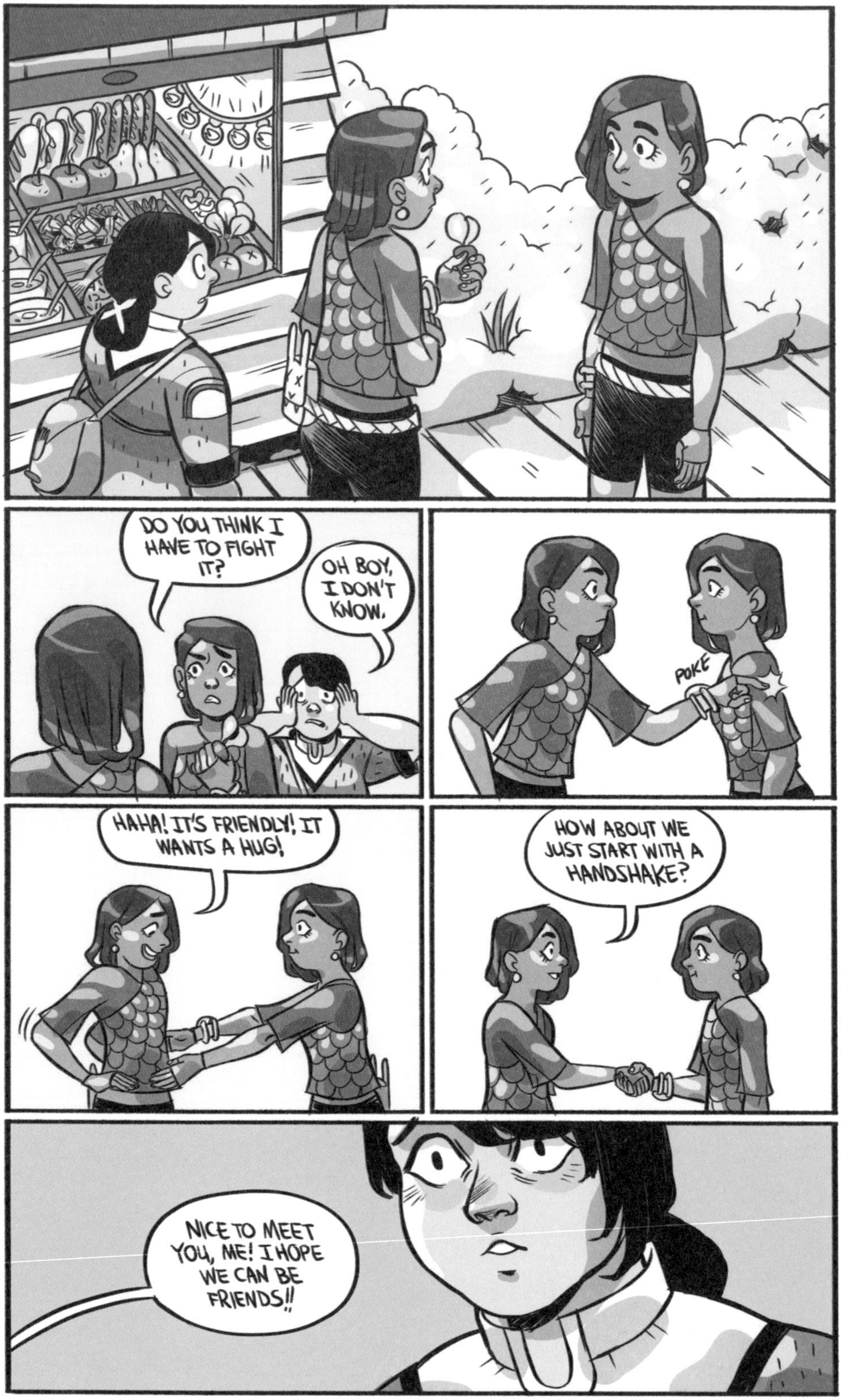
DO YOU THINK I HAVE TO FIGHT IT?
OH BOY, I DON'T KNOW.
POKE
HAHA! IT'S FRIENDLY! IT WANTS A HUG!
HOW ABOUT WE JUST START WITH A HANDSHAKE?
NICE TO MEET YOU, ME! I HOPE WE CAN BE FRIENDS!!

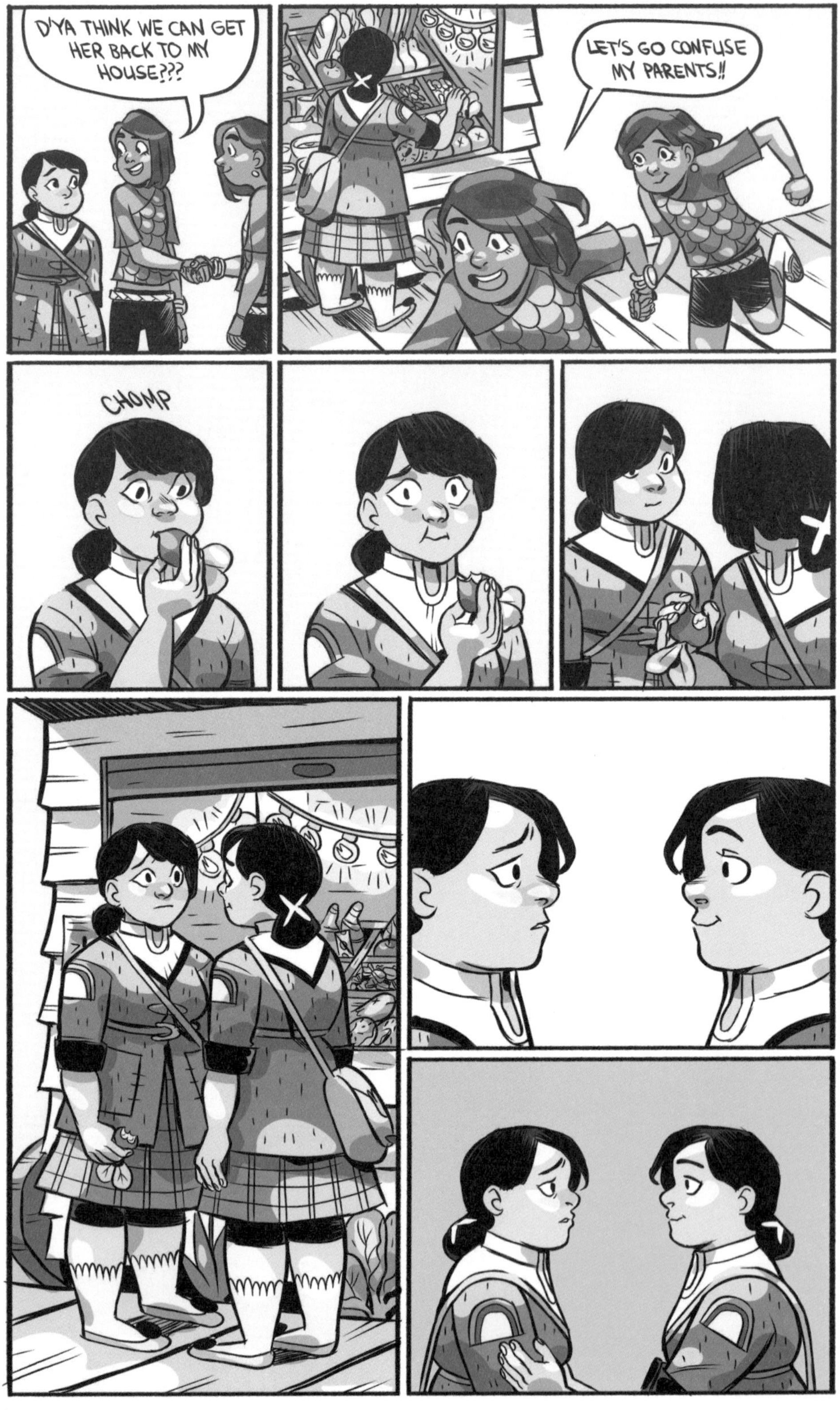
D'YA THINK WE CAN GET HER BACK TO MY HOUSE???
LET'S GO CONFUSE MY PARENTS!!
CHOMP

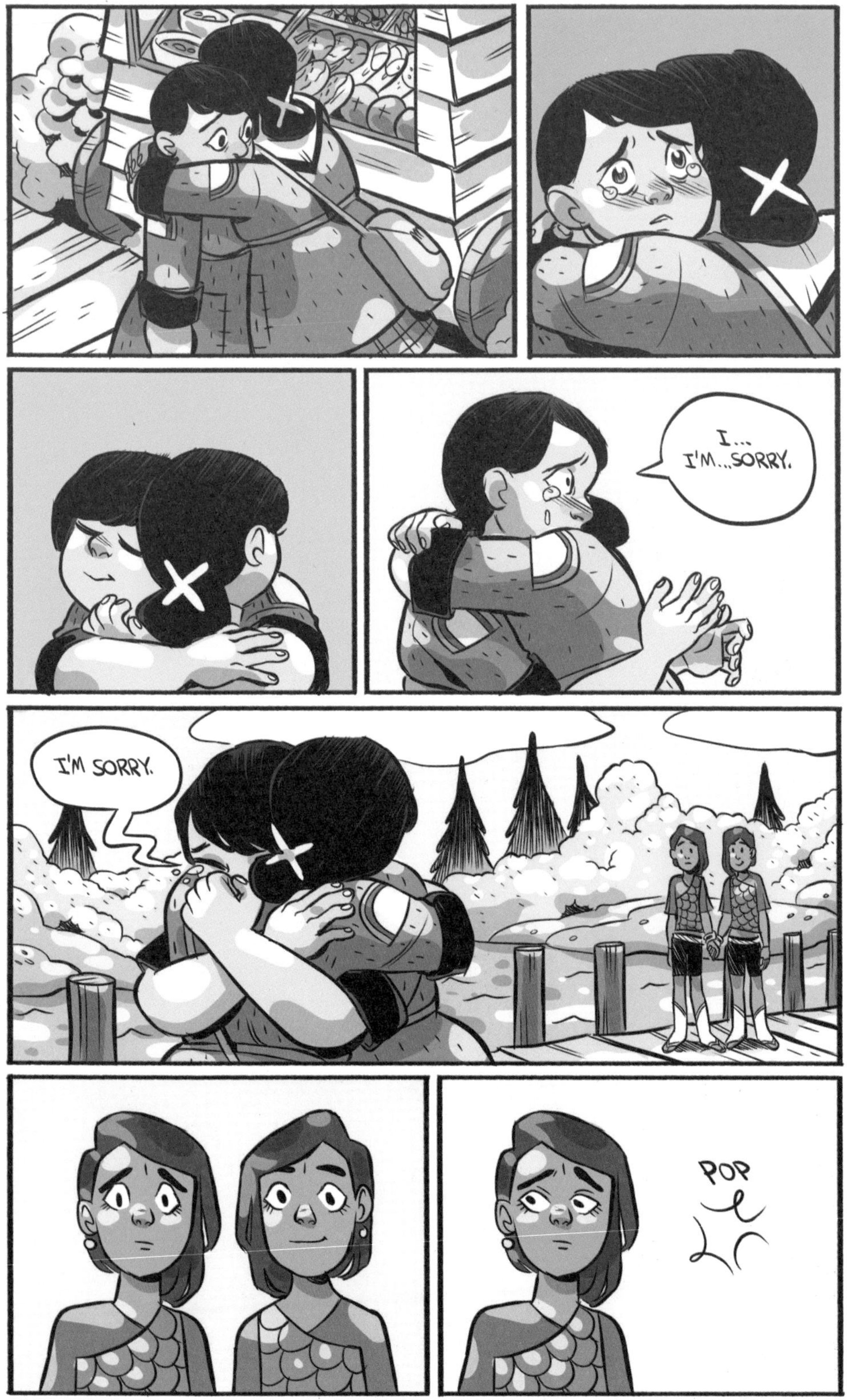
I... I'M...SORRY.
I'M SORRY.
POP

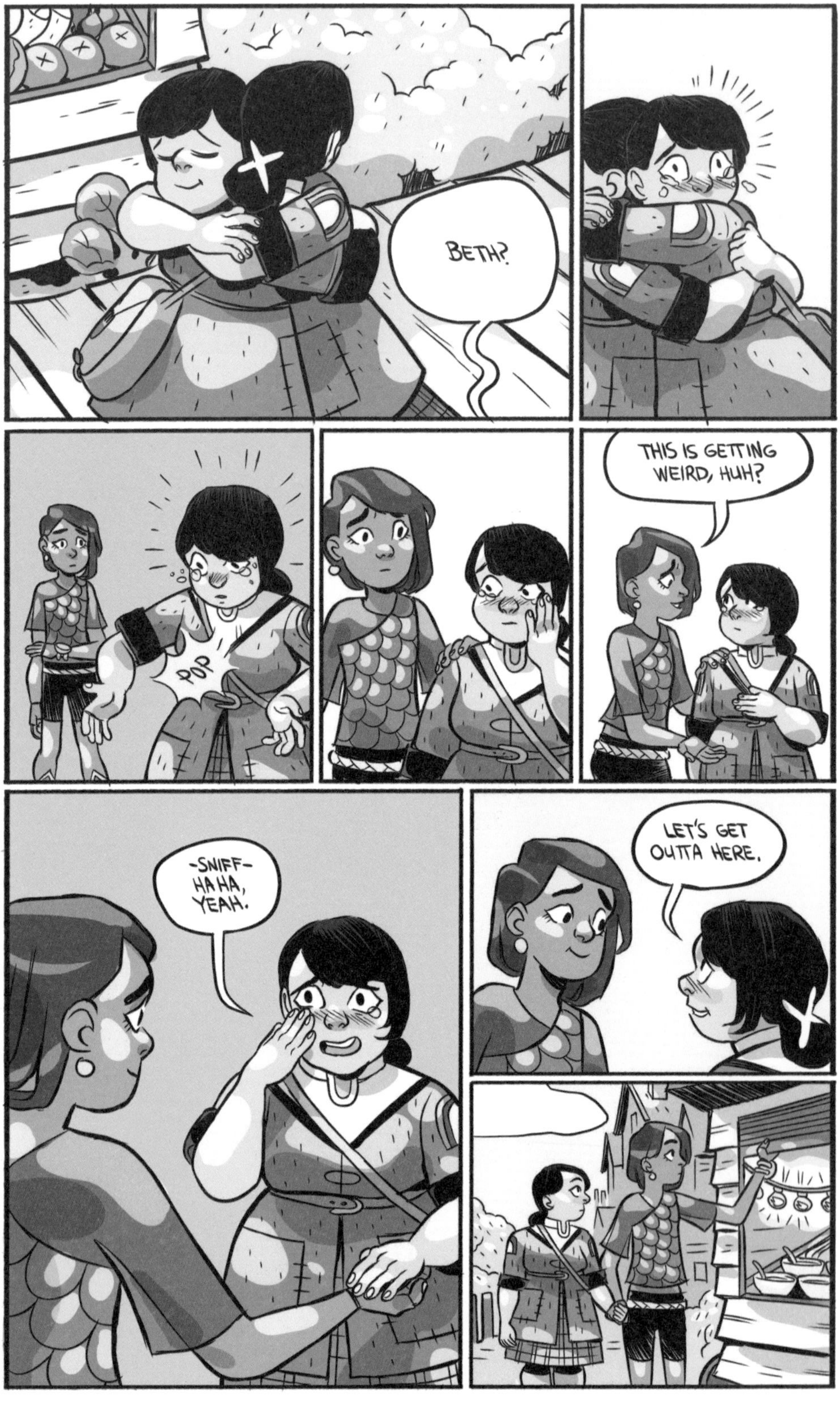
BETH?
POP
THIS IS GETTING WEIRD, HUH?
-SNIFF- HA HA, YEAH.
LET'S GET OUTTA HERE.

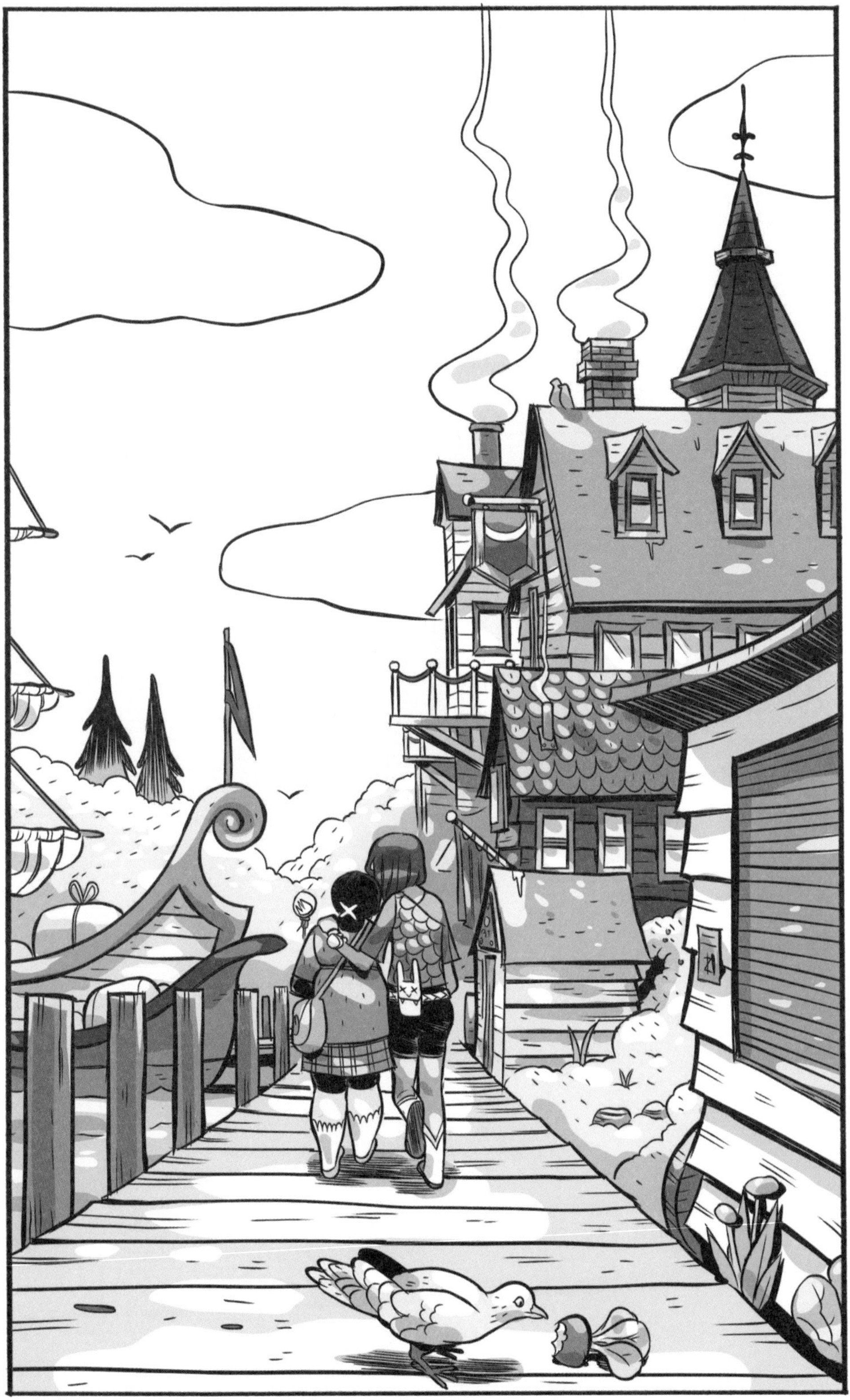

2015

DIANA'S ELECTRIC TONGUE

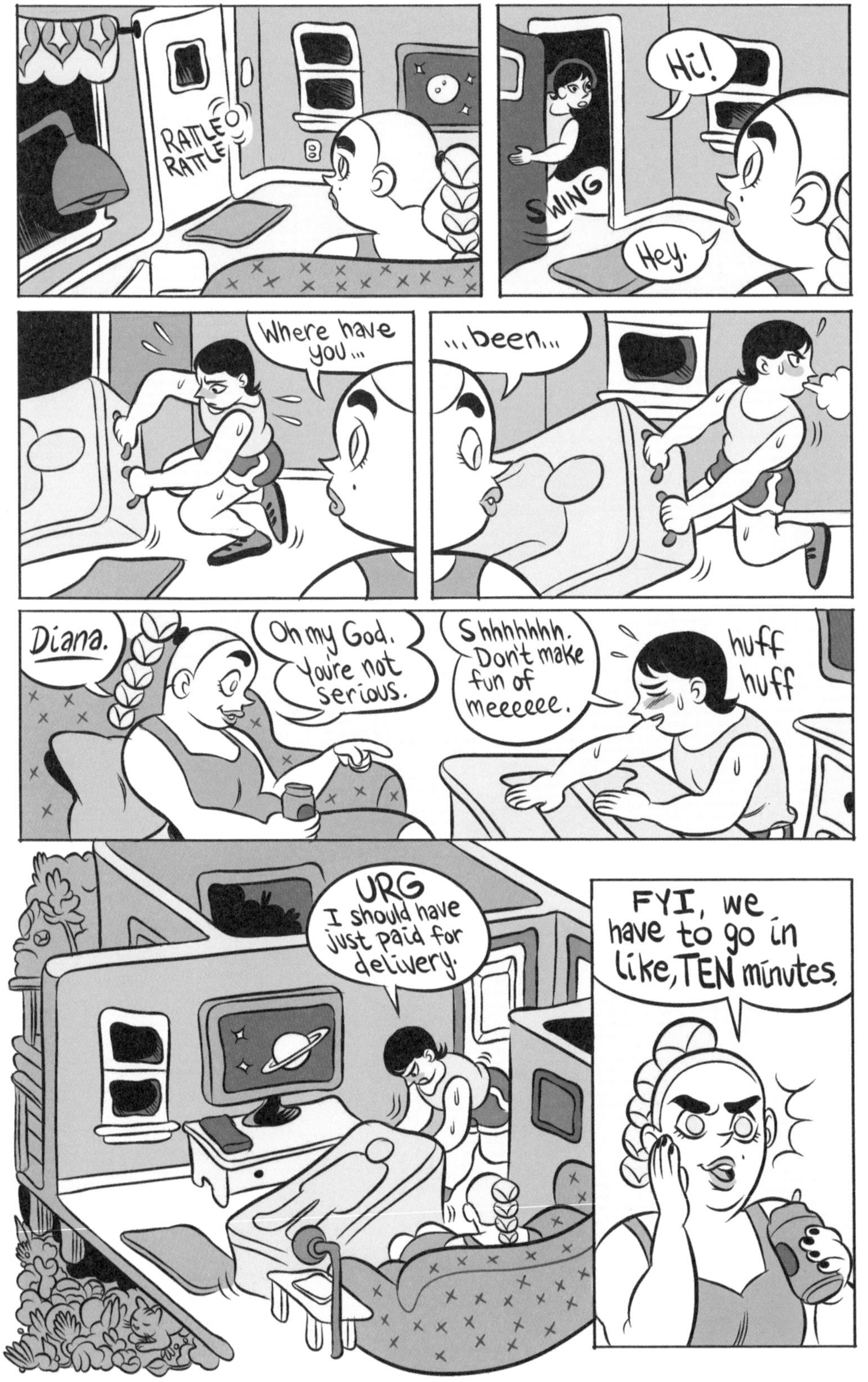
RATTLE RATTLE
Hi!
SWING
Hey.
Where have you...
...been...
Diana.
Oh my God. You're not serious.
Shhhhhhh. Don't make fun of meeeeee.
huff huff
URG I should have just paid for delivery.
FYI, we have to go in like, TEN minutes.

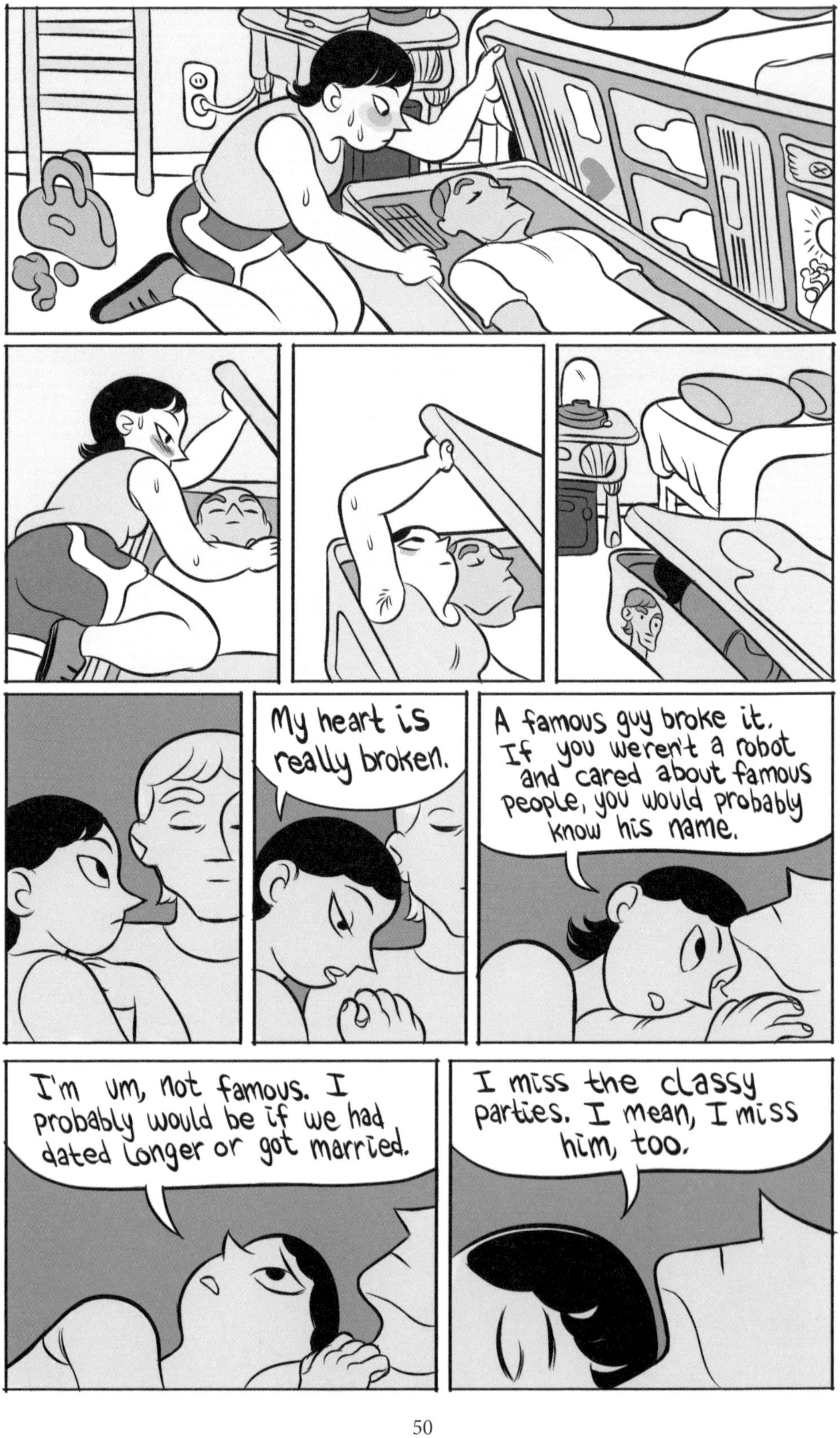

My heart is really broken.
A famous guy broke it. If you weren't a robot and cared about famous people, you would probably know his name.
I'm um, not famous. I probably would be if we had dated longer or got married.
I miss the classy parties. I mean, I miss him, too.

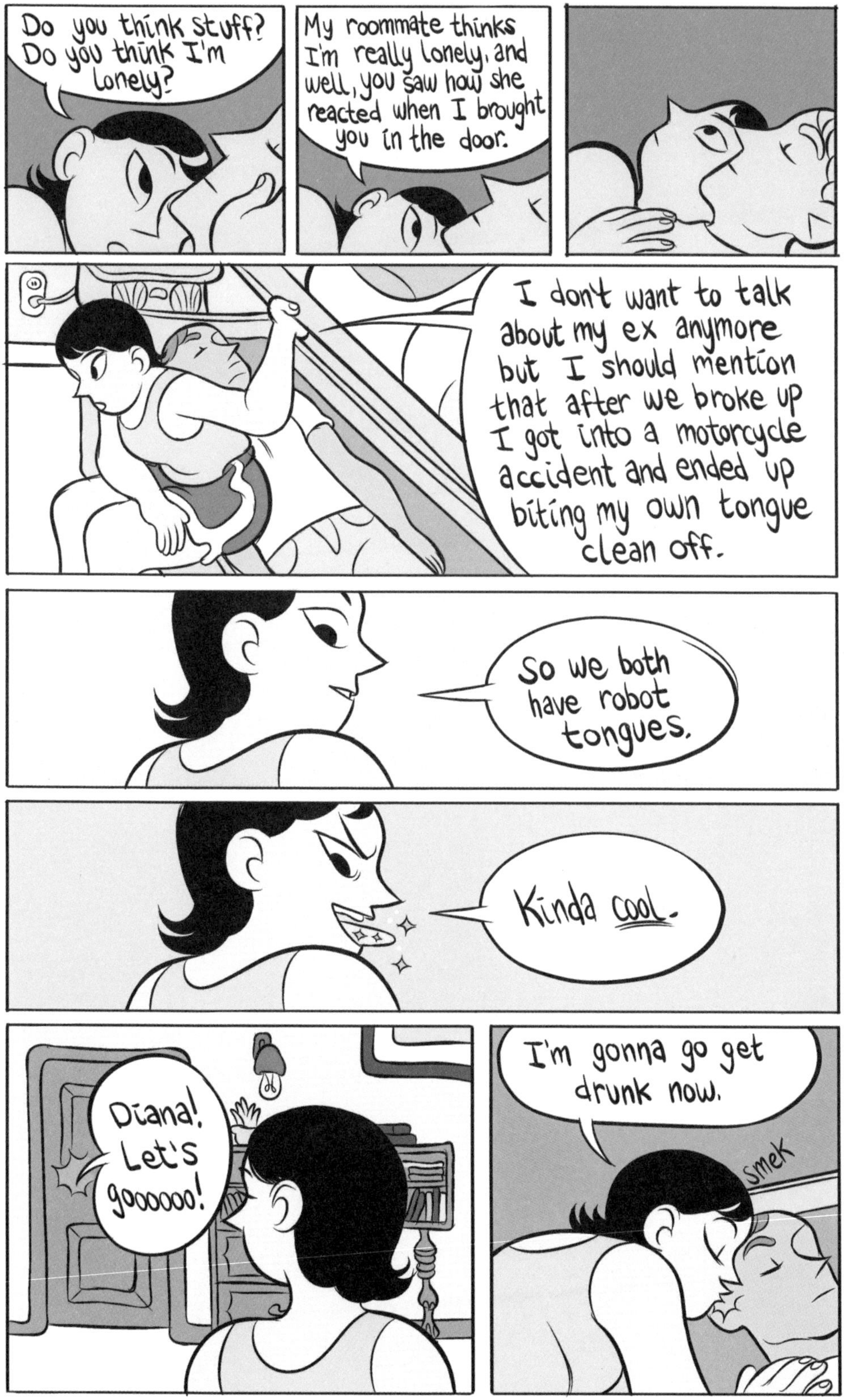
Do you think stuff? Do you think I'm lonely?
My roommate thinks I'm really lonely, and well, you saw how she reacted when I brought you in the door.
I don't want to talk about my ex anymore but I should mention that after we broke up I got into a motorcycle accident and ended up biting my own tongue clean off.
So we both have robot tongues.
Kinda cool.
Diana! Let's goooooo!
I'm gonna go get drunk now.
SMEK

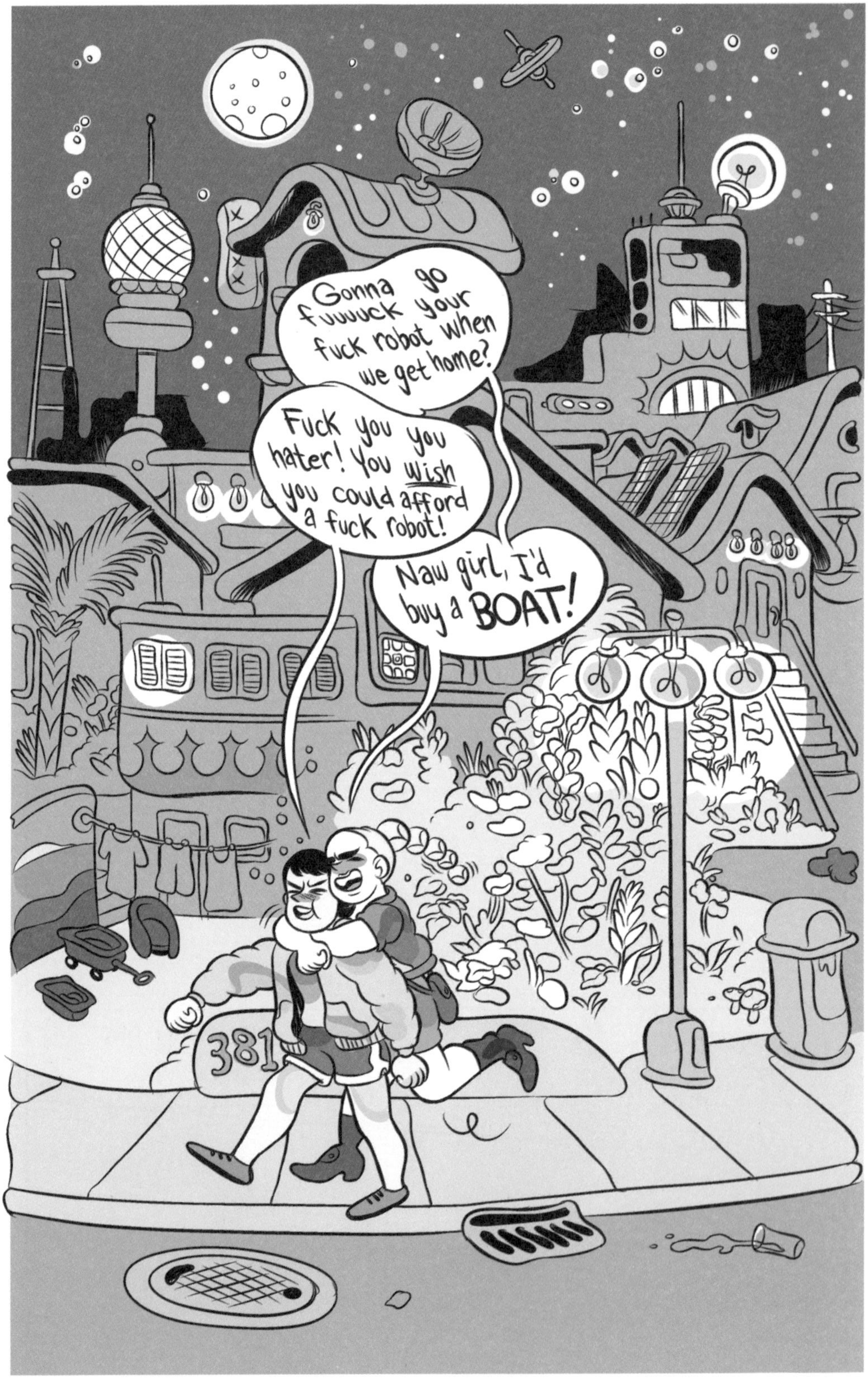
Gonna go fuuuuck your fuck robot when we get home?
Fuck you you hater! You wish you could afford a fuck robot!
Naw girl, I'd buy a BOAT!
381

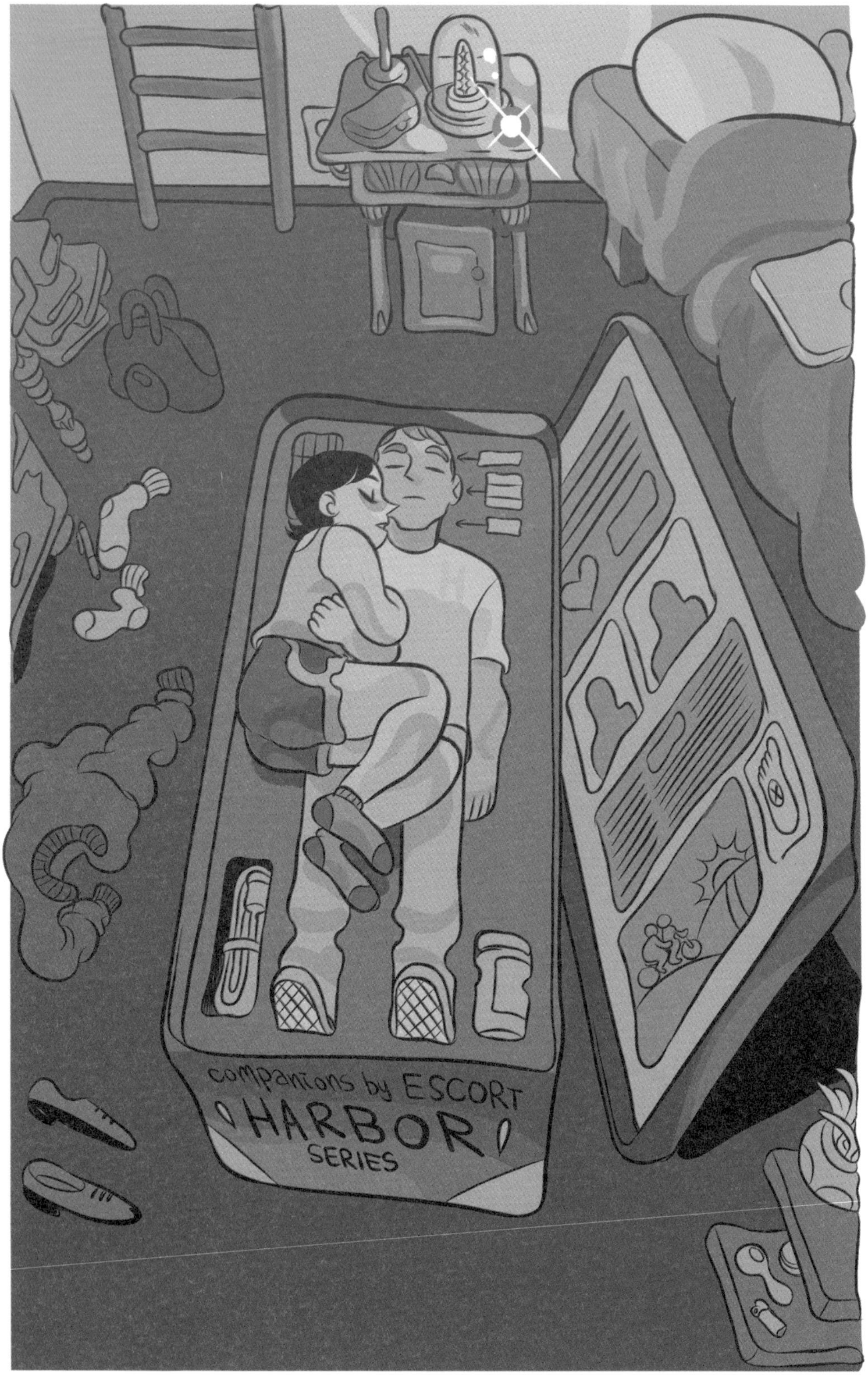
companions by ESCORT
HARBOR
SERIES

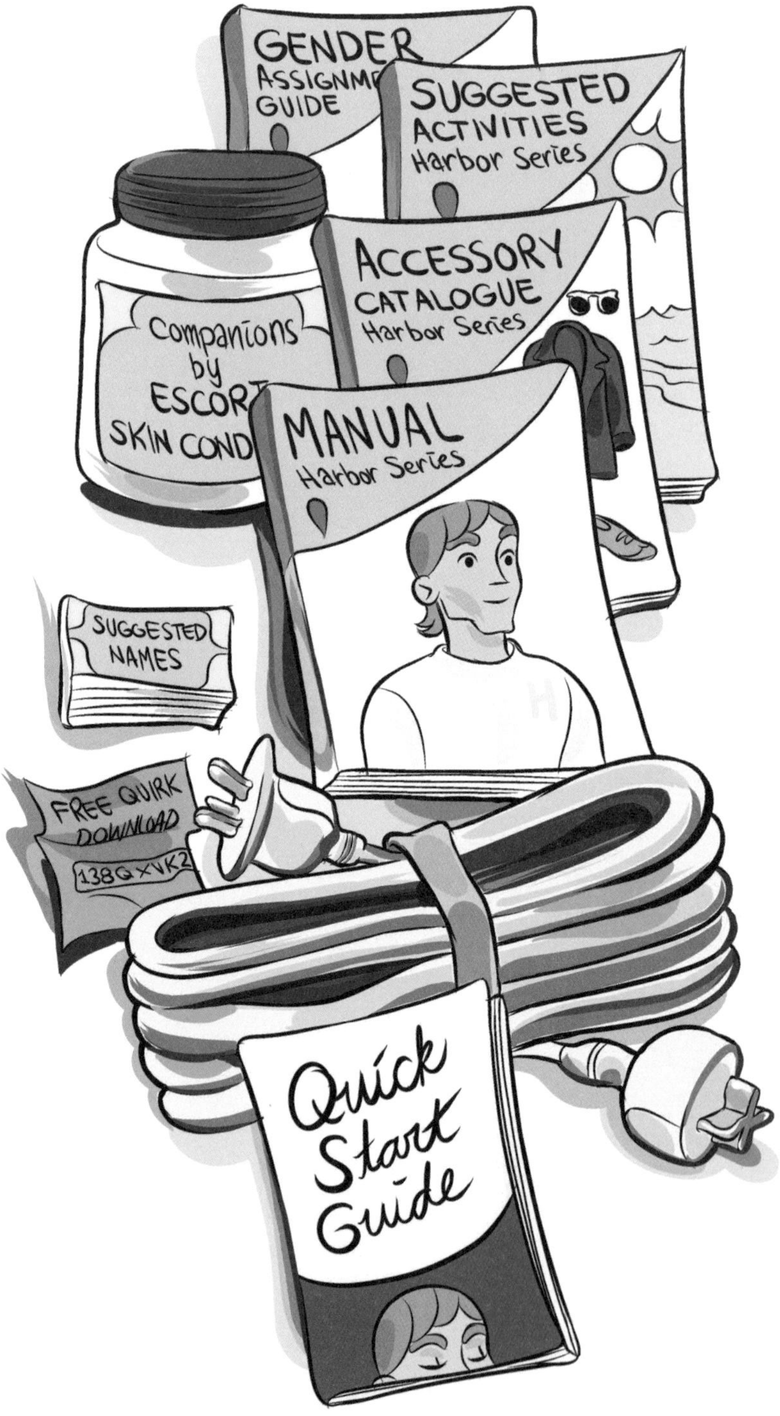
GENDER ASSIGNME
GUIDE
SUGGESTED ACTIVITIES Harbor Series
Companions by ESCORT SKIN COND
ACCESSORY CATALOGUE Harbor Series
MANUAL Harbor Series
SUGGESTED NAMES
FREE QUIRK DOWNLOAD
138GXVK2
Quick Start Guide

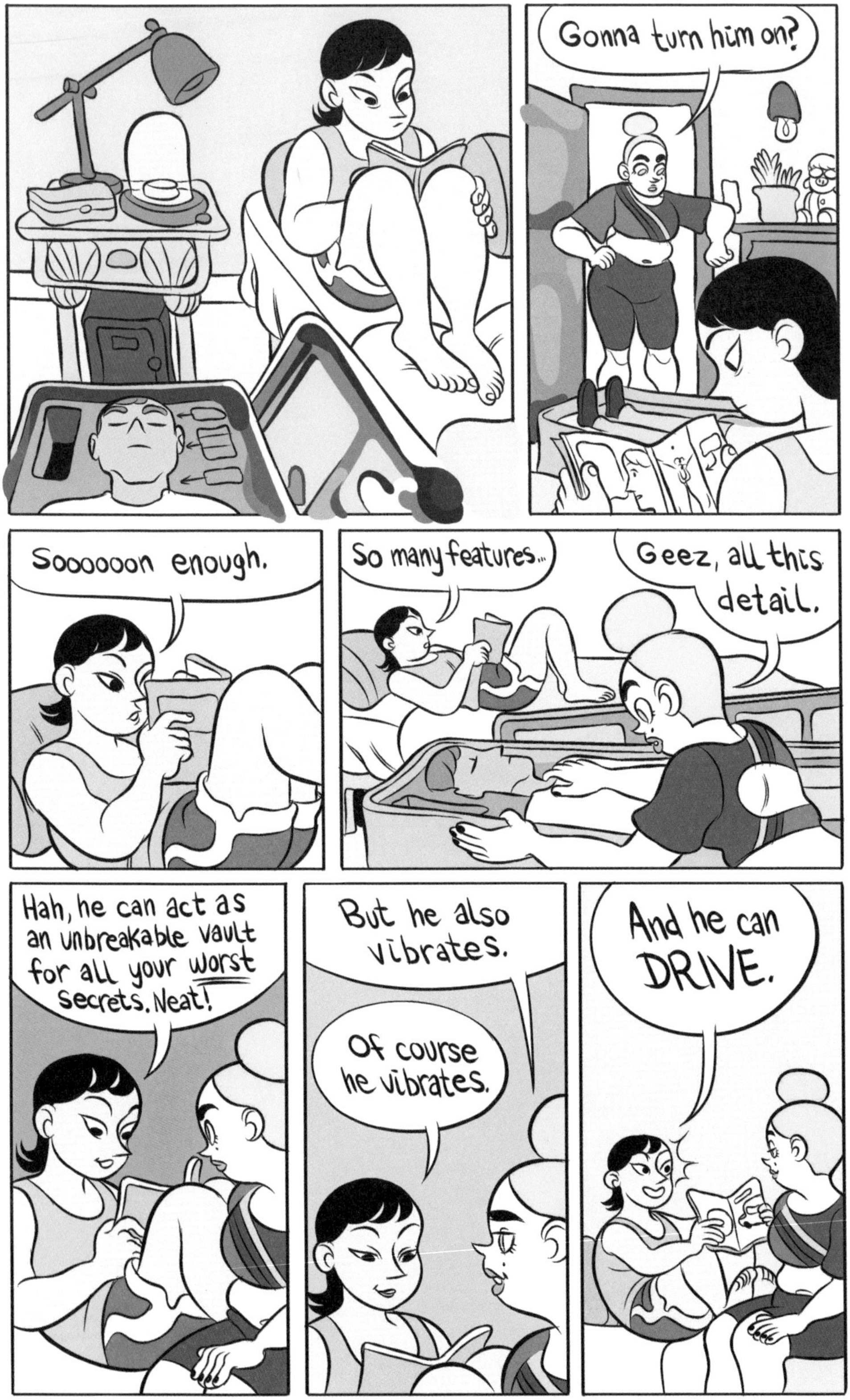
Gonna turn him on?
Soooooon enough.
So many features...
Geez, all this detail.
Hah, he can act as an unbreakable vault for all your worst secrets. Neat!
But he also vibrates.
Of course he vibrates.
And he can DRIVE.

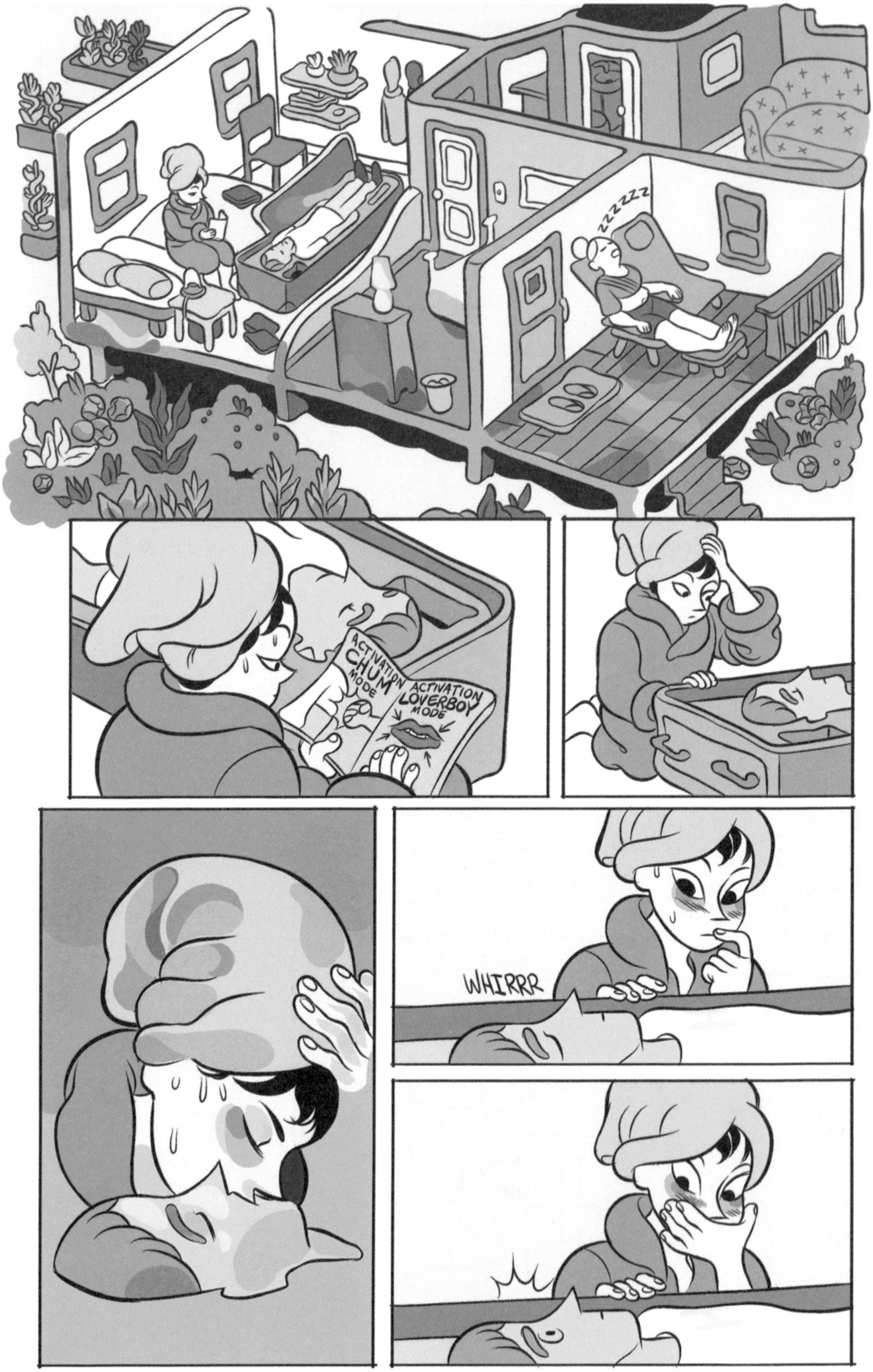
ZZZZZZ
ACTIVATION CHUM MODE
ACTIVATION LOVERBOY MODE
WHIRRR

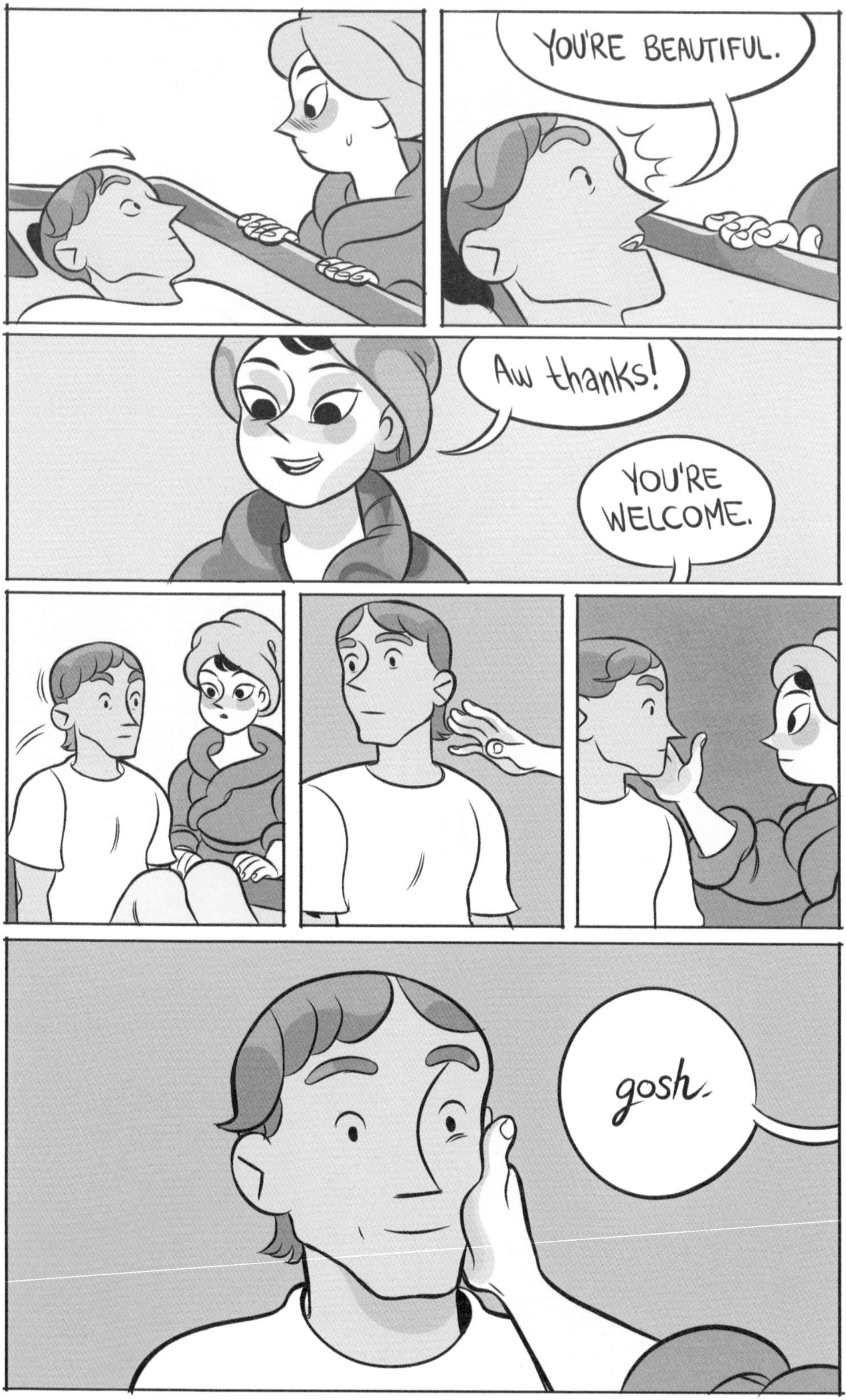
YOU'RE BEAUTIFUL.
Aw thanks!
YOU'RE WELCOME.
gosh.

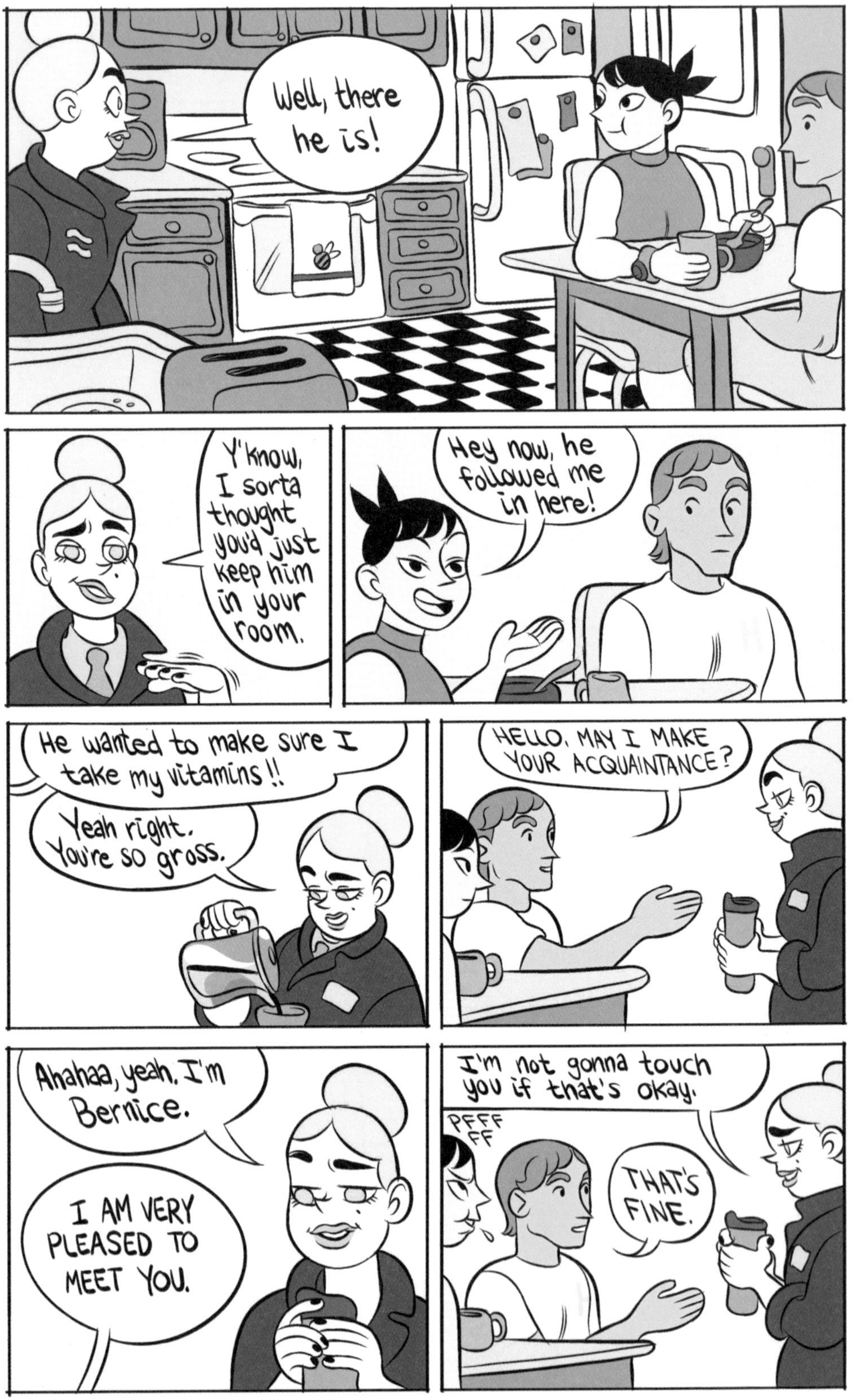
Well, there he is!
Y'know, I sorta thought you'd just keep him in your room.
Hey now, he followed me in here!
He wanted to make sure I take my vitamins !!
Yeah right. You're so gross.
HELLO. MAY I MAKE YOUR ACQUAINTANCE?
Ahahaa, yeah. I'm Bernice.
I AM VERY PLEASED TO MEET YOU.
I'm not gonna touch you if that's okay.
PFFFFF
THAT'S FINE.

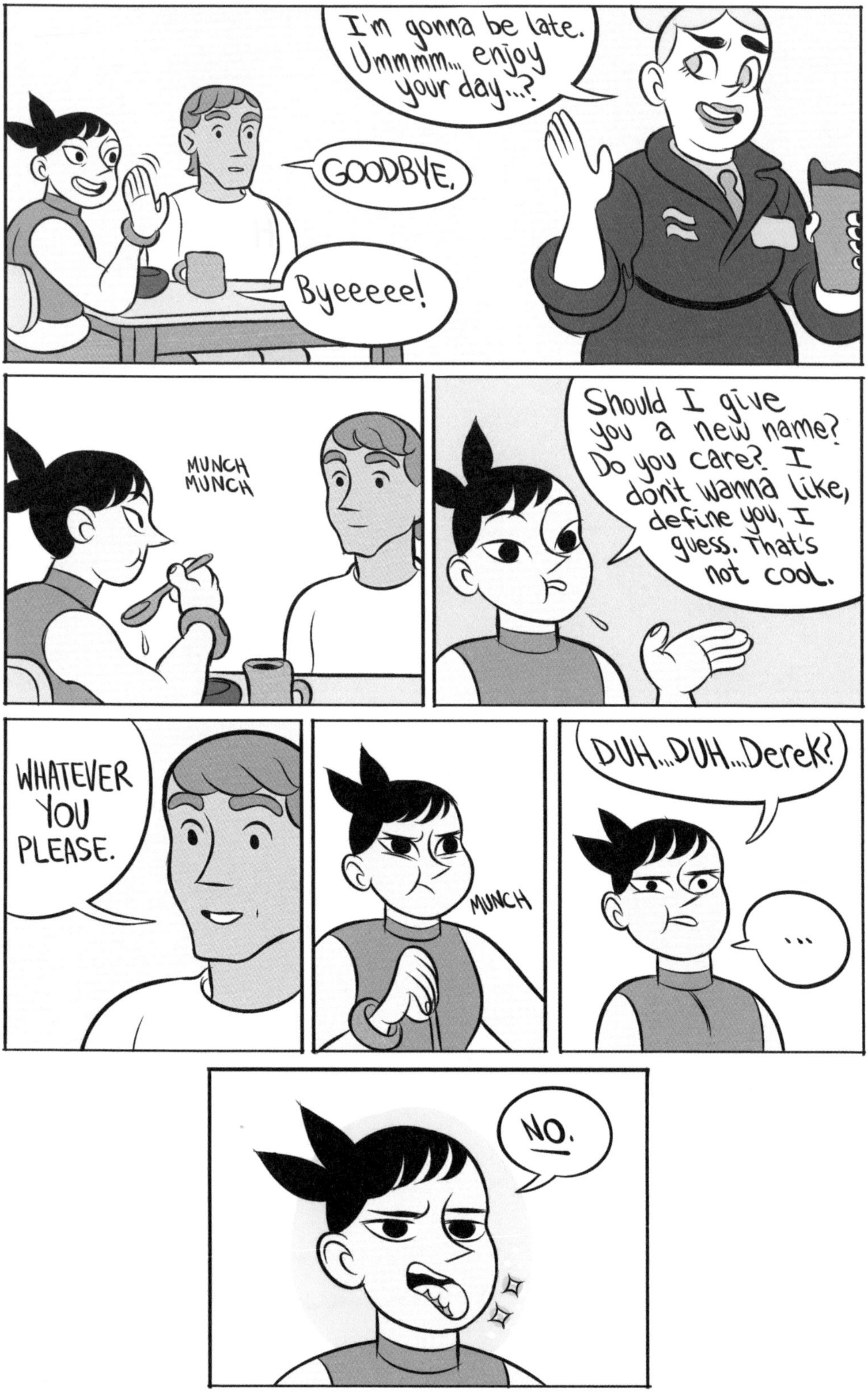
I'm gonna be late. Ummmm... enjoy your day...?
GOODBYE.
Byeeeee!
MUNCH MUNCH
Should I give you a new name? Do you care? I don't wanna like, define you, I guess. That's not cool.
WHATEVER YOU PLEASE.
MUNCH
DUH...DUH...Derek?
...
NO.

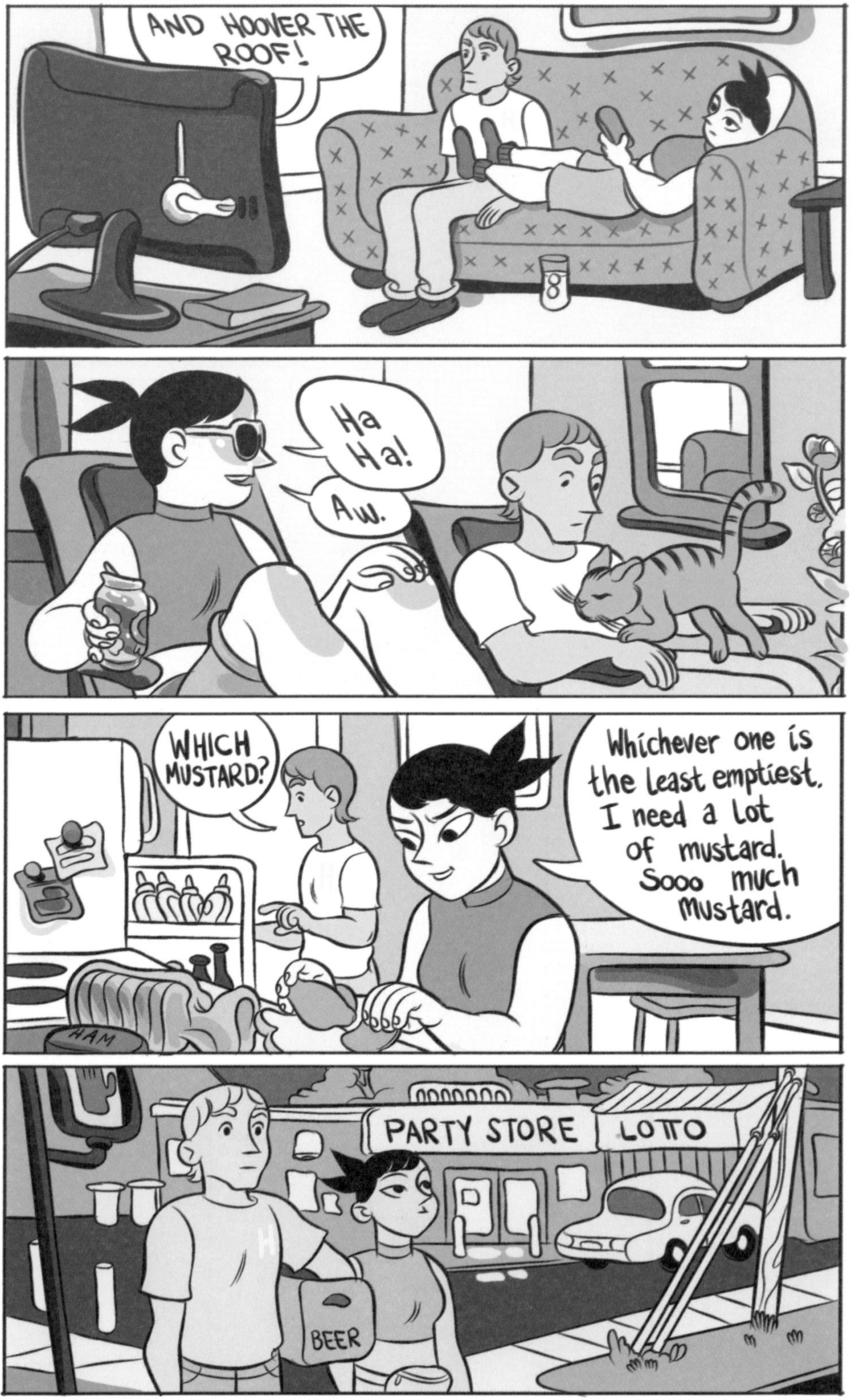
AND HOOVER THE ROOF!
Ha Ha!
Aw.
WHICH MUSTARD?
Whichever one is the least emptiest. I need a lot of mustard. Sooo much mustard.
HAM
PARTY STORE
LOTTO
BEER

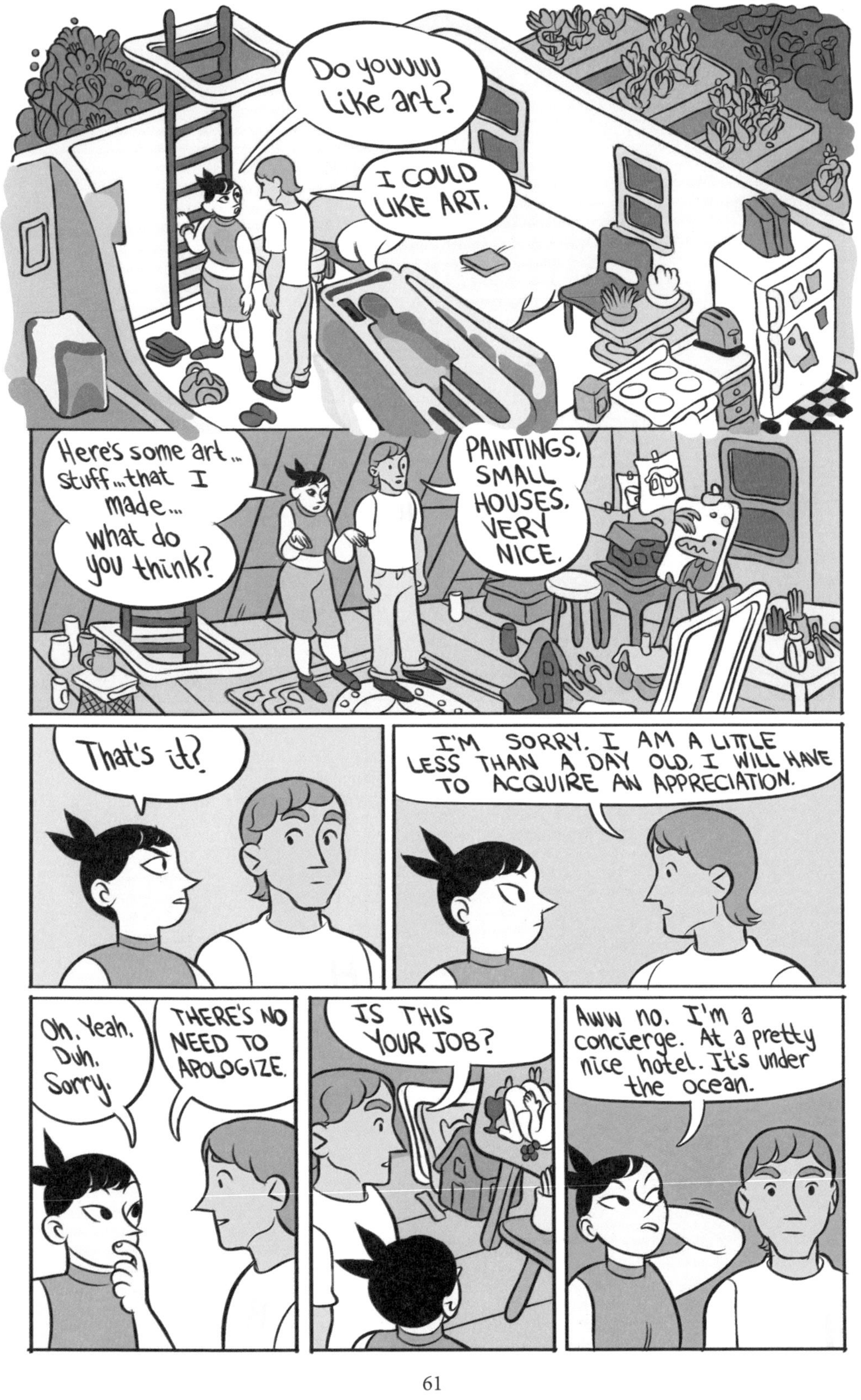
Do youuuu like art?
I COULD LIKE ART.
Here's some art... stuff...that I made...
what do you think?
PAINTINGS, SMALL HOUSES. VERY NICE.
That's it?
I'M SORRY. I AM A LITTLE LESS THAN A DAY OLD. I WILL HAVE TO ACQUIRE AN APPRECIATION.
Oh. Yeah. Duh. Sorry.
THERE'S NO NEED TO APOLOGIZE.
IS THIS YOUR JOB?
Aww no. I'm a concierge. At a pretty nice hotel. It's under the ocean.

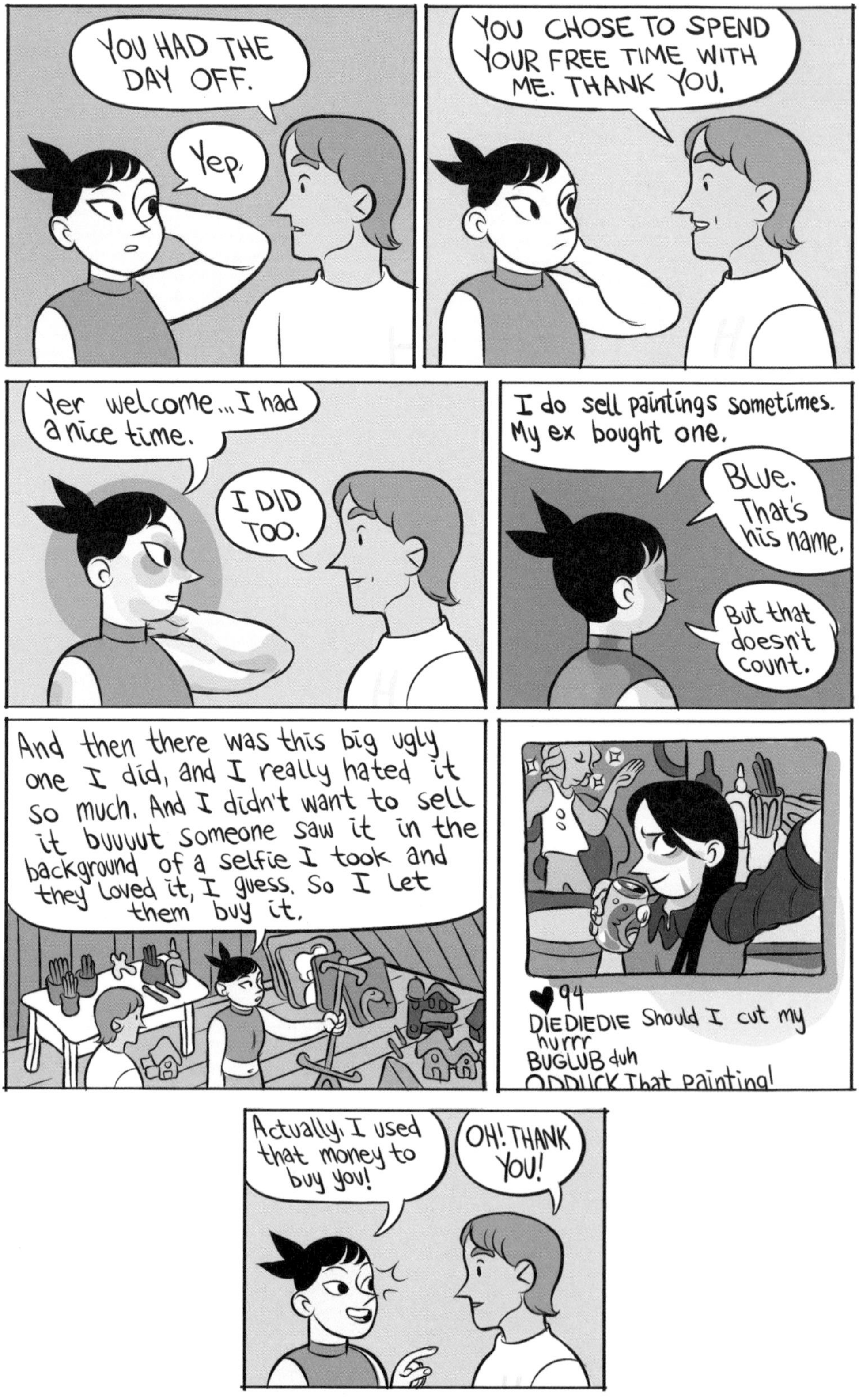
YOU HAD THE DAY OFF.
Yep.
YOU CHOSE TO SPEND YOUR FREE TIME WITH ME. THANK YOU.
Yer welcome... I had a nice time.
I DID TOO.
I do sell paintings sometimes. My ex bought one.
Blue. That's his name.
But that doesn't count.
And then there was this big ugly one I did, and I really hated it so much. And I didn't want to sell it buuuut someone saw it in the background of a selfie I took and they loved it, I guess. So I let them buy it.
94
DIEDIEDIE Should I cut my hurrr
BUGLUB duh
ODDUCK That painting!
Actually, I used that money to buy you!
OH! THANK YOU!

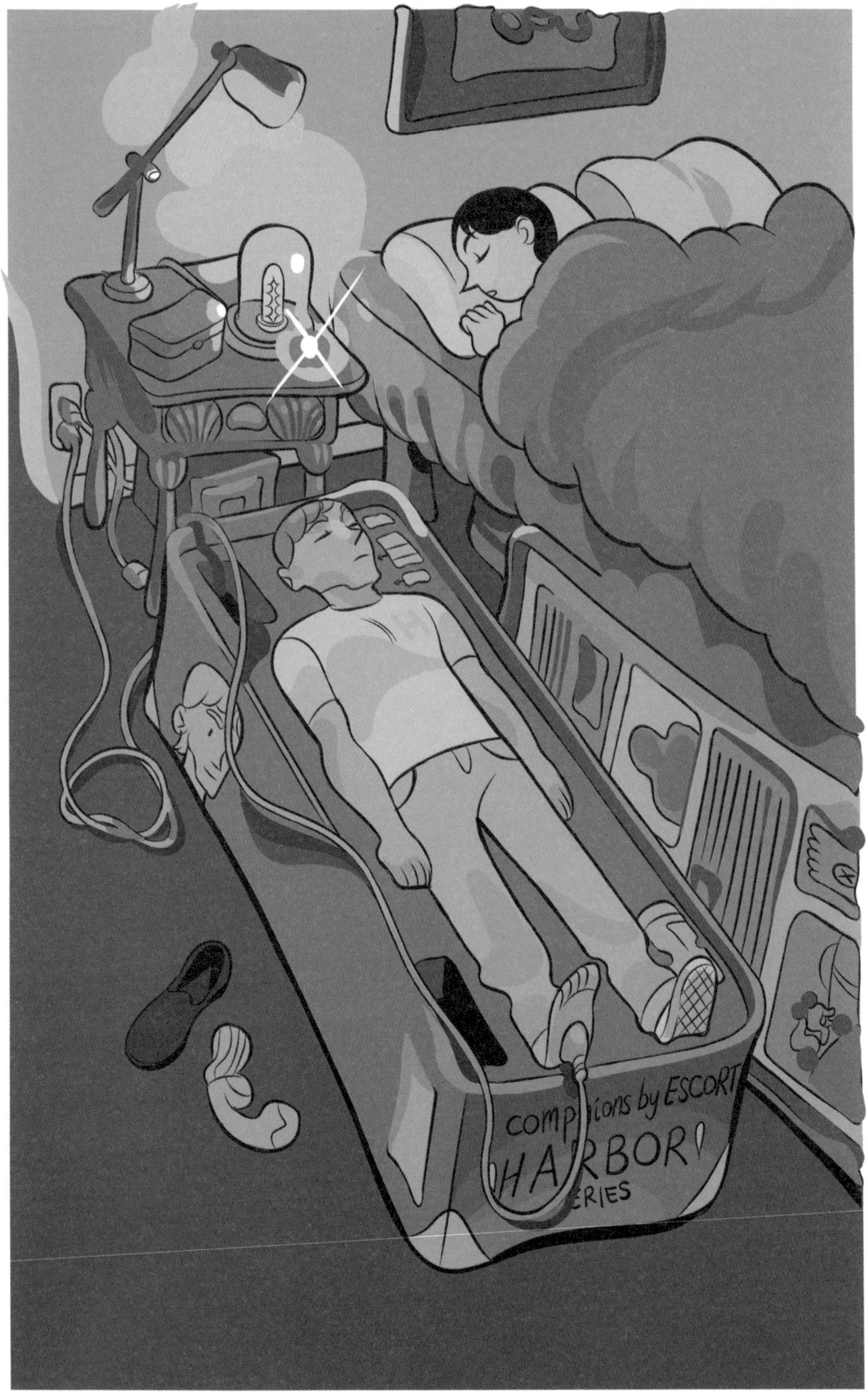
comp ions by ESCORT
HA RBOR
ERIES

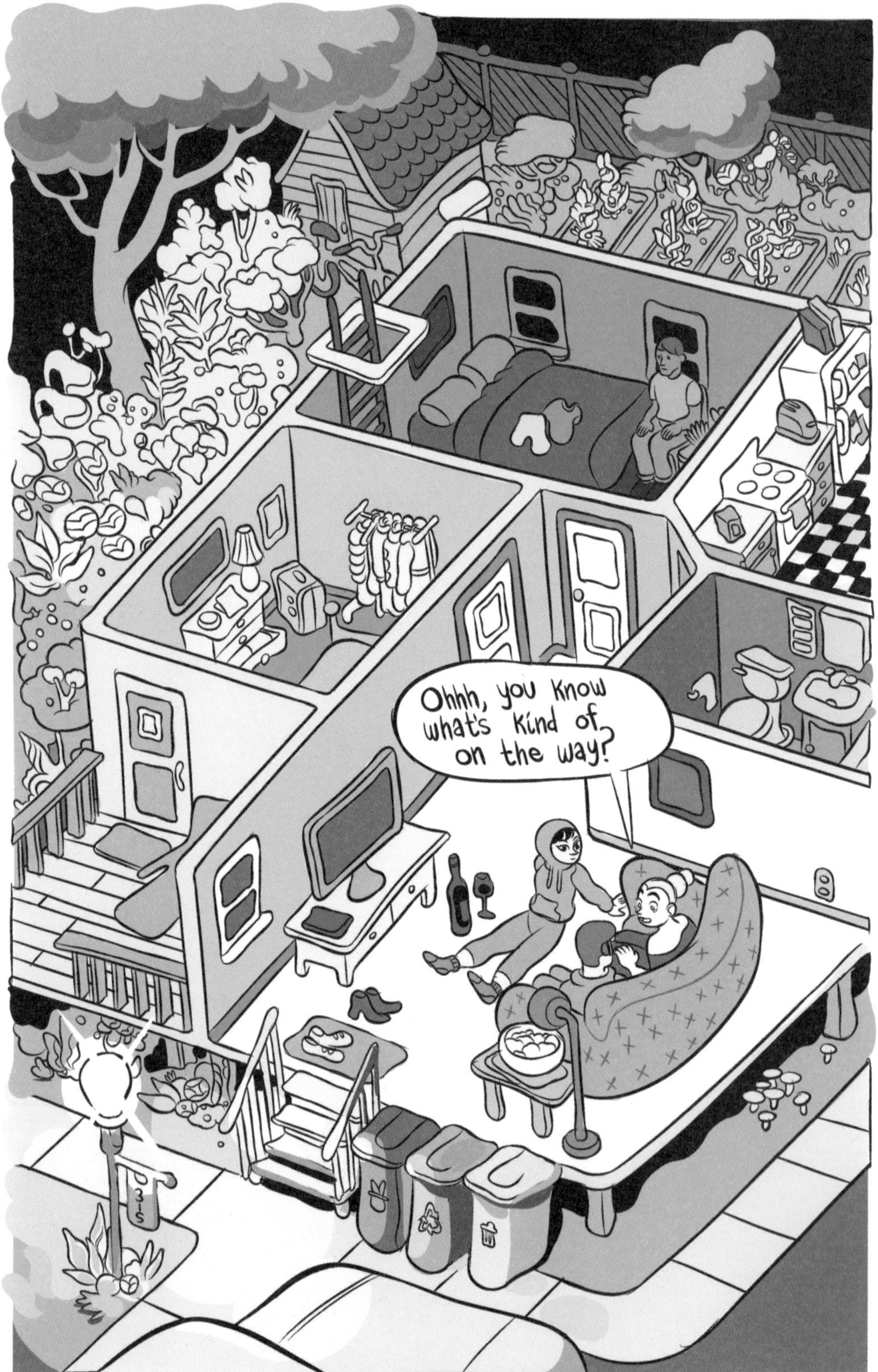
Ohhh, you know what's kind of on the way?
315

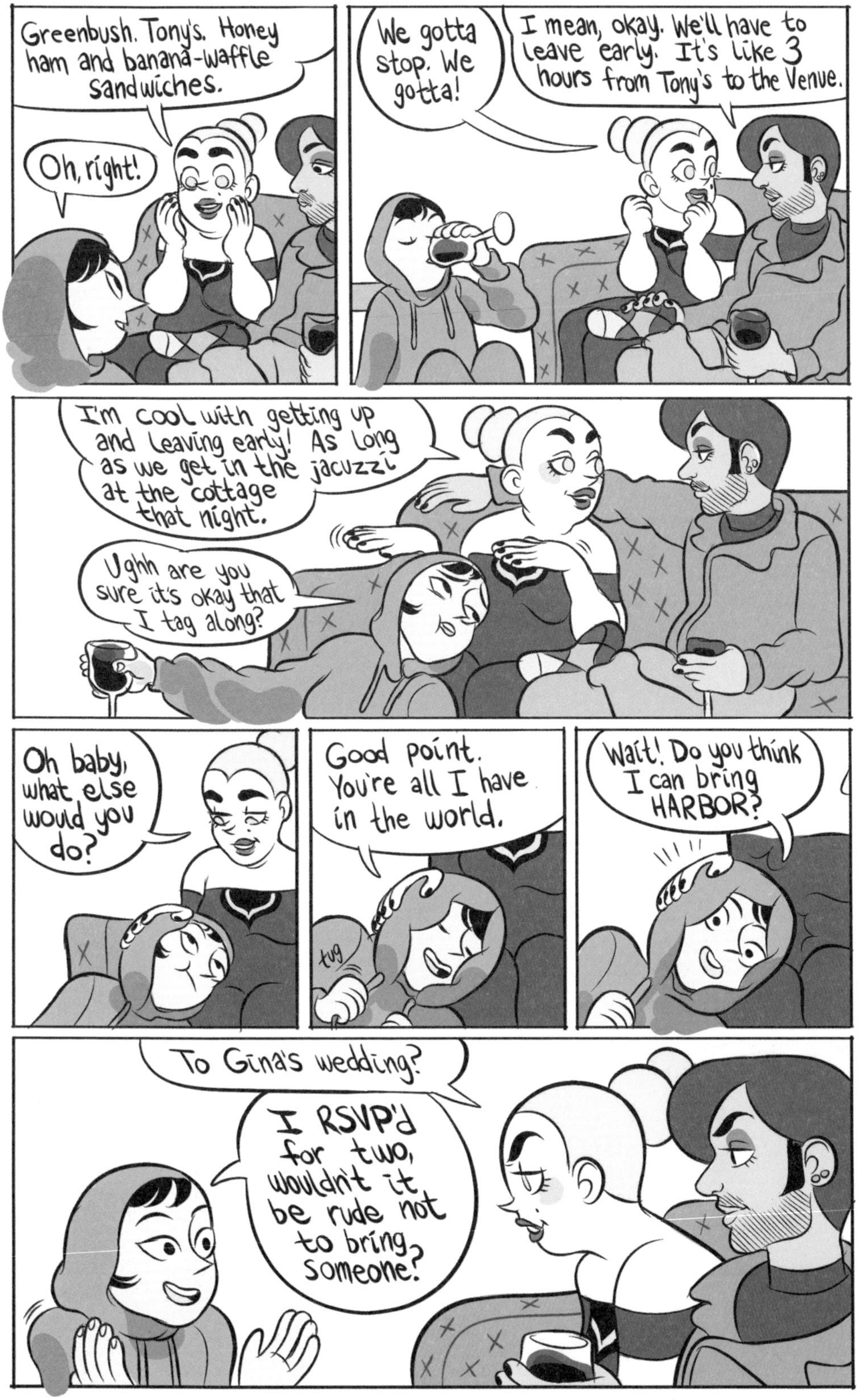
Greenbush. Tony's. Honey ham and banana-waffle sandwiches.
Oh, right!
We gotta stop. We gotta!
I mean, okay. We'll have to leave early. It's like 3 hours from Tony's to the Venue.
I'm cool with getting up and leaving early! As long as we get in the jacuzzi at the cottage that night.
Ughh are you sure it's okay that I tag along?
Oh baby, what else would you do?
Good point. You're all I have in the world.
tug
Wait! Do you think I can bring HARBOR?
To Gina's wedding?
I RSVP'd for two, wouldn't it be rude not to bring someone?

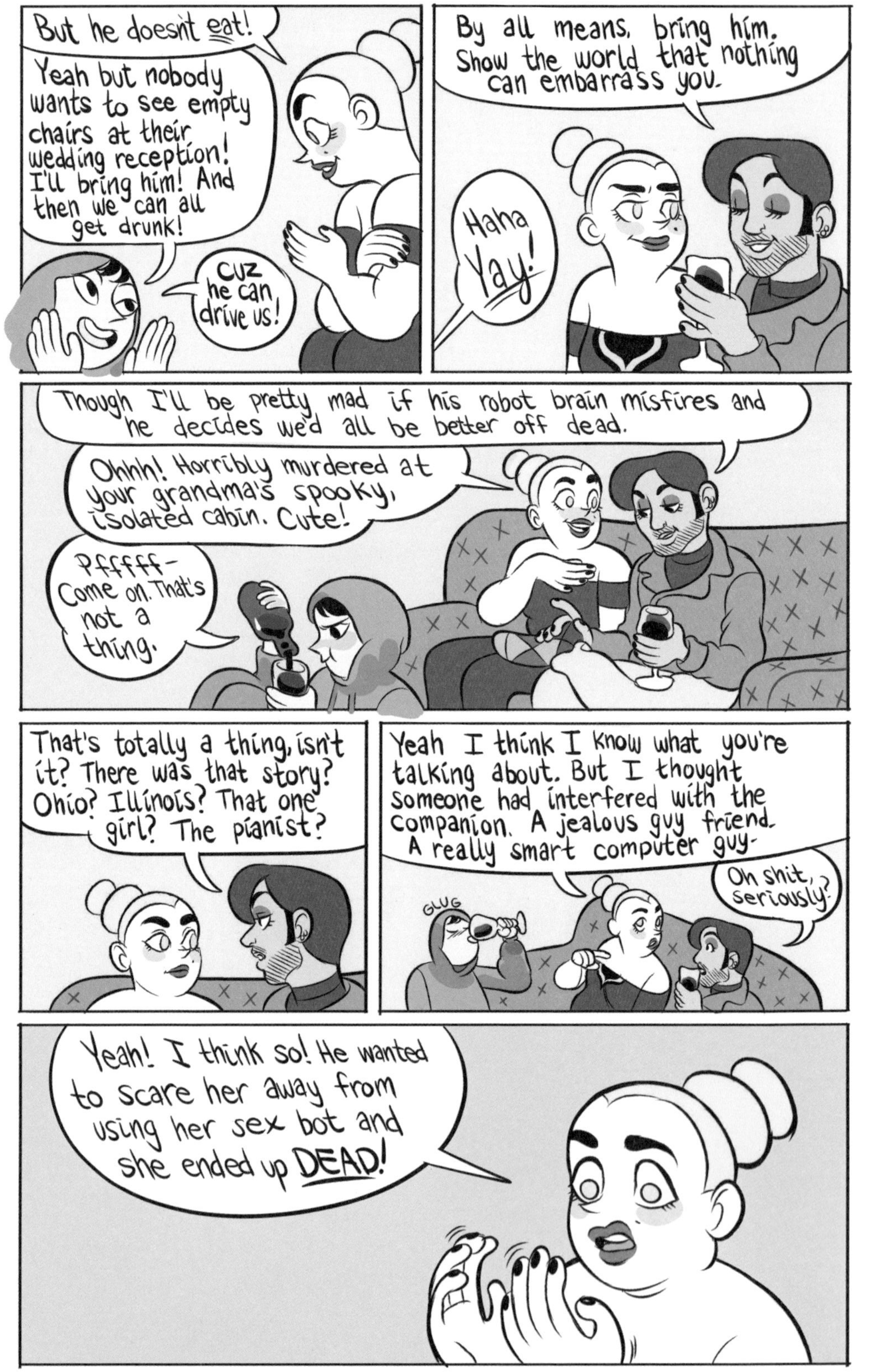

But he doesn't eat!
Yeah but nobody wants to see empty chairs at their wedding reception! I'll bring him! And then we can all get drunk!
CUZ he can drive us!
By all means, bring him. Show the world that nothing can embarrass you.
Haha Yay!
Though I'll be pretty mad if his robot brain misfires and he decides we'd all be better off dead.
Ohhh! Horribly murdered at your grandma's spooky, isolated cabin. Cute!
Pfffff- Come on. That's not a thing.
That's totally a thing, isn't it? There was that story? Ohio? Illinois? That one girl? The pianist?
Yeah I think I know what you're talking about. But I thought someone had interfered with the companion. A jealous guy friend. A really smart computer guy-
GLUG
Oh shit, seriously?
Yeah! I think so! He wanted to scare her away from using her sex bot and she ended up DEAD!

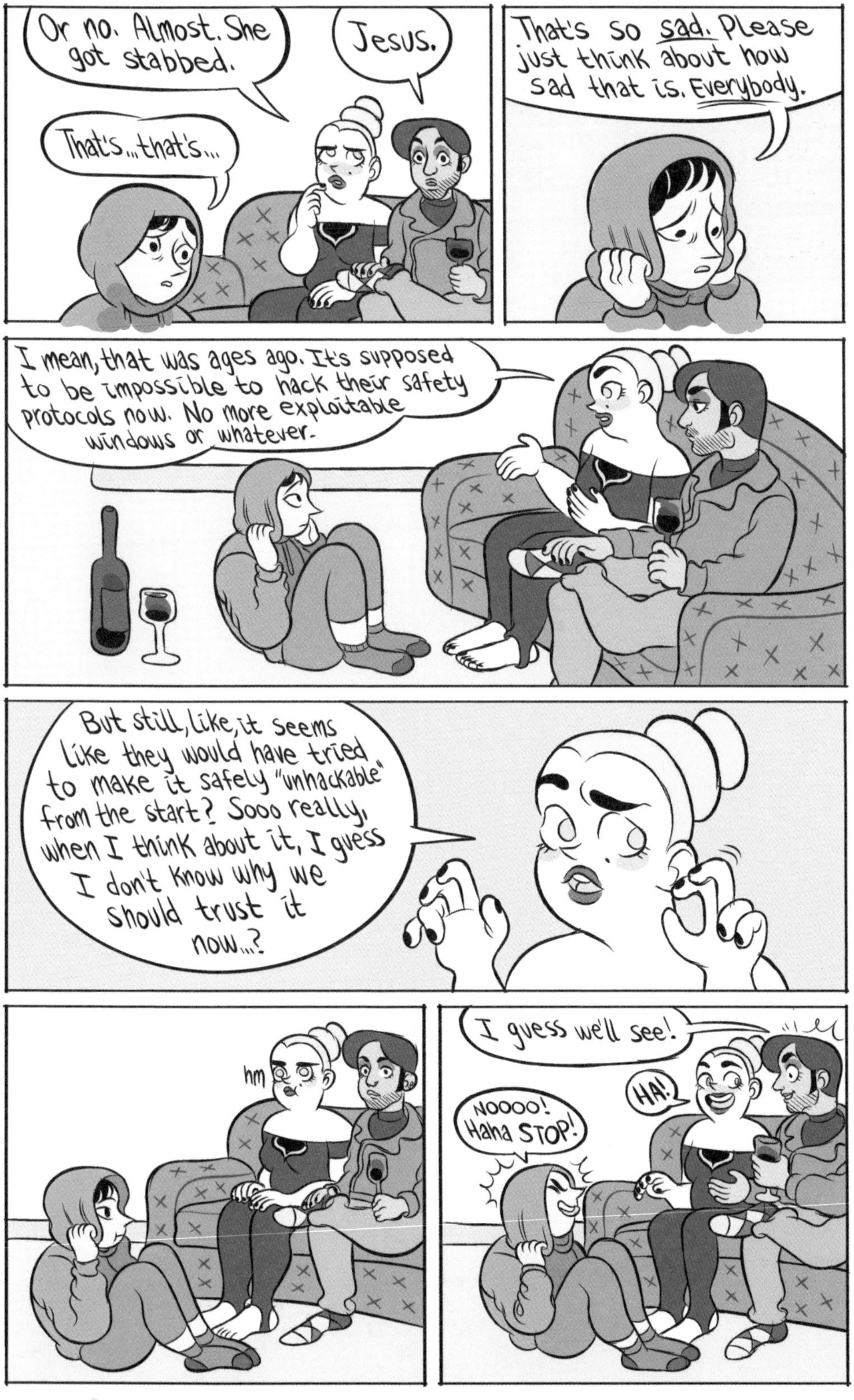
Or no. Almost. She got stabbed.
Jesus.
That's... that's...
That's so sad. Please just think about how sad that is. Everybody.
I mean, that was ages ago. It's supposed to be impossible to hack their safety protocols now. No more exploitable windows or whatever.
But still, like, it seems like they would have tried to make it safely "unhackable" from the start? Sooo really, when I think about it, I guess I don't know why we should trust it now...?
hm
I guess we'll see!
HA!
NOOOO! Haha STOP!

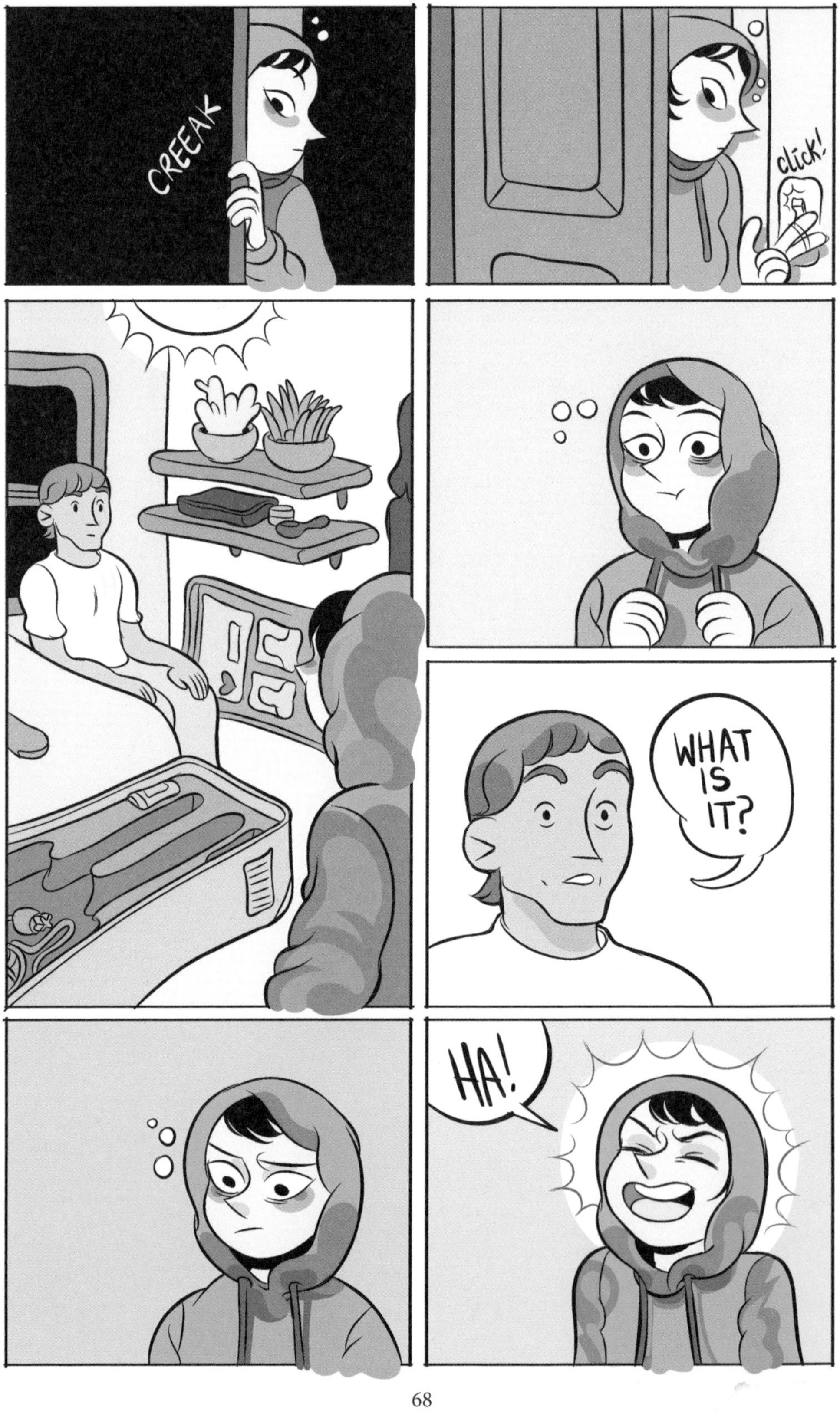
CREEAK
click!
WHAT IS IT?
HA!

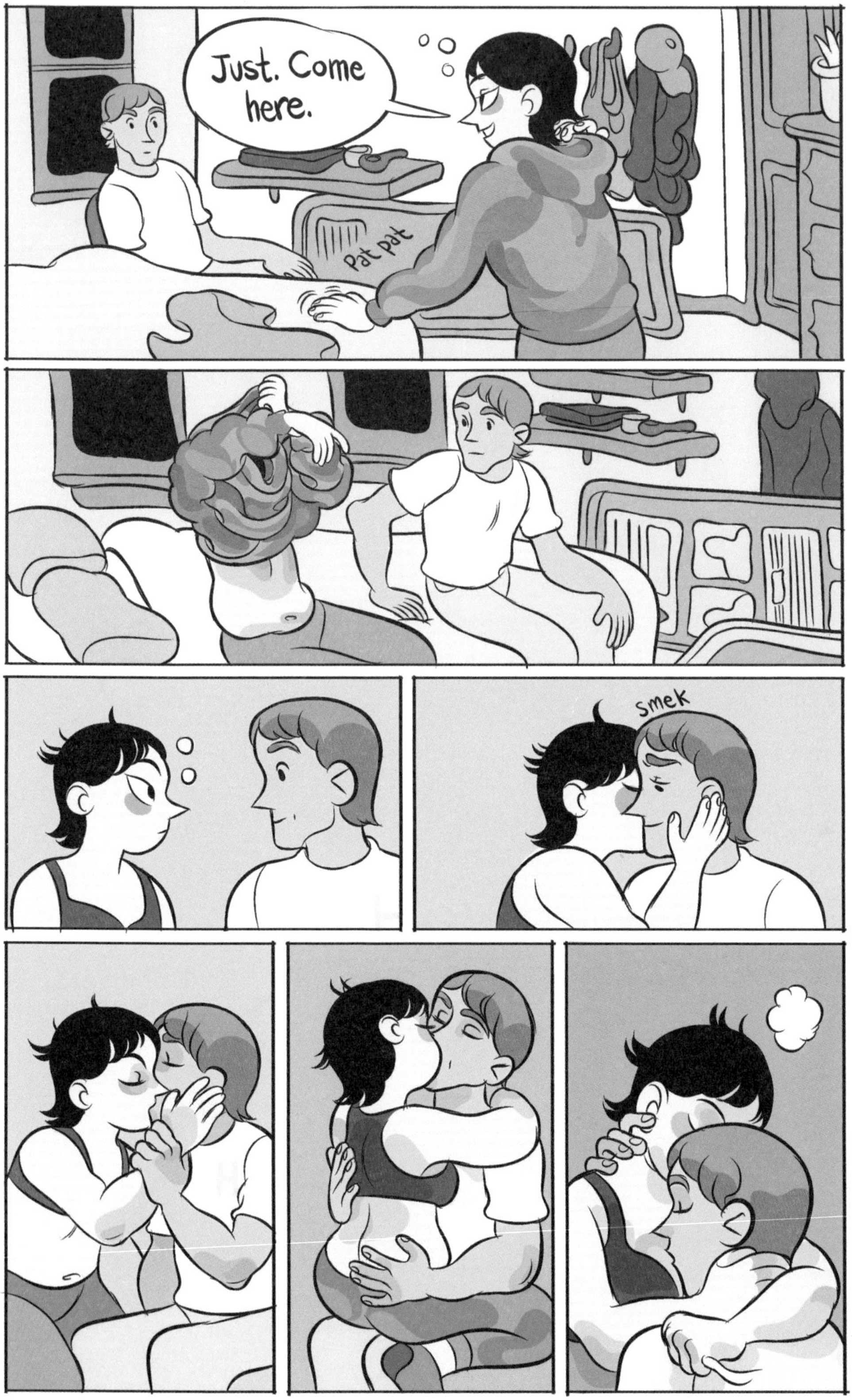
Just. Come here.
pat pat
smek

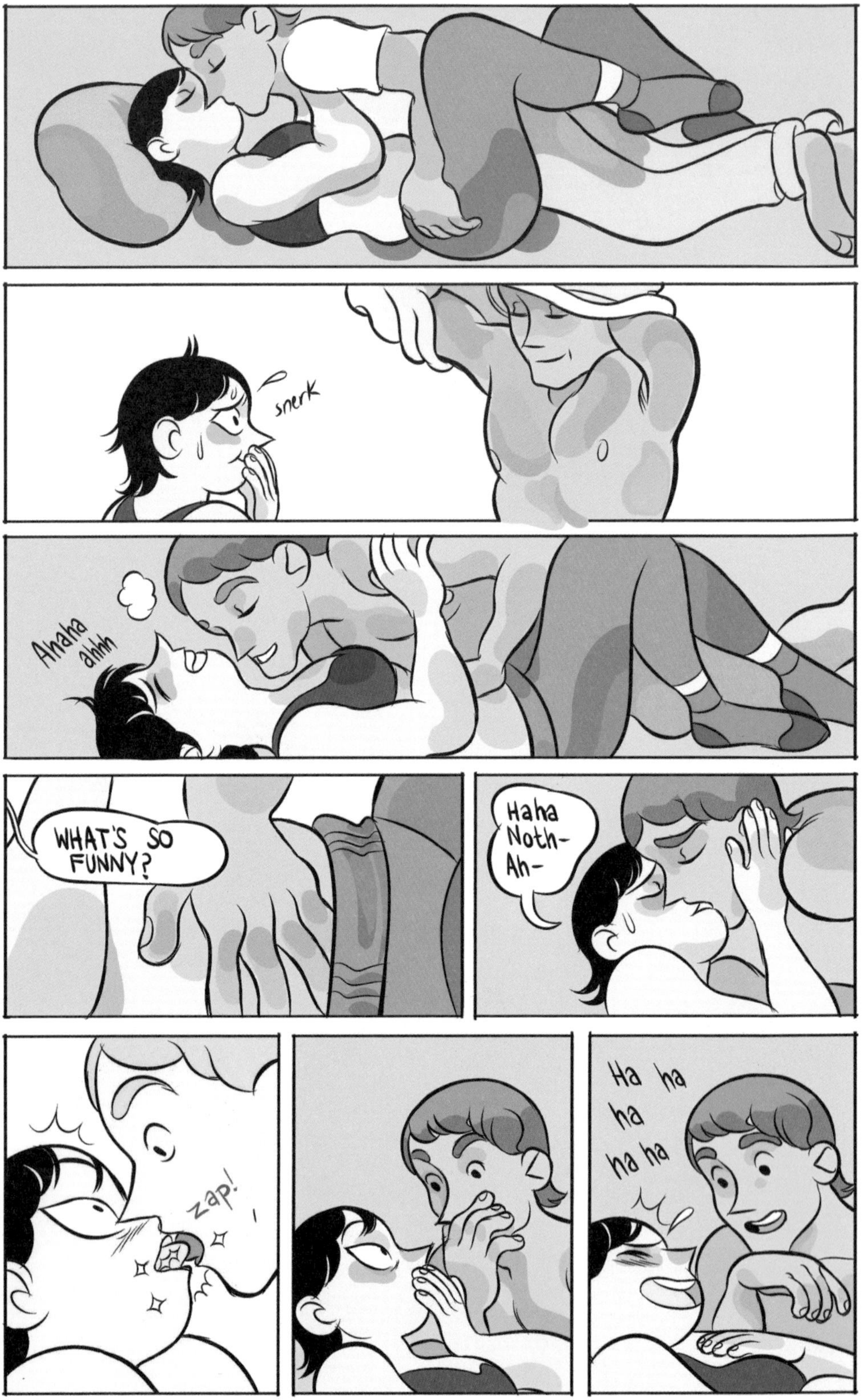
snerk
Ahaha ahhh
WHAT'S SO FUNNY?
Haha Noth- Ah-
zap!
Ha ha ha ha ha

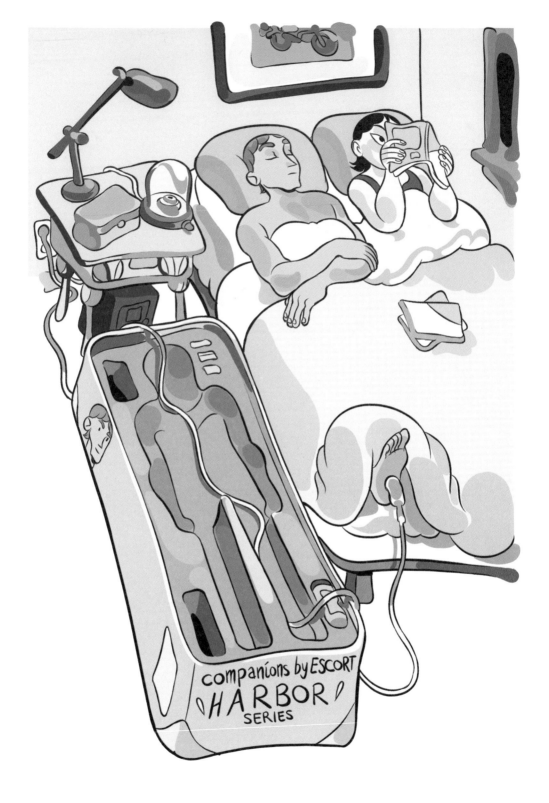

companions by ESCORT
HARBOR
SERIES

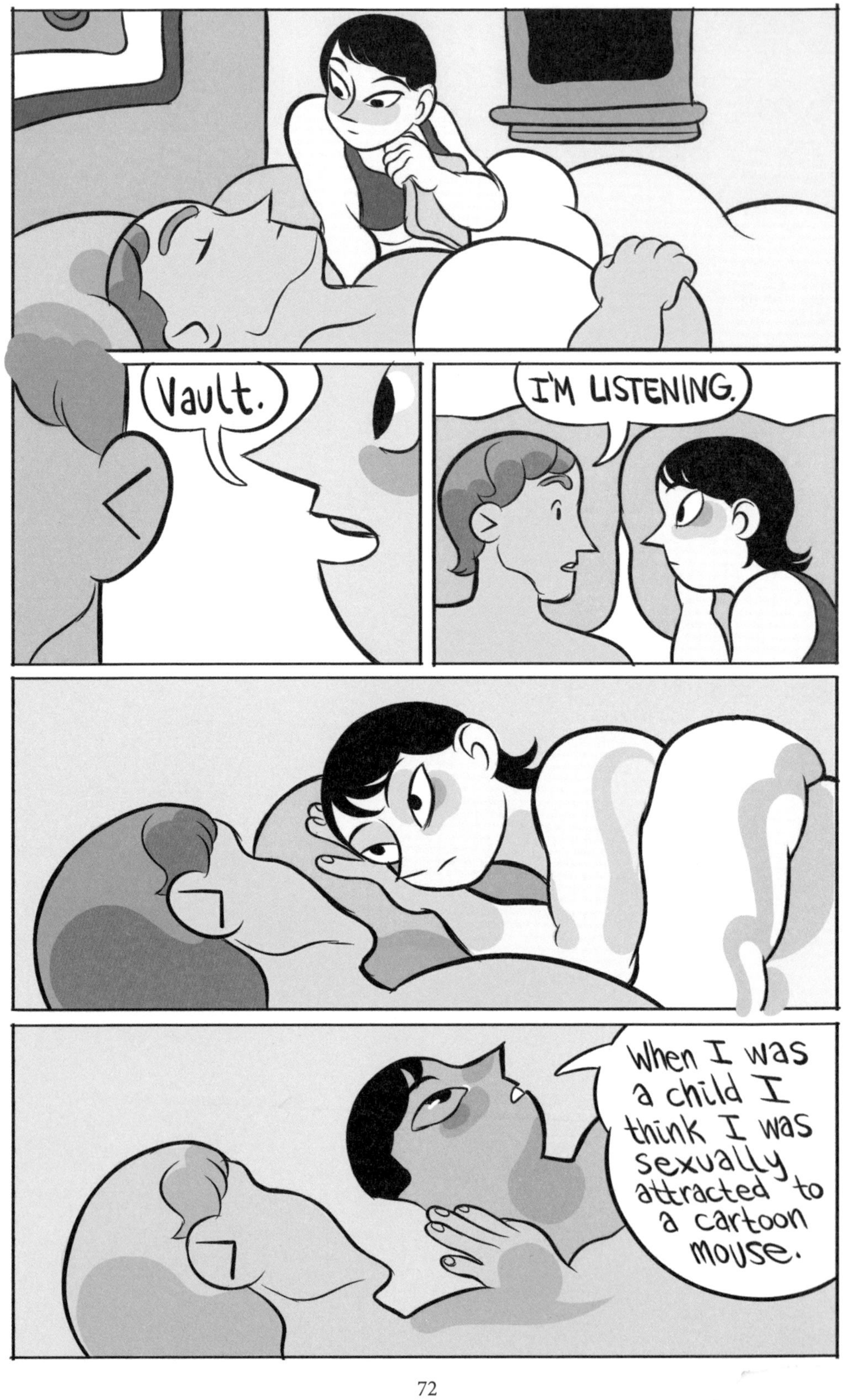
Vault.
I'M LISTENING.
When I was a child I think I was sexually attracted to a cartoon mouse.

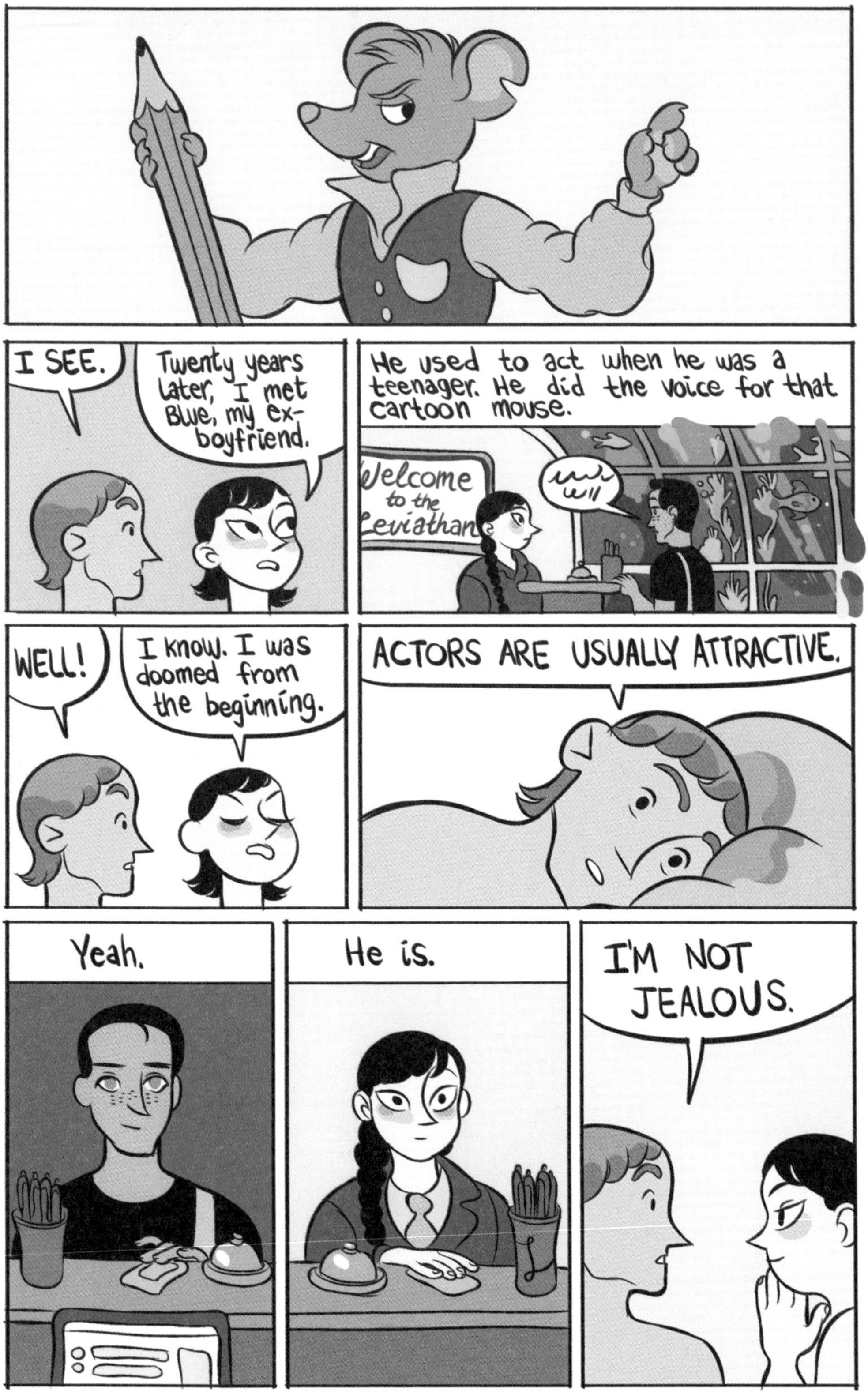
I SEE.
Twenty years later, I met Blue, my ex-boyfriend.
He used to act when he was a teenager. He did the voice for that cartoon mouse.
Welcome to the Leviathan
WELL!
I know. I was doomed from the beginning.
ACTORS ARE USUALLY ATTRACTIVE.
Yeah.
He is.
I'M NOT JEALOUS.

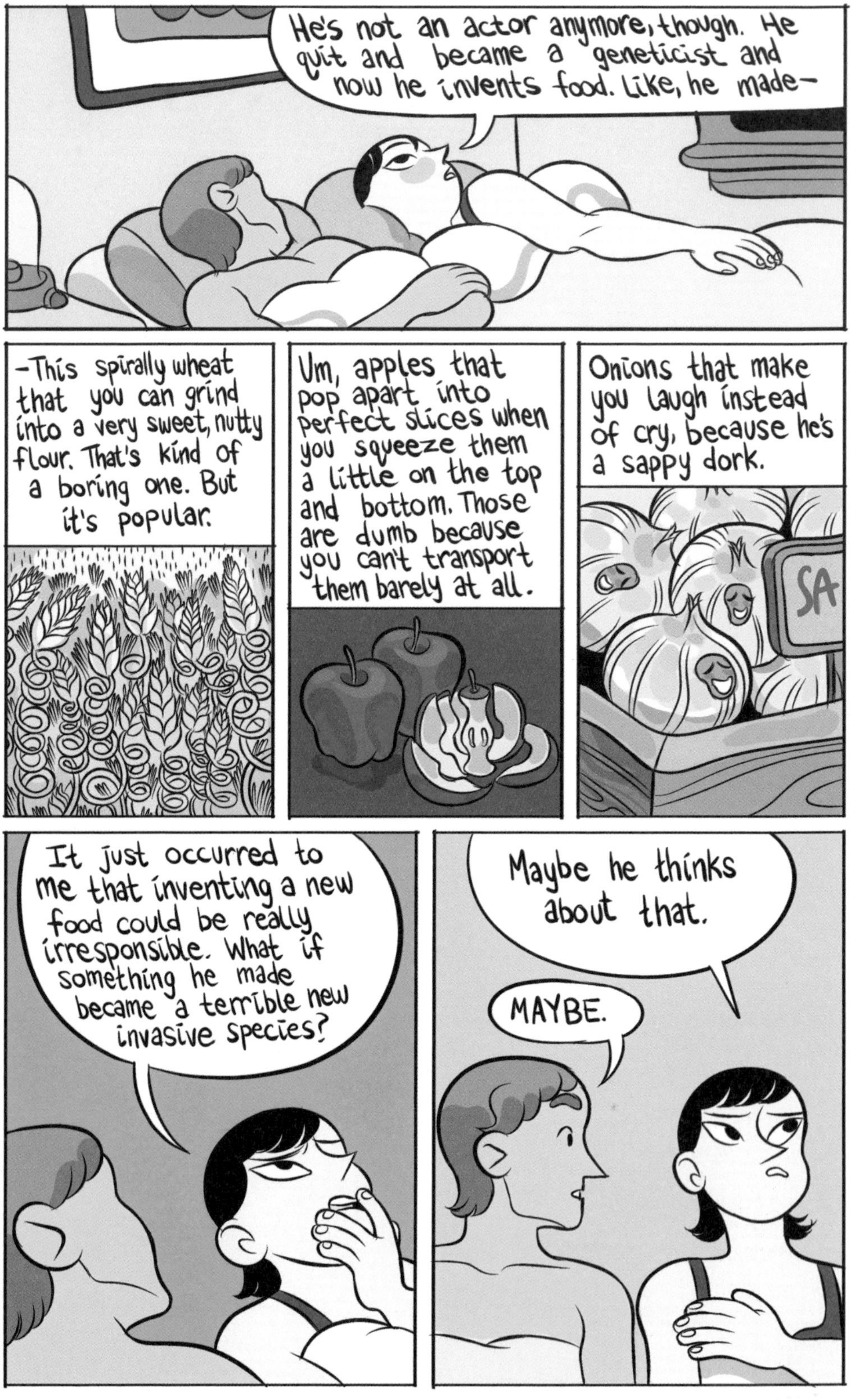
He's not an actor anymore, though. He quit and became a geneticist and now he invents food. Like, he made—
—This spirally wheat that you can grind into a very sweet, nutty flour. That's kind of a boring one. But it's popular.
Um, apples that pop apart into perfect slices when you squeeze them a little on the top and bottom. Those are dumb because you can't transport them barely at all.
Onions that make you laugh instead of cry, because he's a sappy dork.
SA
It just occurred to me that inventing a new food could be really irresponsible. What if something he made became a terrible new invasive species?
Maybe he thinks about that.
MAYBE.

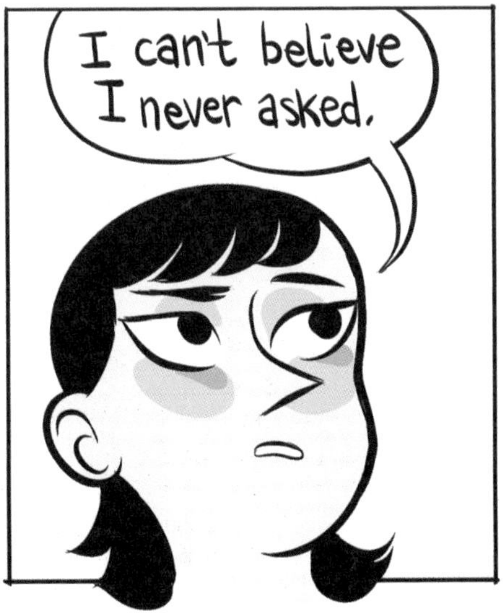
I can't believe I never asked.

TWO

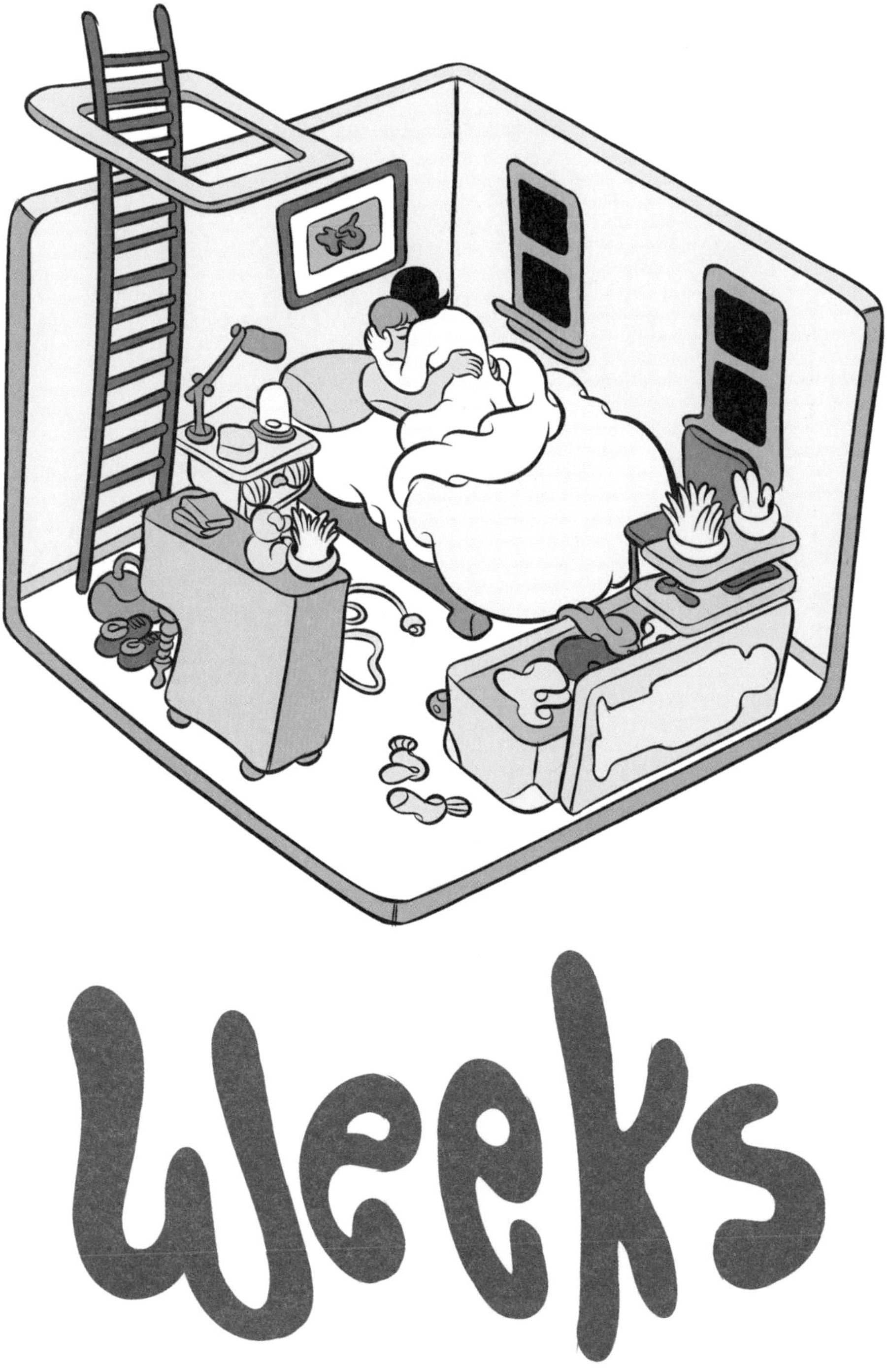

Weeks

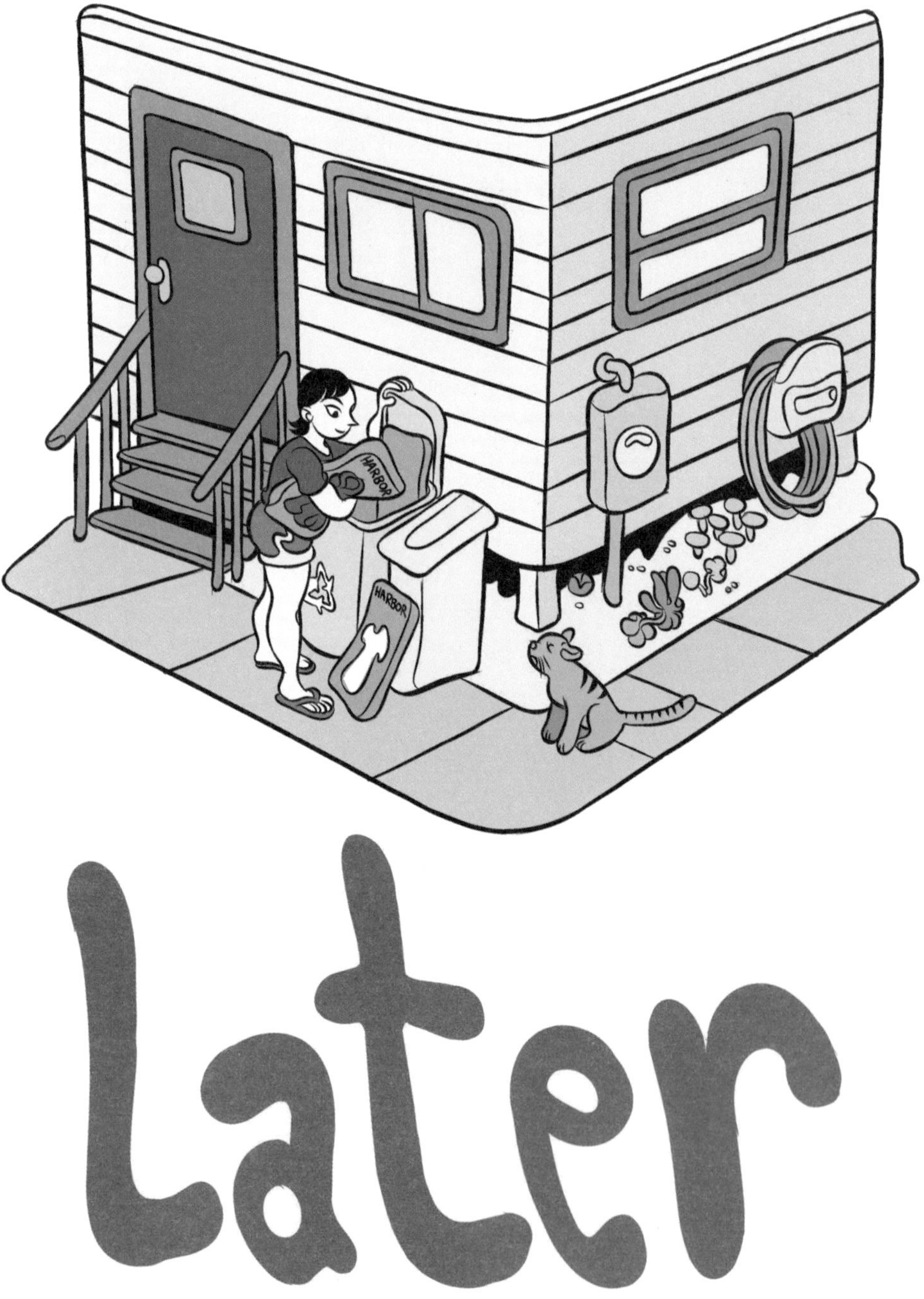
HARBOR
HARBOR

Later

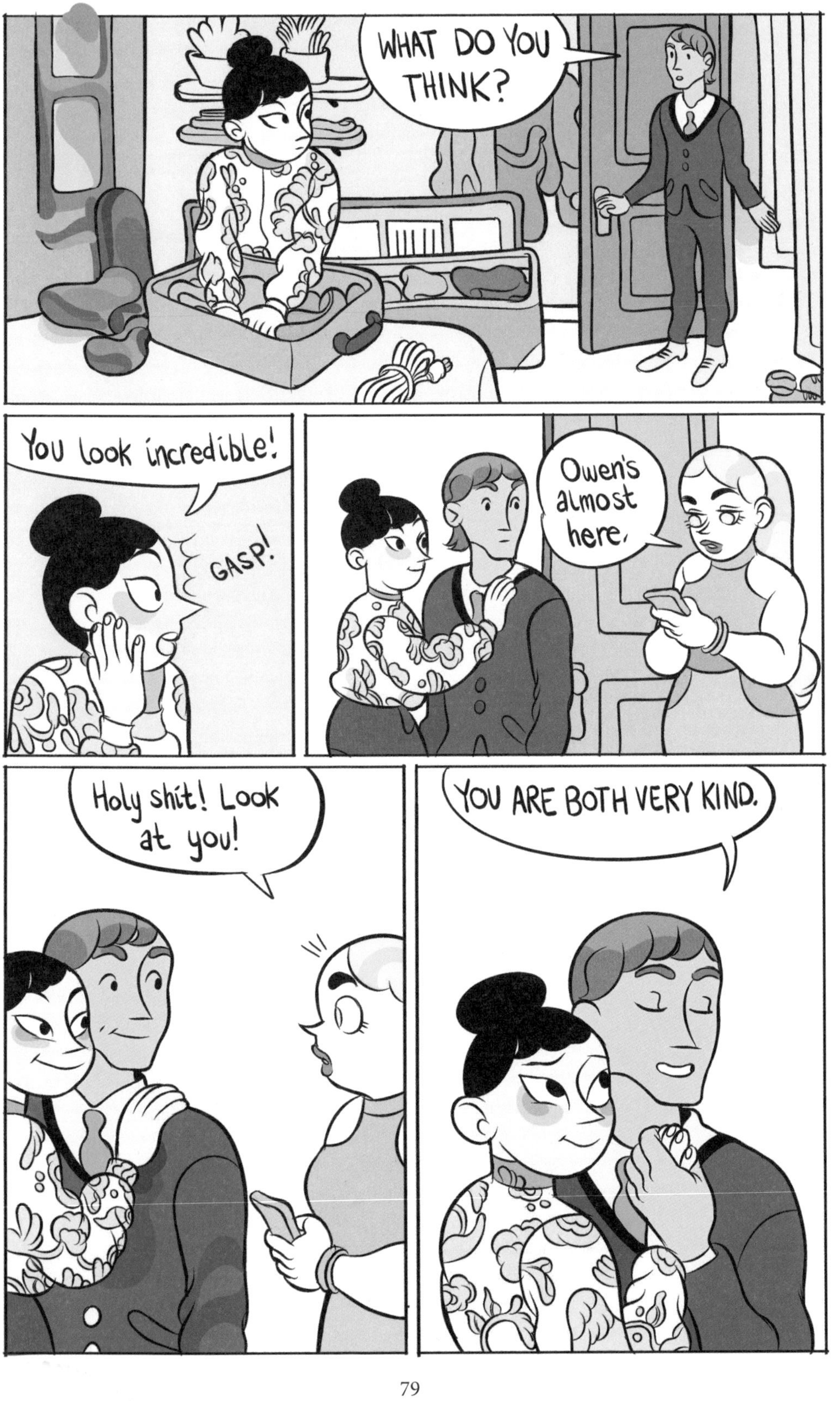
WHAT DO YOU THINK?
You look incredible!
GASP!
Owen's almost here.
Holy shit! Look at you!
YOU ARE BOTH VERY KIND.

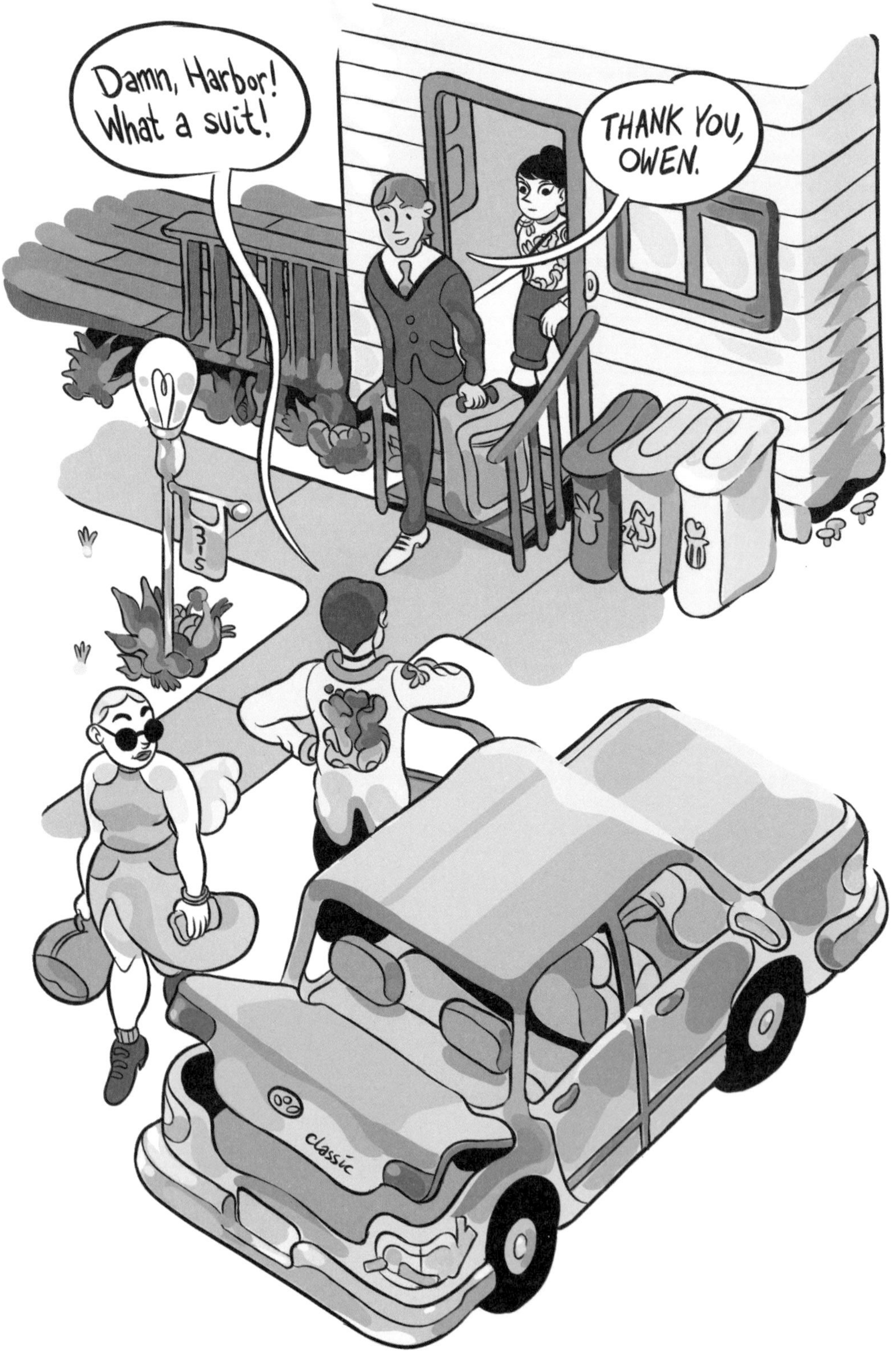
Damn, Harbor! What a suit!
THANK YOU, OWEN.
315
classic

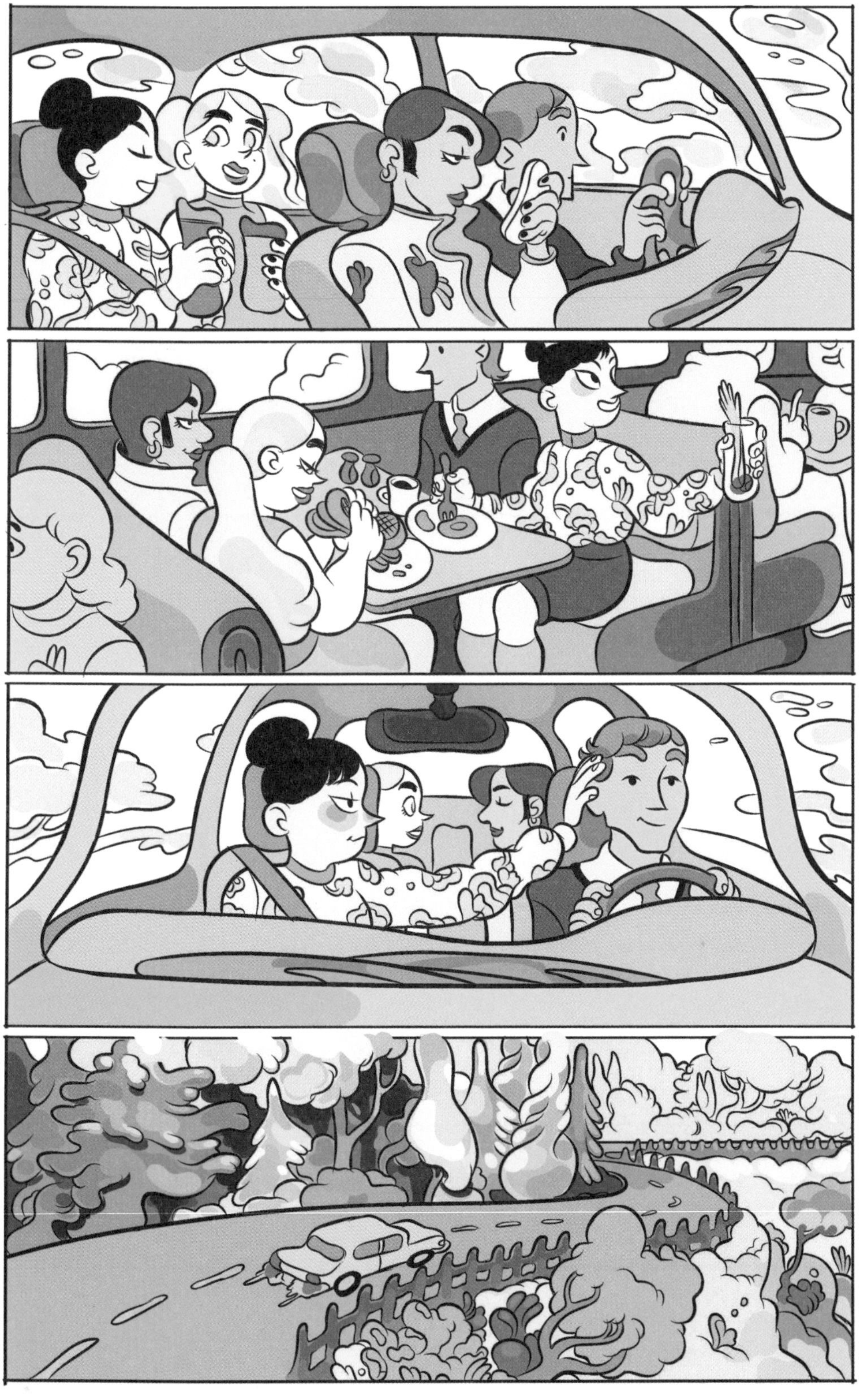

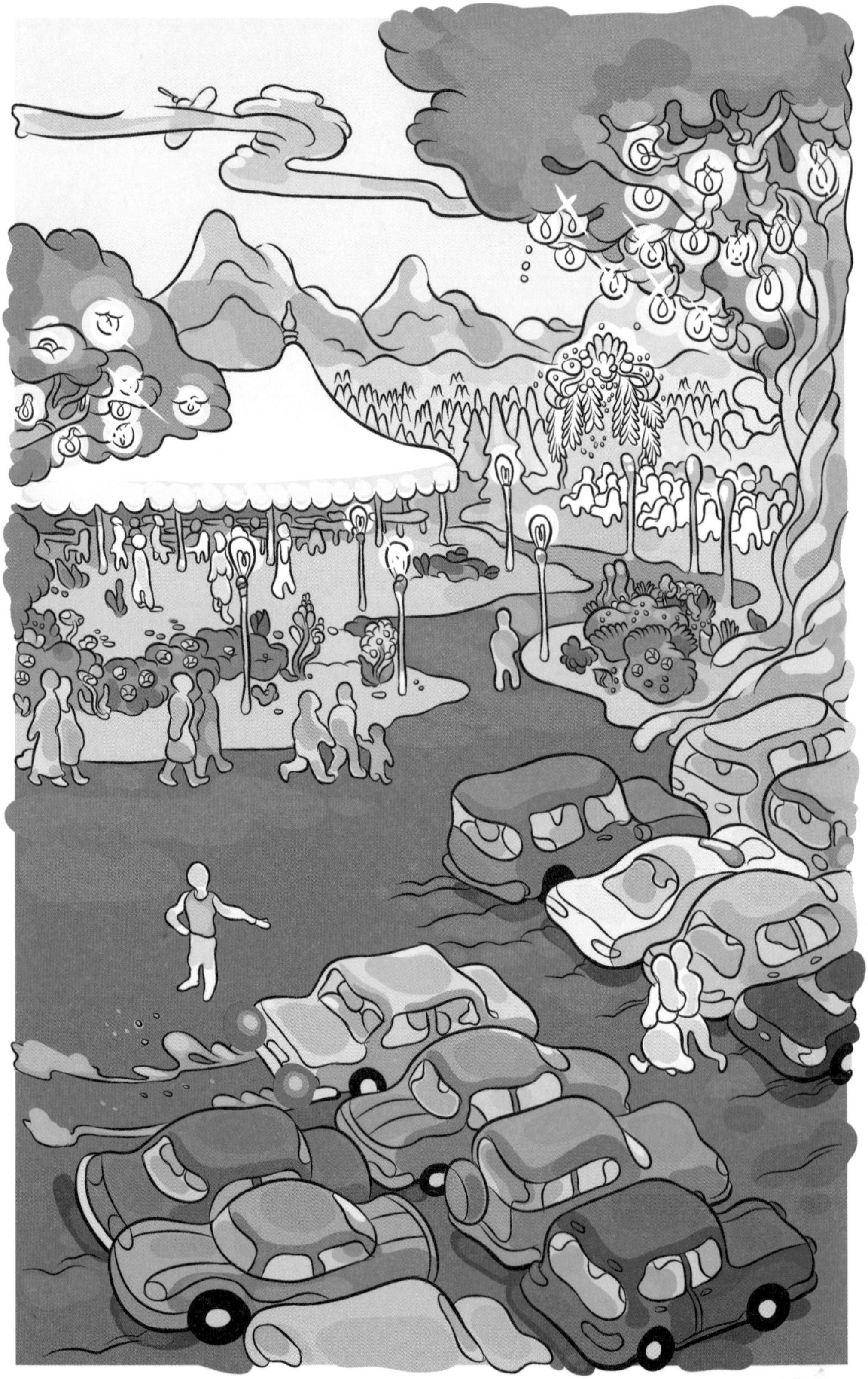

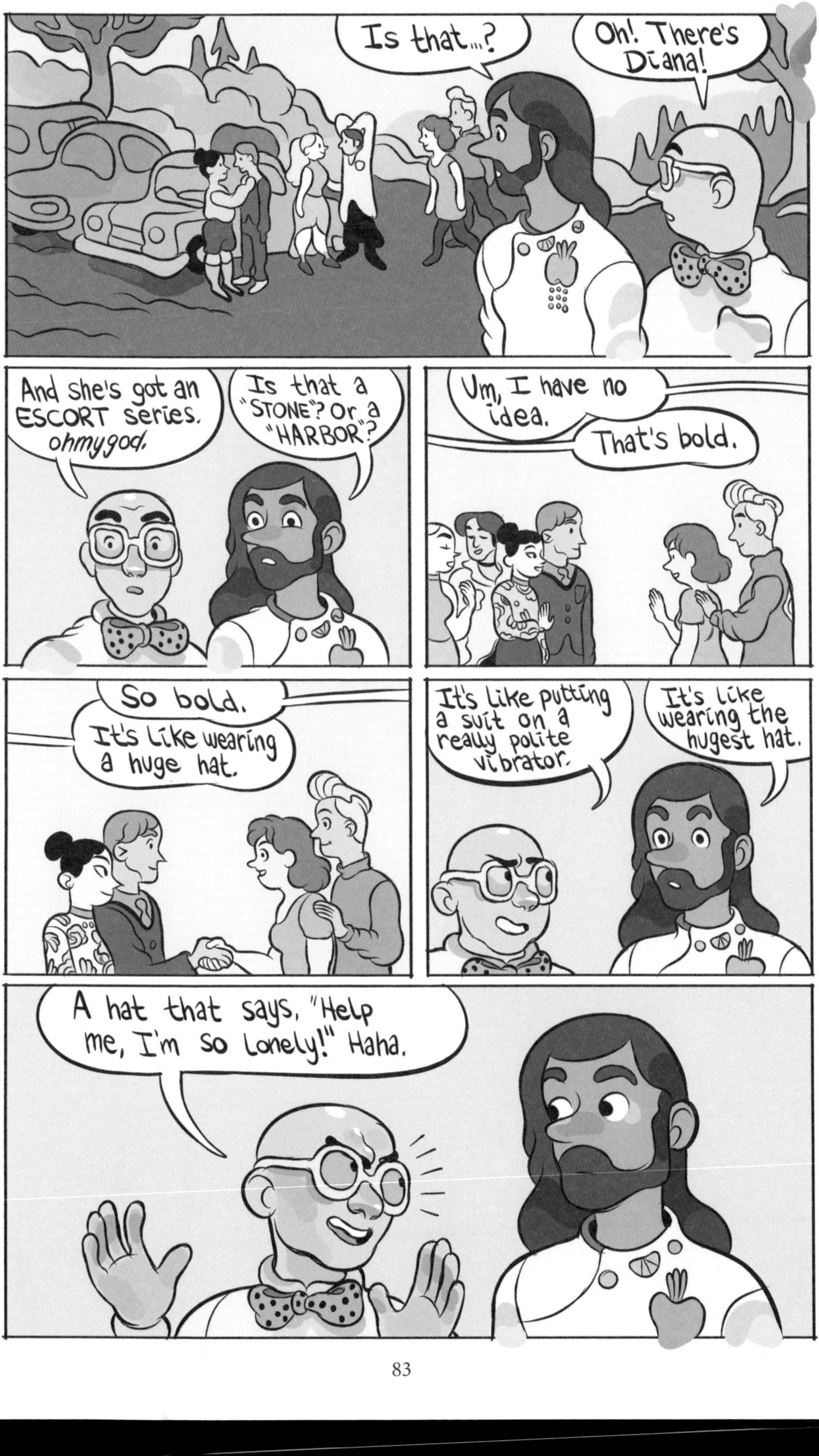

Is that...?
Oh! There's Diana!
And she's got an ESCORT series. ohmygod.
Is that a "STONE"? Or a "HARBOR"?
Um, I have no idea.
That's bold.
So bold.
It's like wearing a huge hat.
It's like putting a suit on a really polite vibrator.
It's like wearing the hugest hat.
A hat that says, "Help me, I'm so lonely!" Haha.

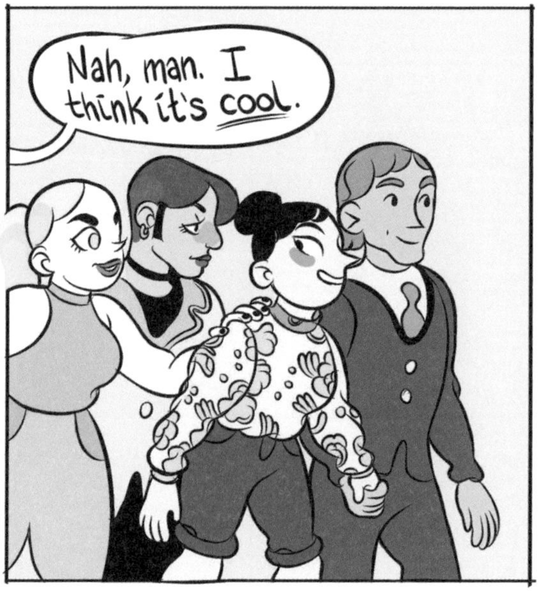
Nah, man. I think it's cool.

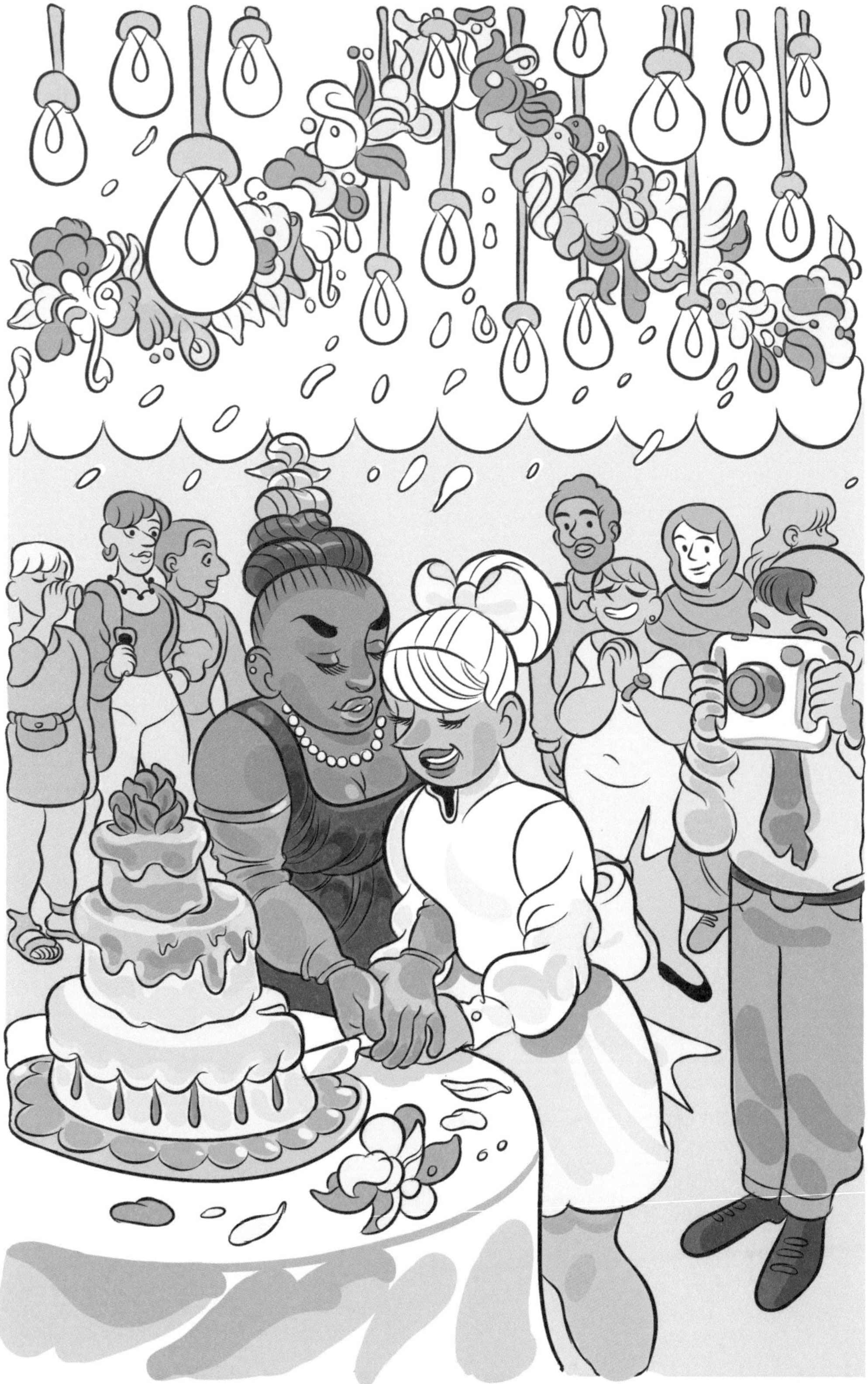

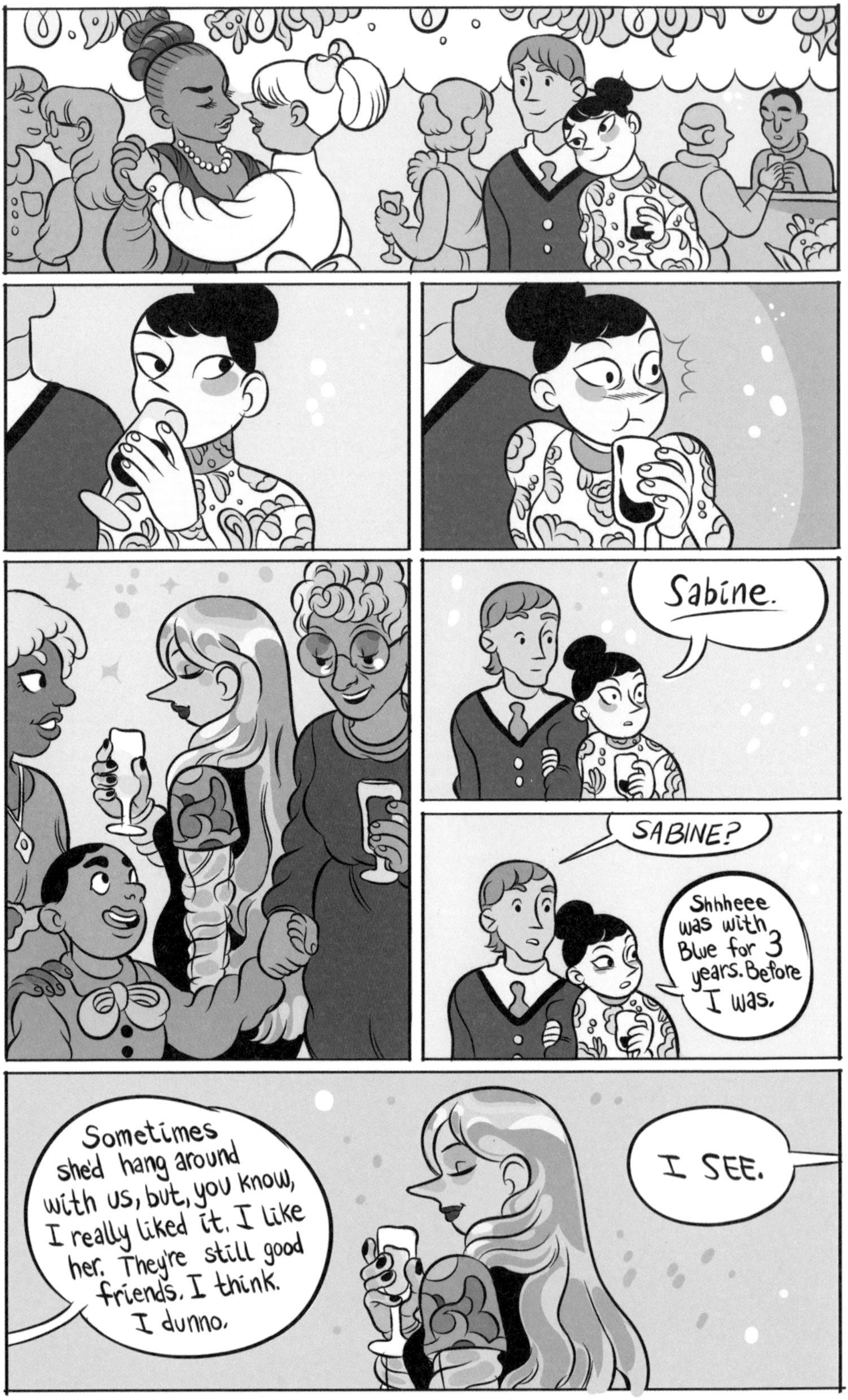
Sabine.
SABINE?
Shhheee was with Blue for 3 years. Before I was.
Sometimes she'd hang around with us, but, you know, I really liked it. I like her. They're still good friends. I think. I dunno.
I SEE.

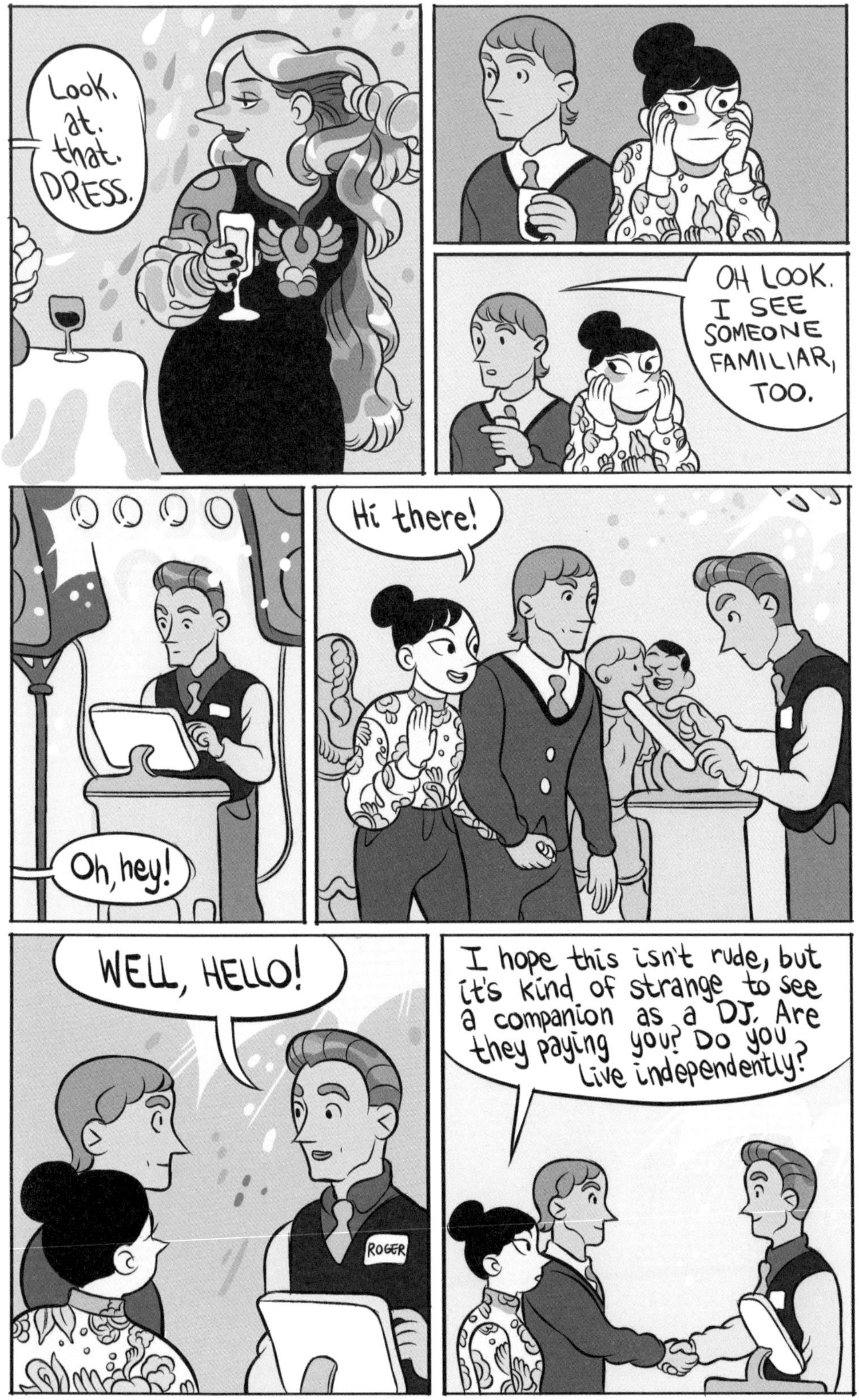
Look. at. that. DRESS.
OH LOOK. I SEE SOMEONE FAMILIAR, TOO.
Oh, hey!
Hi there!
WELL, HELLO!
ROGER
I hope this isn't rude, but it's kind of strange to see a companion as a DJ. Are they paying you? Do you live independently?

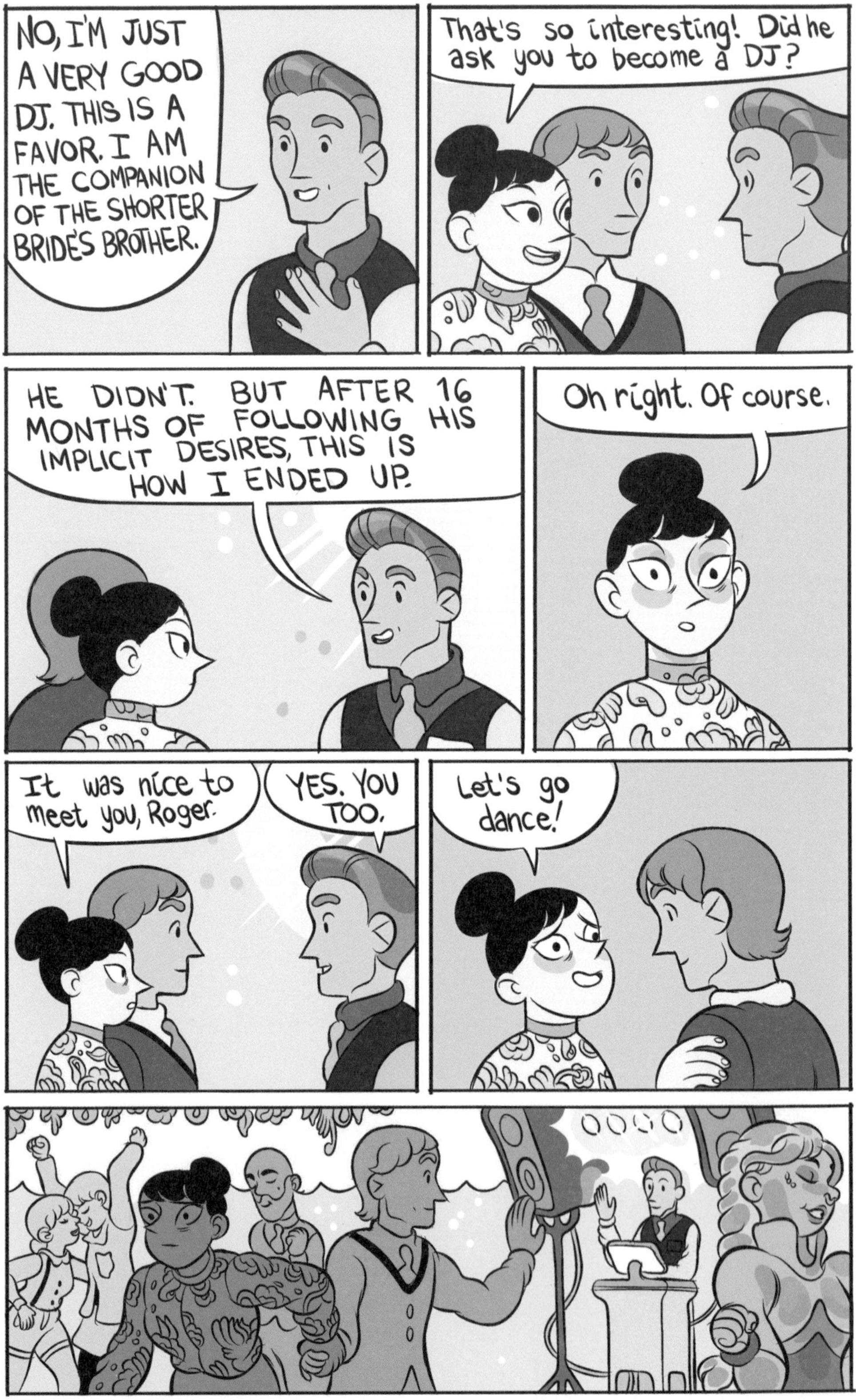
NO, I'M JUST A VERY GOOD DJ. THIS IS A FAVOR. I AM THE COMPANION OF THE SHORTER BRIDE'S BROTHER.
That's so interesting! Did he ask you to become a DJ?
HE DIDN'T. BUT AFTER 16 MONTHS OF FOLLOWING HIS IMPLICIT DESIRES, THIS IS HOW I ENDED UP.
Oh right. Of course.
It was nice to meet you, Roger.
YES. YOU TOO.
Let's go dance!

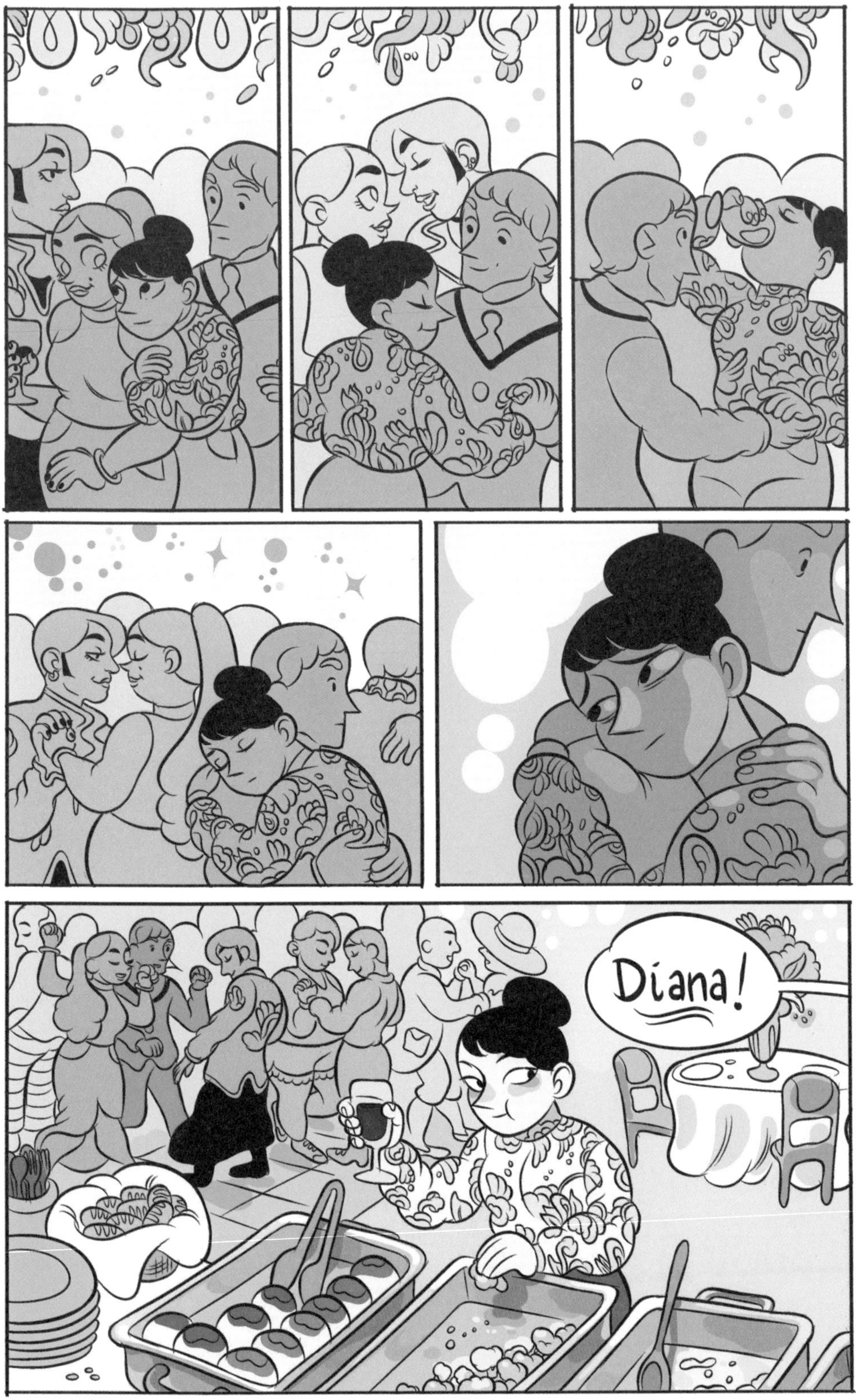
Diana!

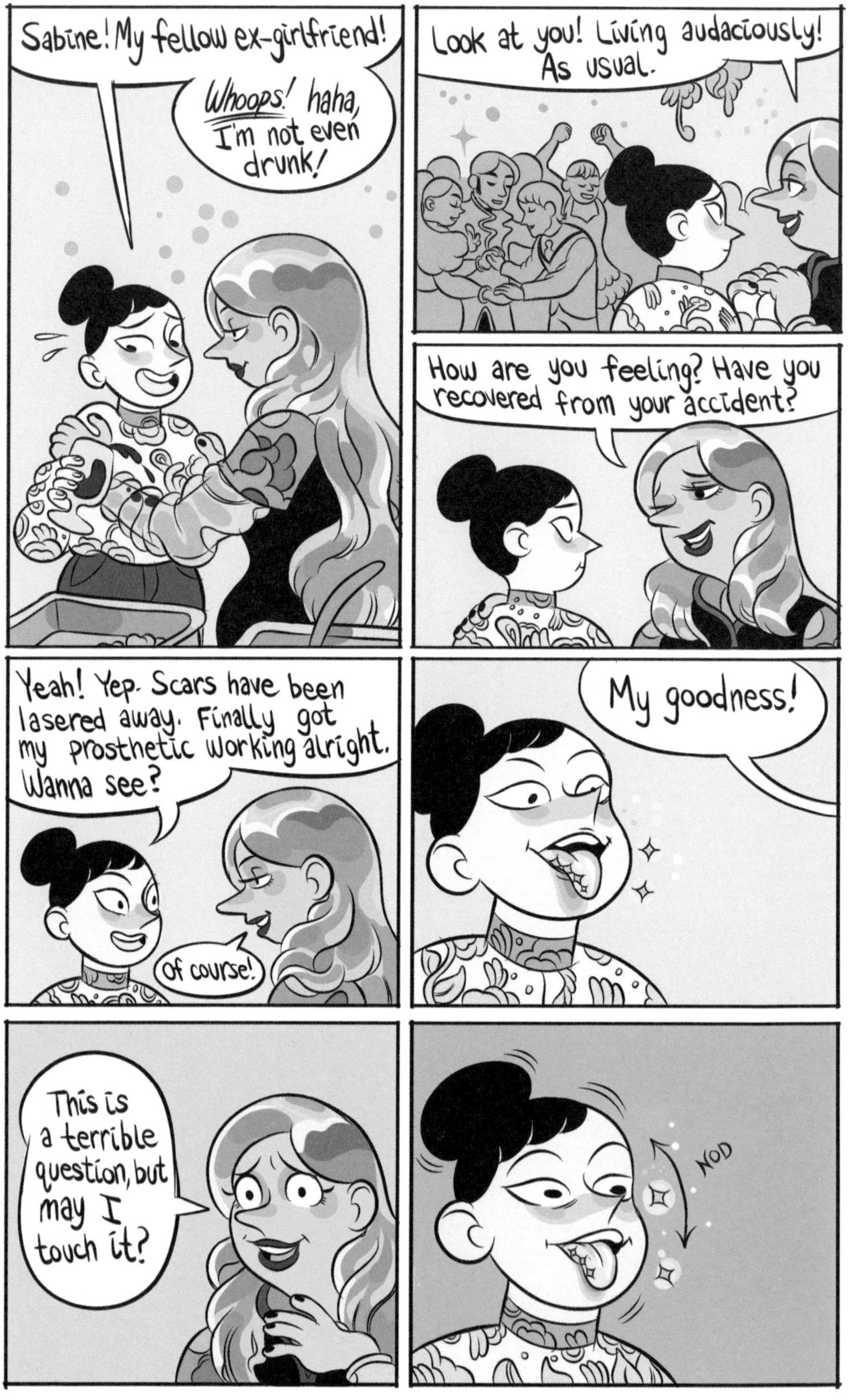

Sabine! My fellow ex-girlfriend!
Whoops! haha, I'm not even drunk!
Look at you! Living audaciously! As usual.
How are you feeling? Have you recovered from your accident?
Yeah! Yep. Scars have been lasered away. Finally got my prosthetic working alright. Wanna see?
Of course!
My goodness!
This is a terrible question, but may I touch it?
NOD

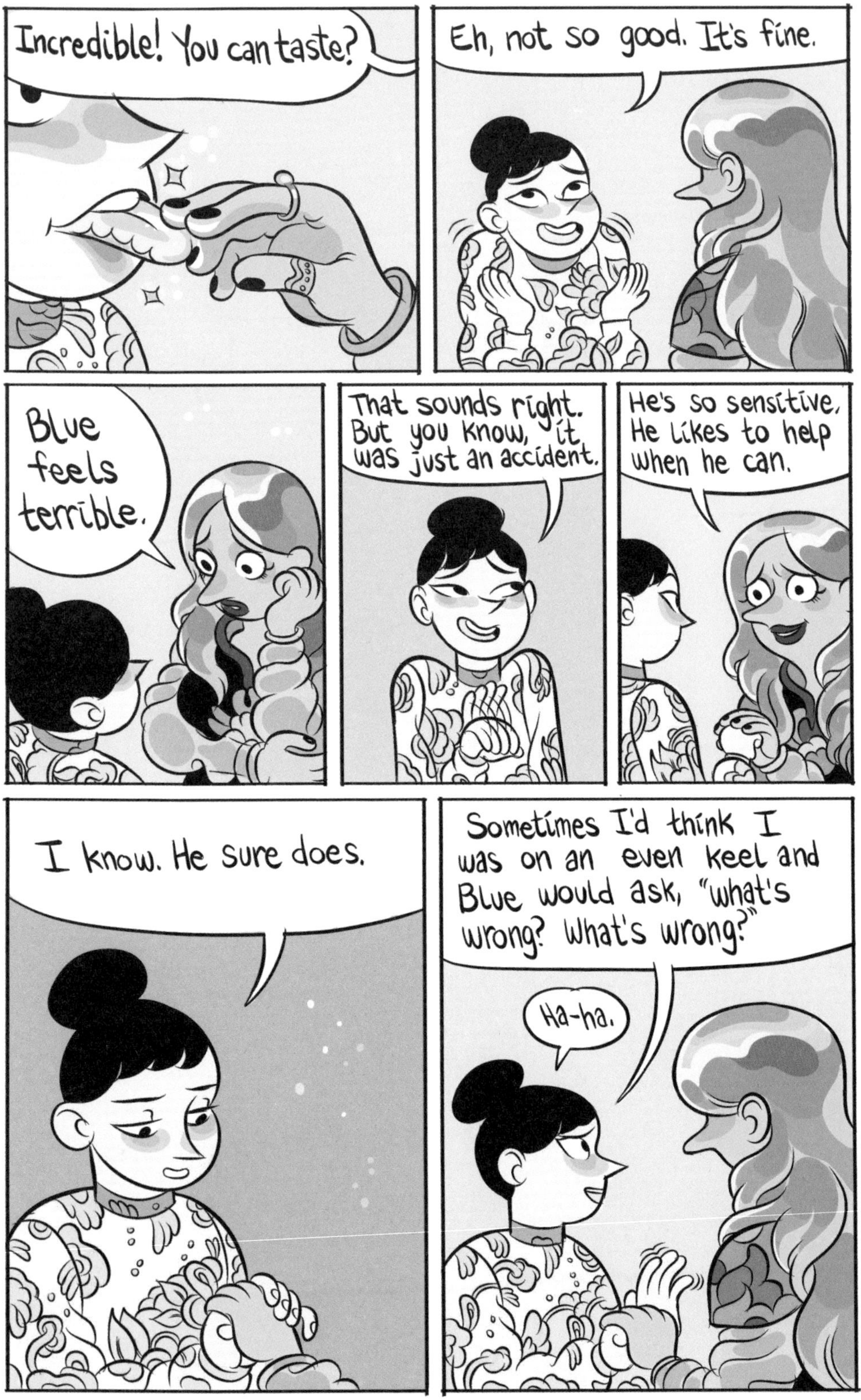
Incredible! You can taste?
Eh, not so good. It's fine.
Blue feels terrible.
That sounds right. But you know, it was just an accident.
He's so sensitive, He likes to help when he can.
I know. He sure does.
Sometimes I'd think I was on an even keel and Blue would ask, "what's wrong? What's wrong?"
Ha-ha.

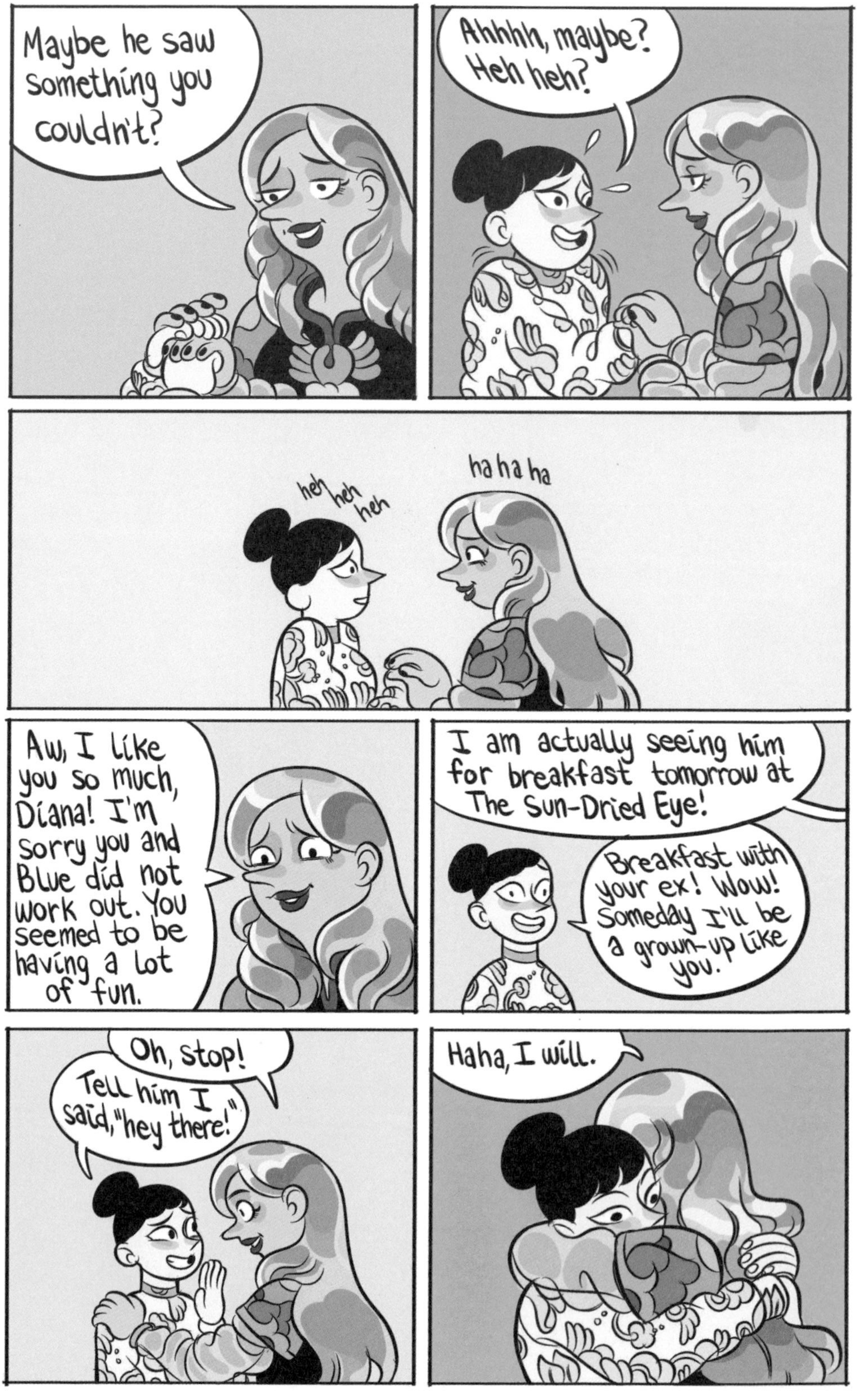

Maybe he saw something you couldn't?
Ahhhh, maybe? Heh heh?
heh heh heh
ha ha ha
Aw, I like you so much, Diana! I'm sorry you and Blue did not work out. You seemed to be having a lot of fun.
I am actually seeing him for breakfast tomorrow at The Sun-Dried Eye!
Breakfast with your ex! Wow! Someday I'll be a grown-up like you.
Oh, stop!
Tell him I said, "hey there!"
Haha, I will.

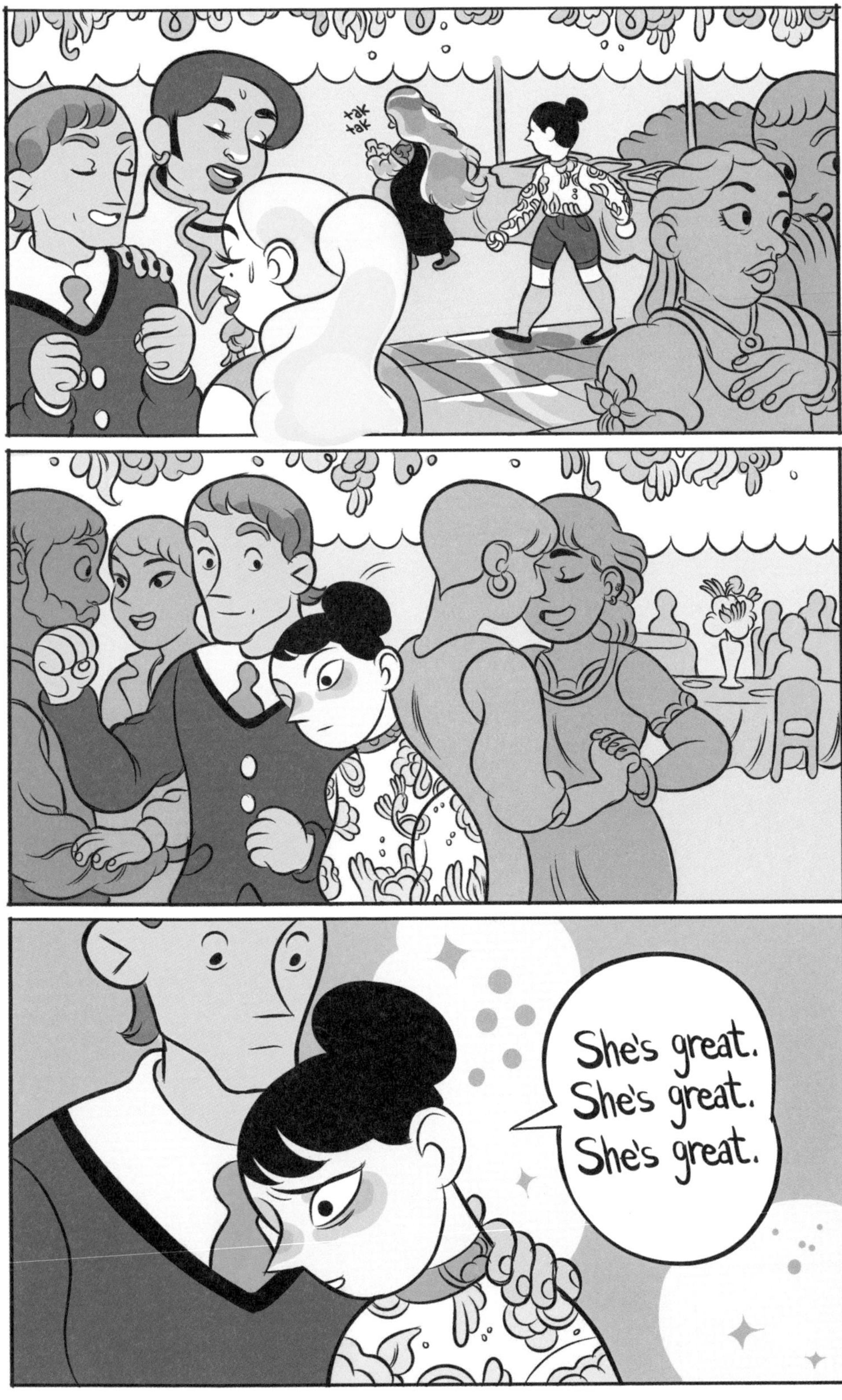
tak tak
She's great.
She's great.
She's great.

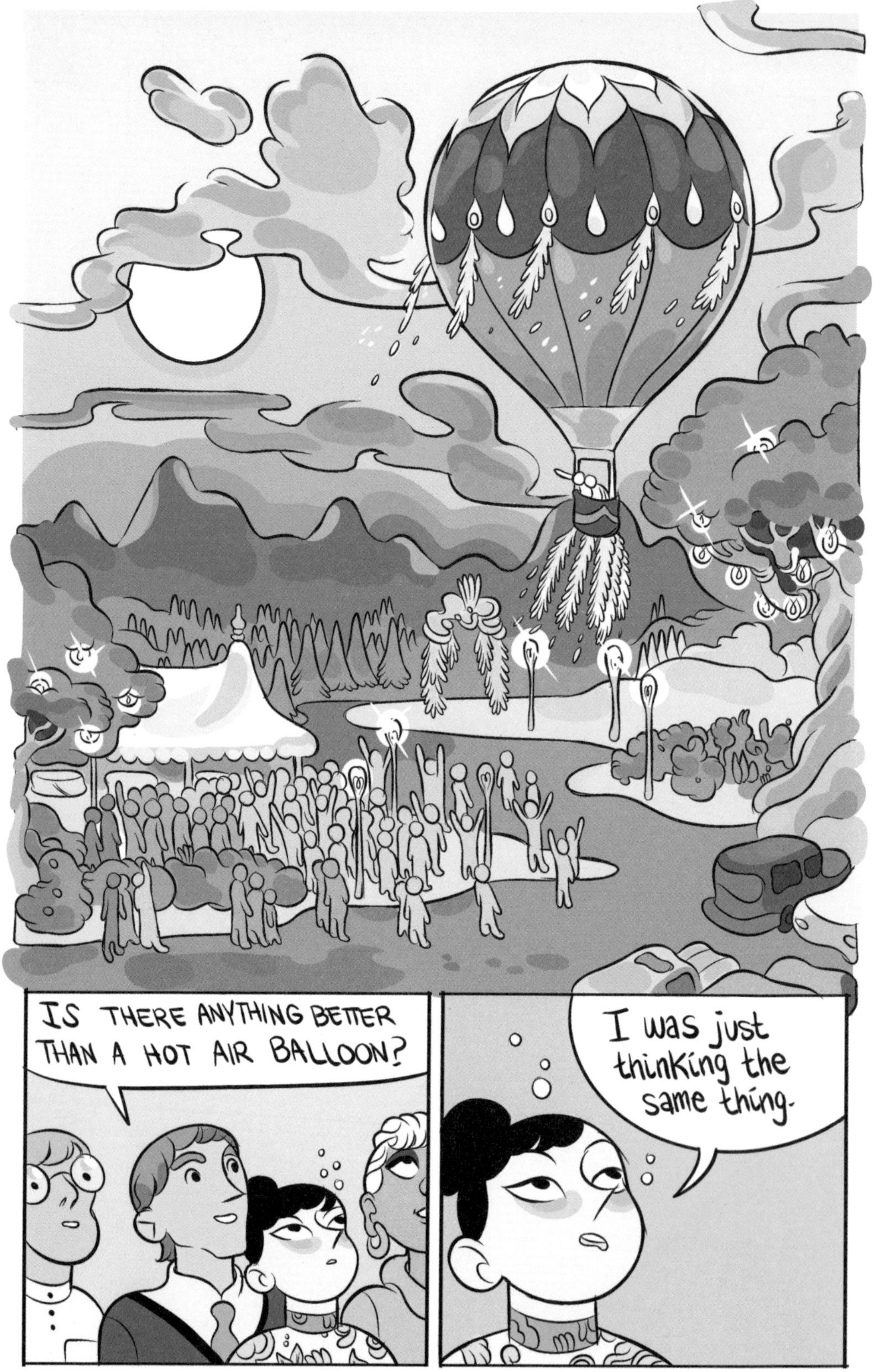
IS THERE ANYTHING BETTER THAN A HOT AIR BALLOON?
I was just thinking the same thing.

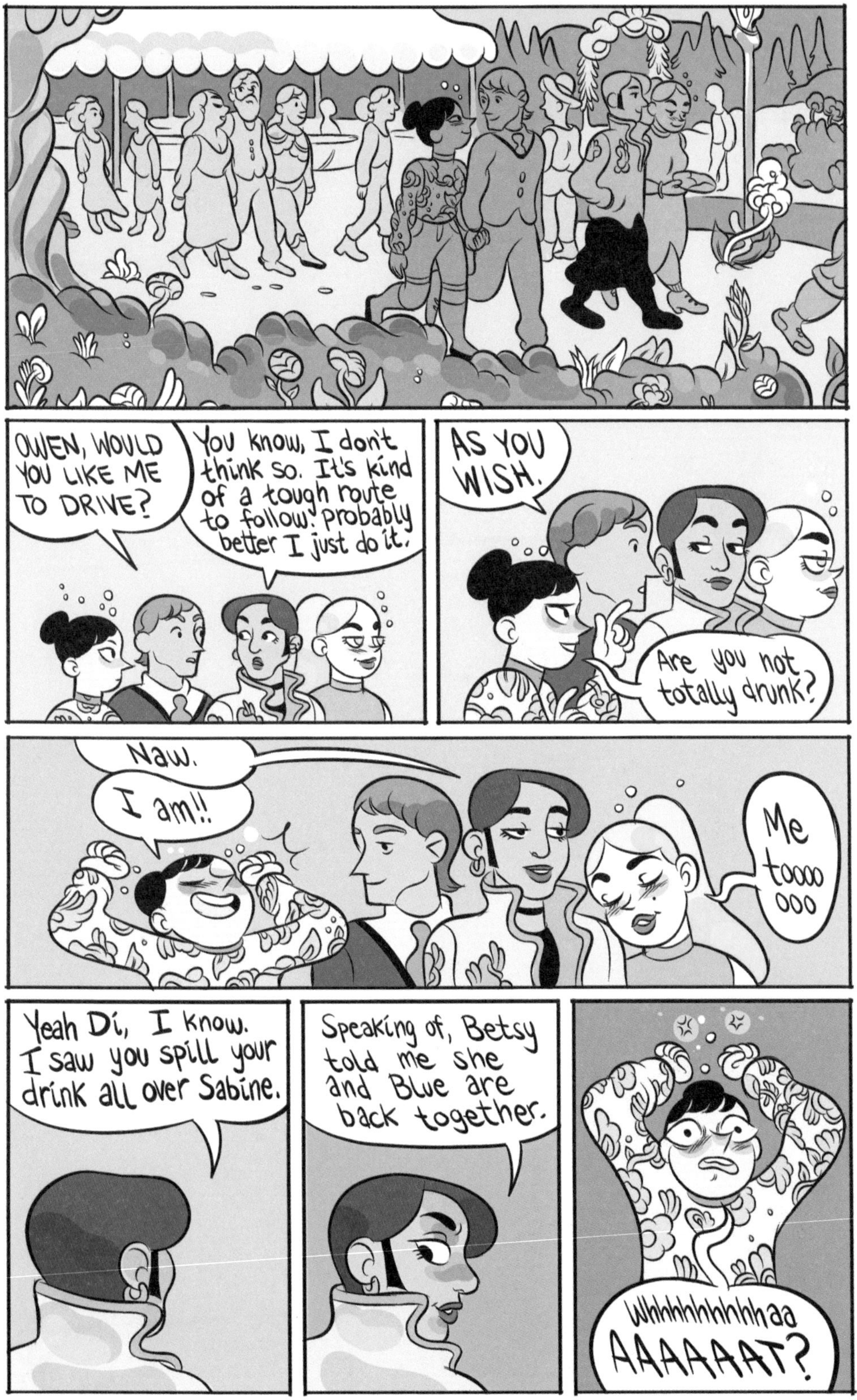
OWEN, WOULD YOU LIKE ME TO DRIVE?
You know, I don't think so. It's kind of a tough route to follow. probably better I just do it.
AS YOU WISH.
Are you not totally drunk?
Naw.
I am!!
Me tooooooo
Yeah Di, I know. I saw you spill your drink all over Sabine.
Speaking of, Betsy told me she and Blue are back together.
Whhhhhhhhhhaa AAAAAAT?

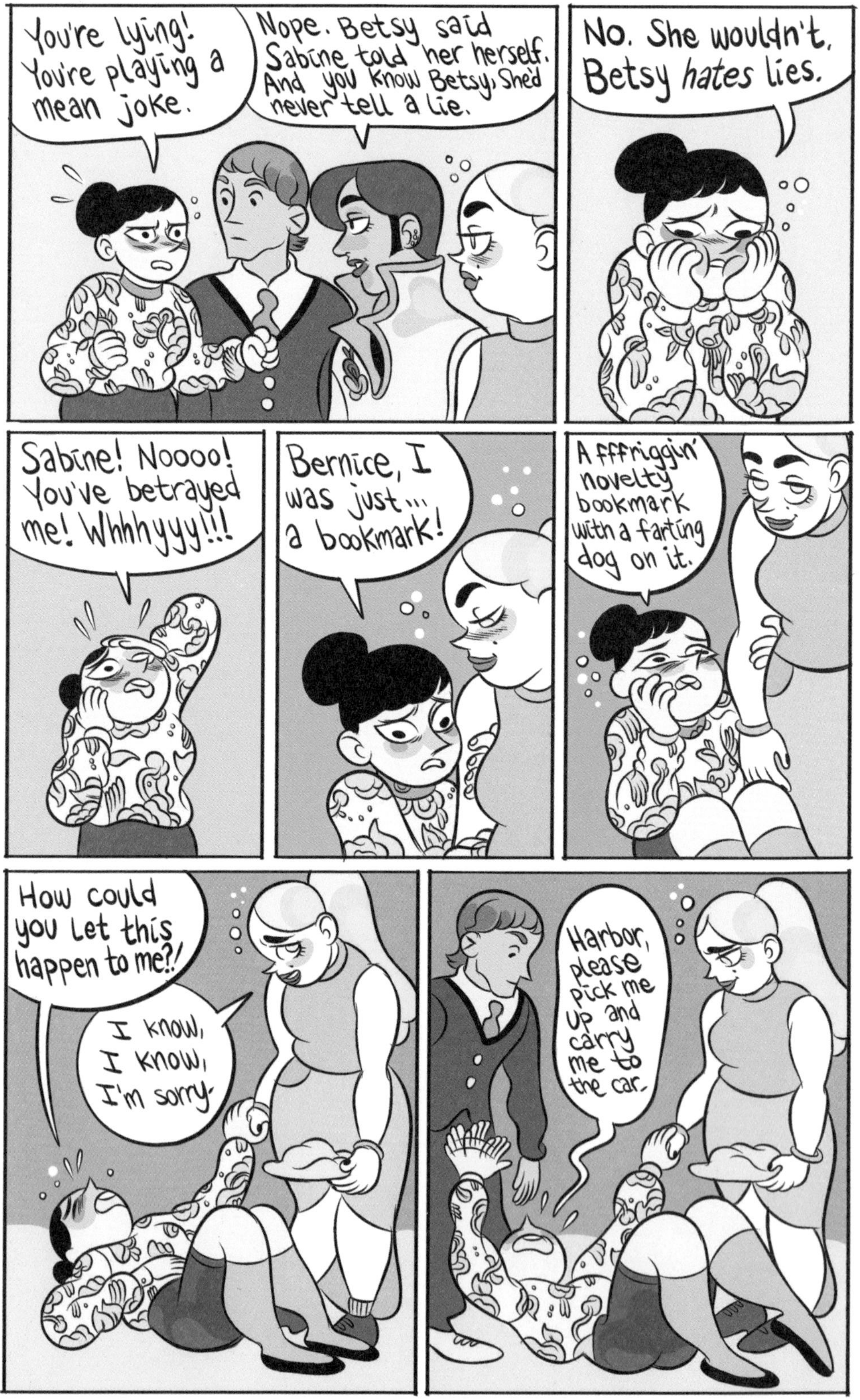
You're lying! You're playing a mean joke.
Nope. Betsy said Sabine told her herself. And you know Betsy, She'd never tell a lie.
No. She wouldn't. Betsy *hates* lies.
Sabine! Noooo! You've betrayed me! Whhhyyy!!!
Bernice, I was just... a bookmark!
A fffriggin' novelty bookmark with a farting dog on it.
How could you let this happen to me?!
I know, I know, I'm sorry.
Harbor, please pick me up and carry me to the car.

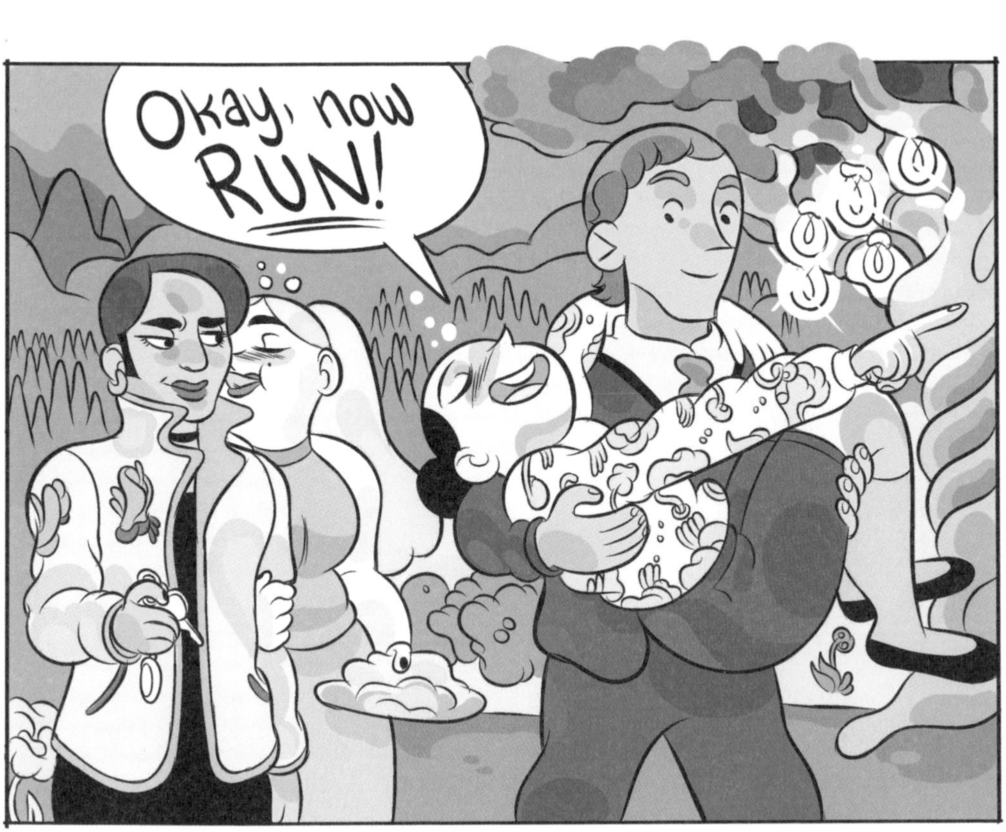
Okay, now RUN!

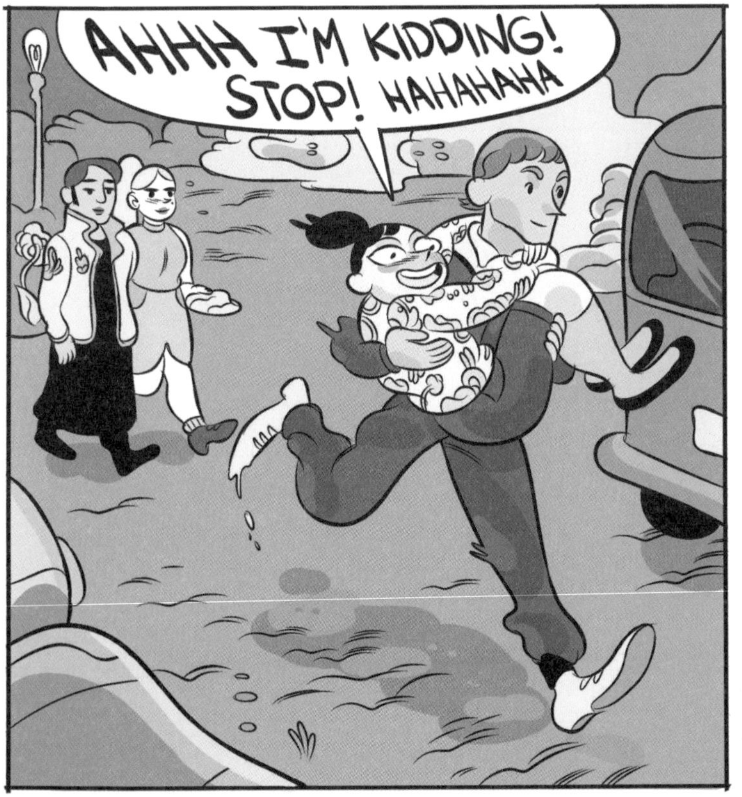
AHHH I'M KIDDING! STOP! HAHAHAHA

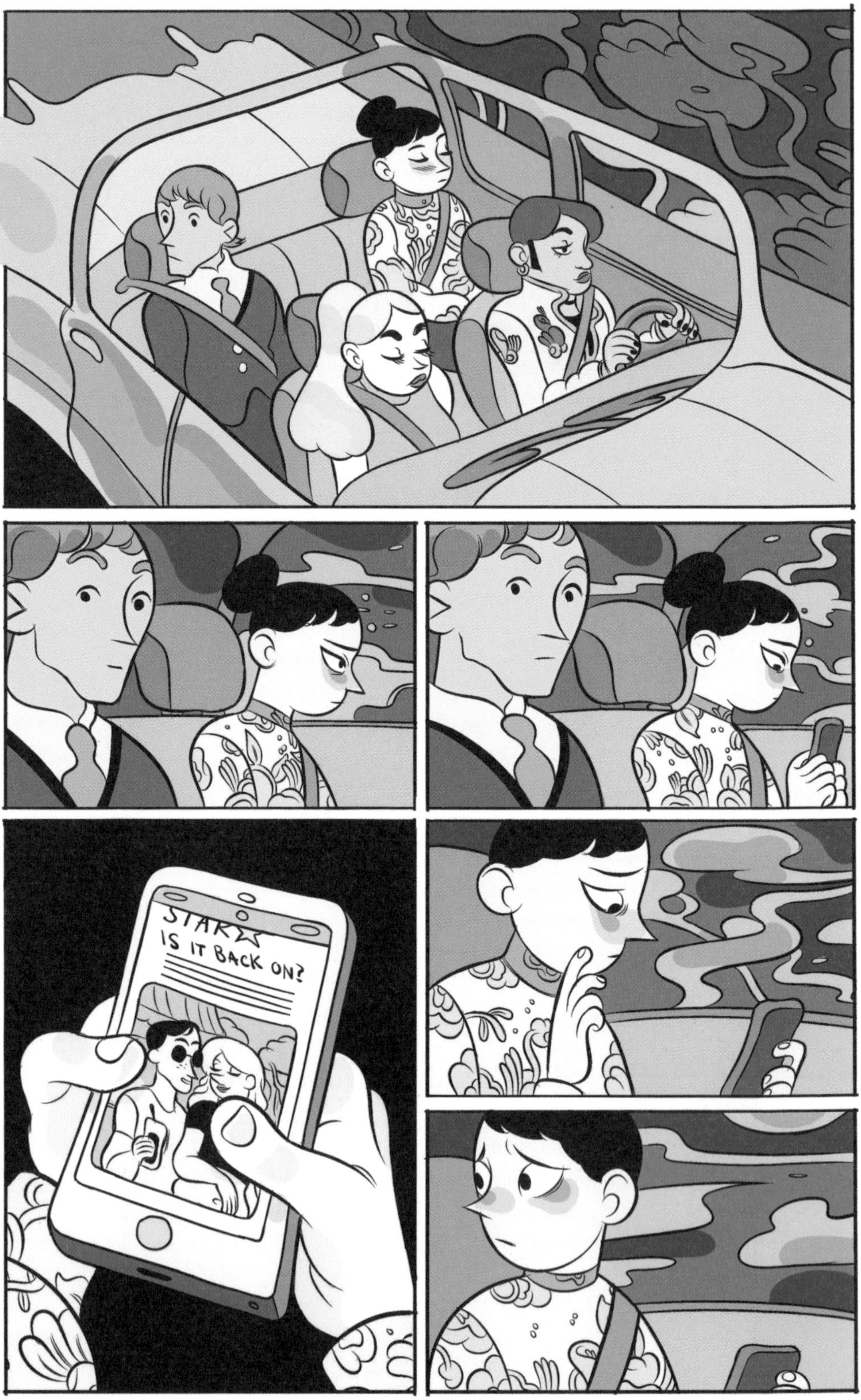
STAR☆
IS IT BACK ON?

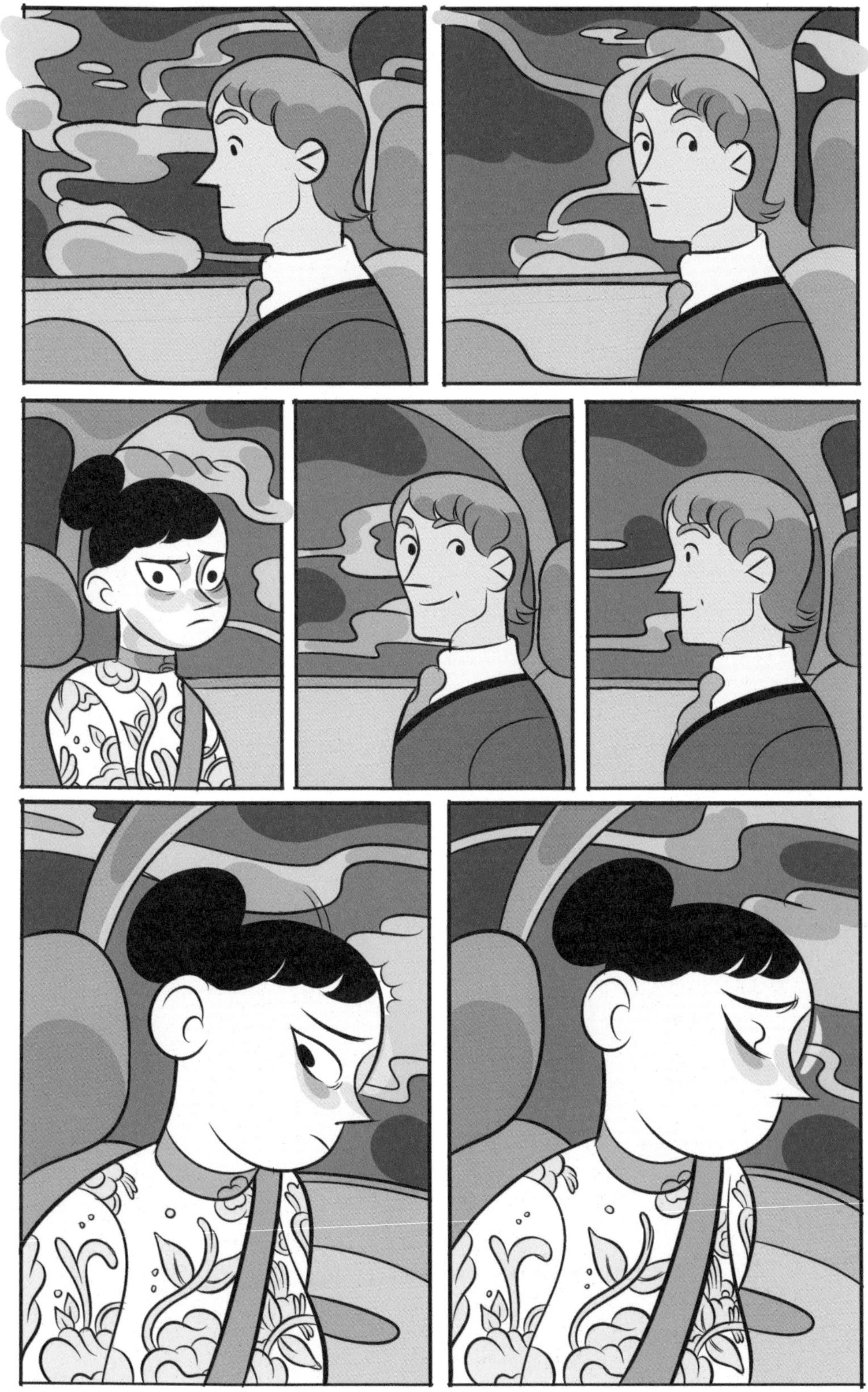

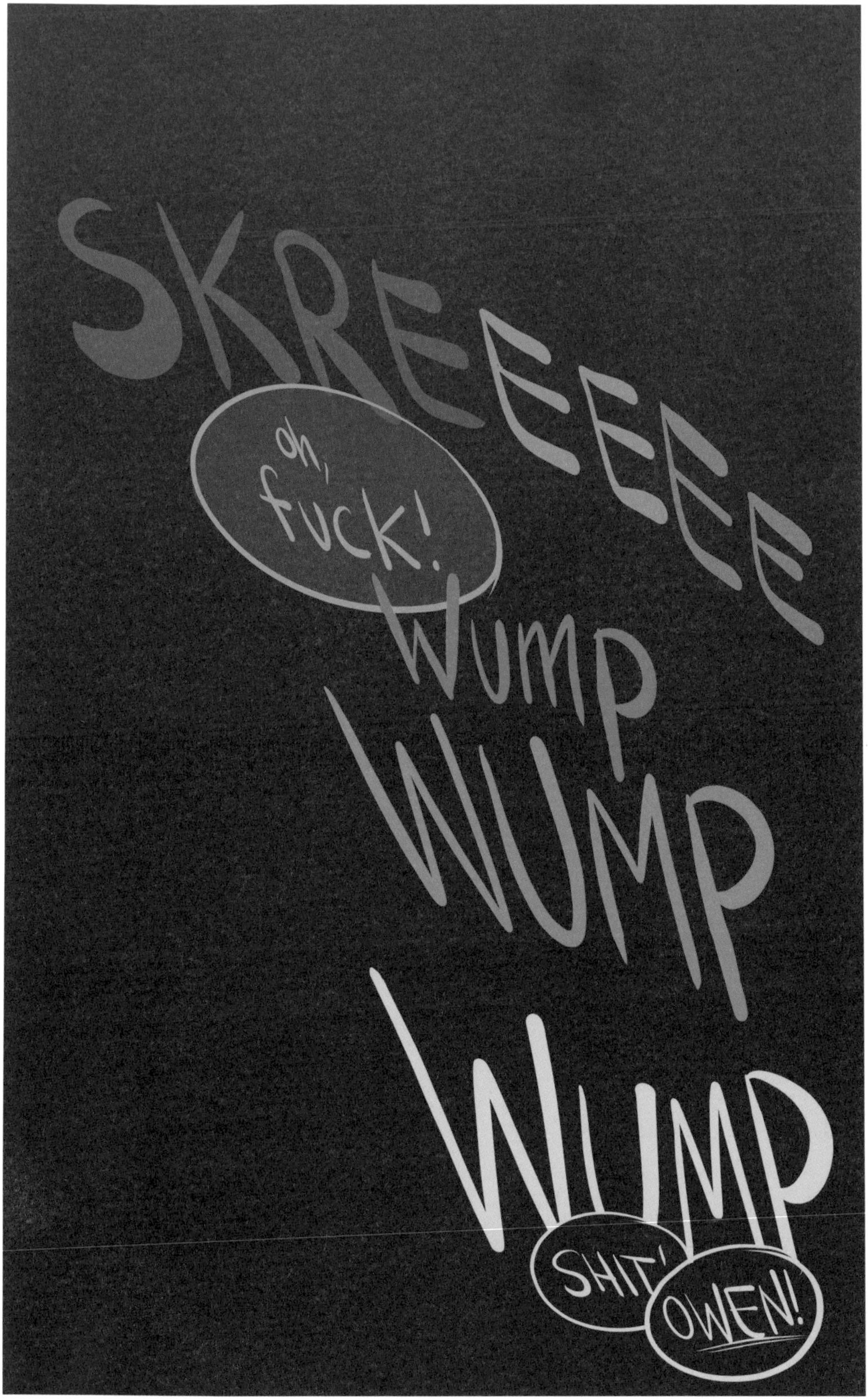
SKREEEEEE
oh, fuck!
Wump
WUMP
WUMP
SHIT'
OWEN!

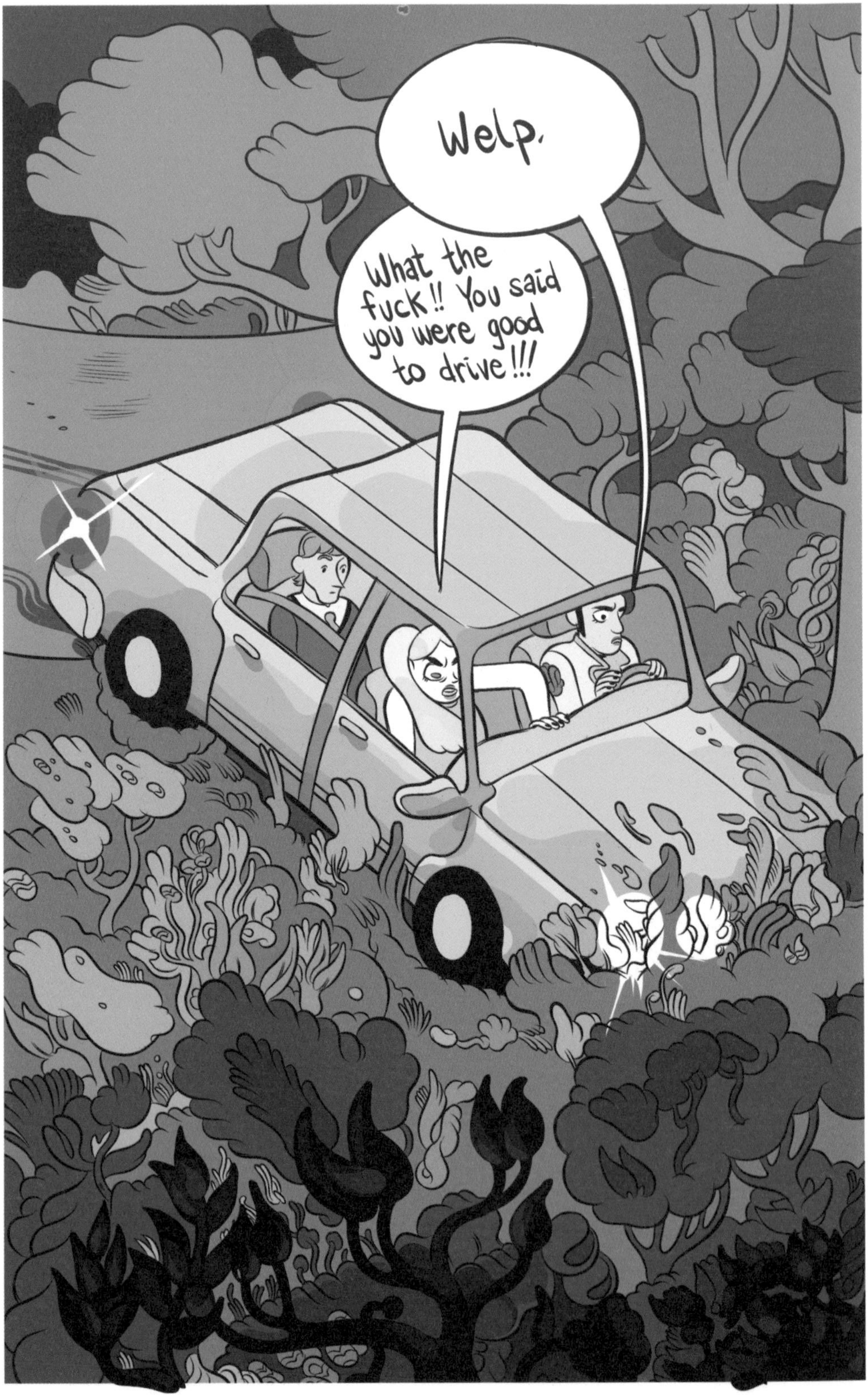
Welp.
What the fuck!! You said you were good to drive!!!

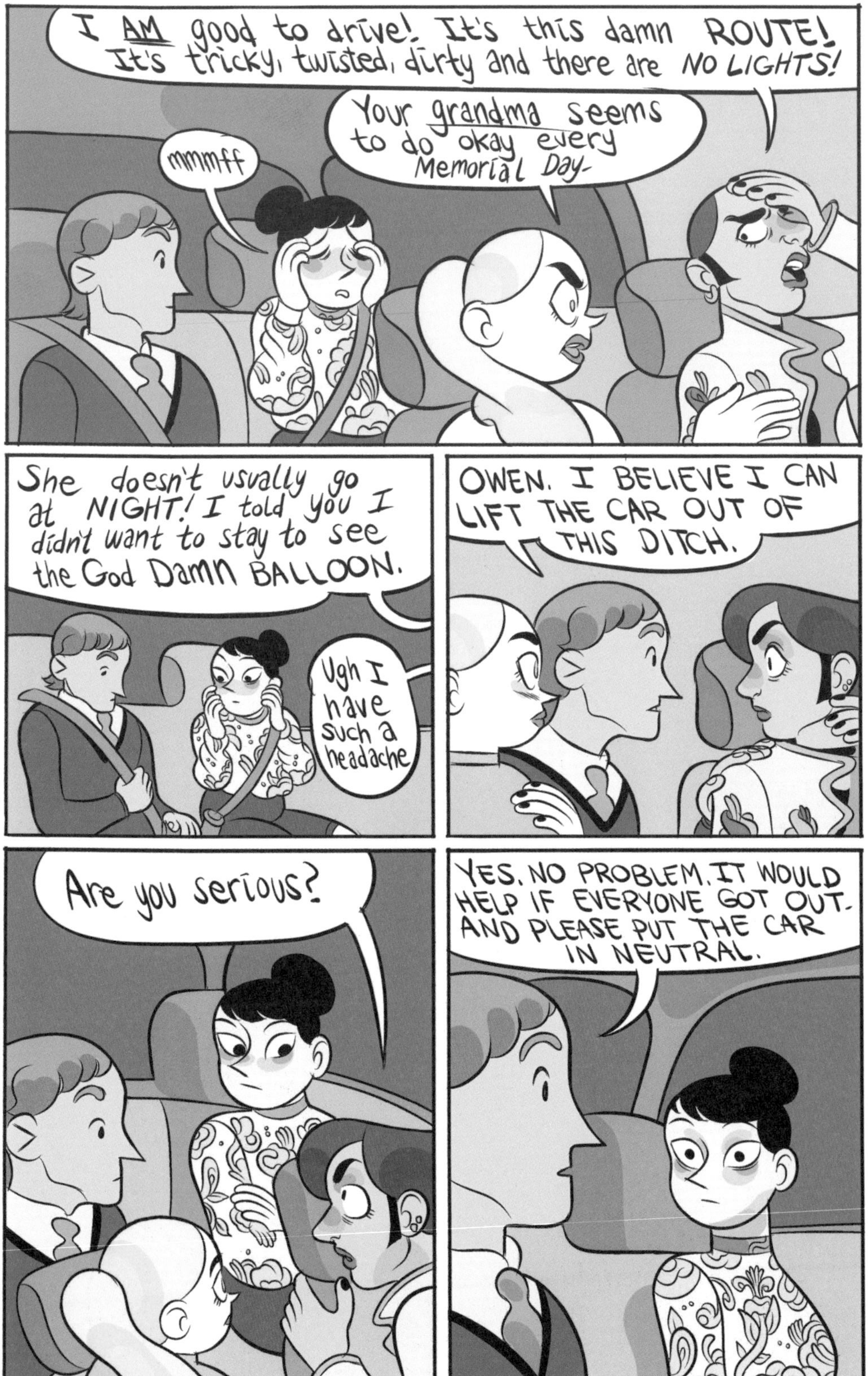
I AM good to drive! It's this damn ROUTE! It's tricky, twisted, dirty and there are NO LIGHTS!
mmmff
Your grandma seems to do okay every Memorial Day-
She doesn't usually go at NIGHT! I told you I didn't want to stay to see the God Damn BALLOON.
Ugh I have such a headache
OWEN. I BELIEVE I CAN LIFT THE CAR OUT OF THIS DITCH.
Are you serious?
YES. NO PROBLEM. IT WOULD HELP IF EVERYONE GOT OUT. AND PLEASE PUT THE CAR IN NEUTRAL.

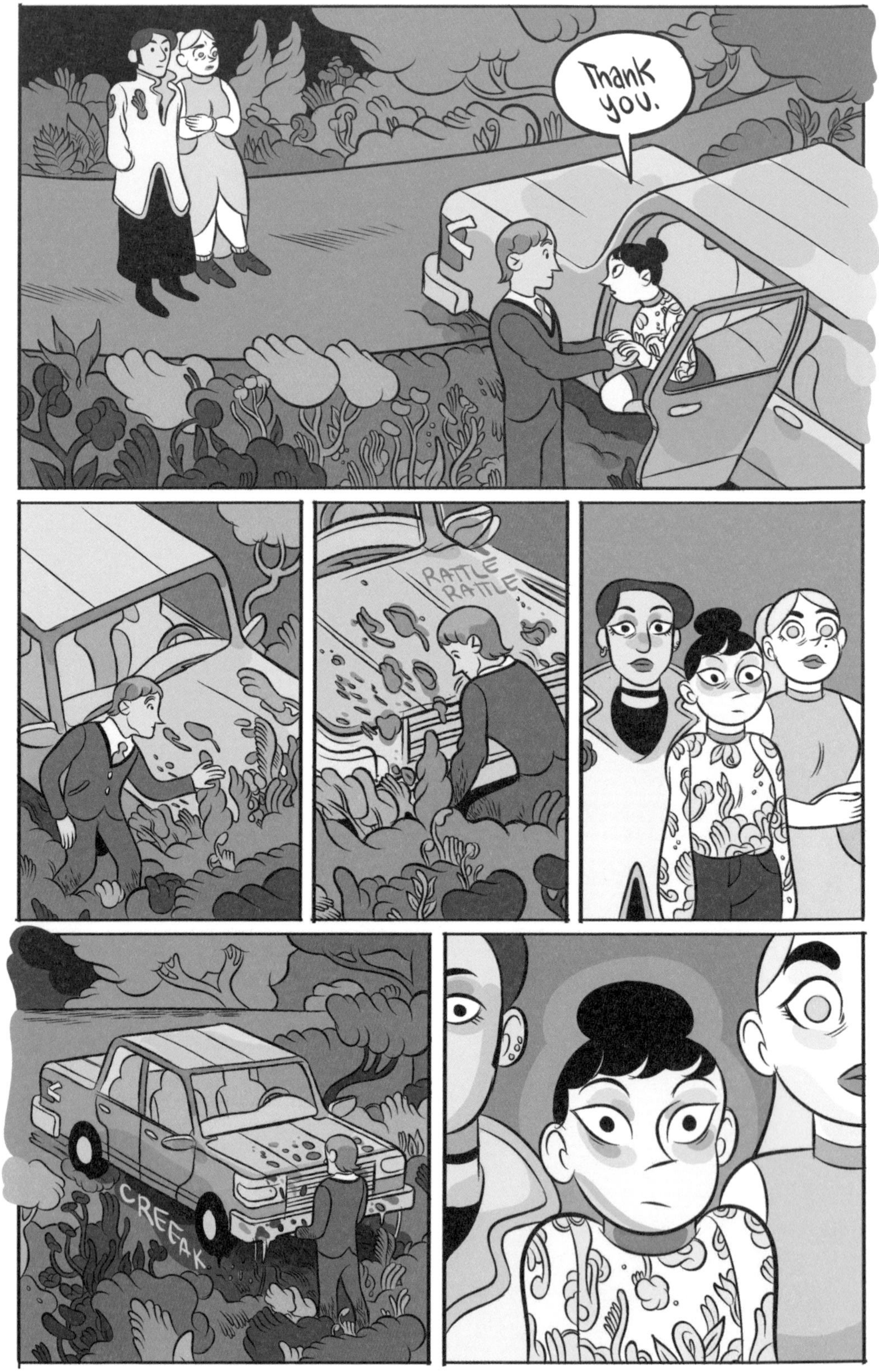

Thank you.
RATTLE RATTLE
CREEAK

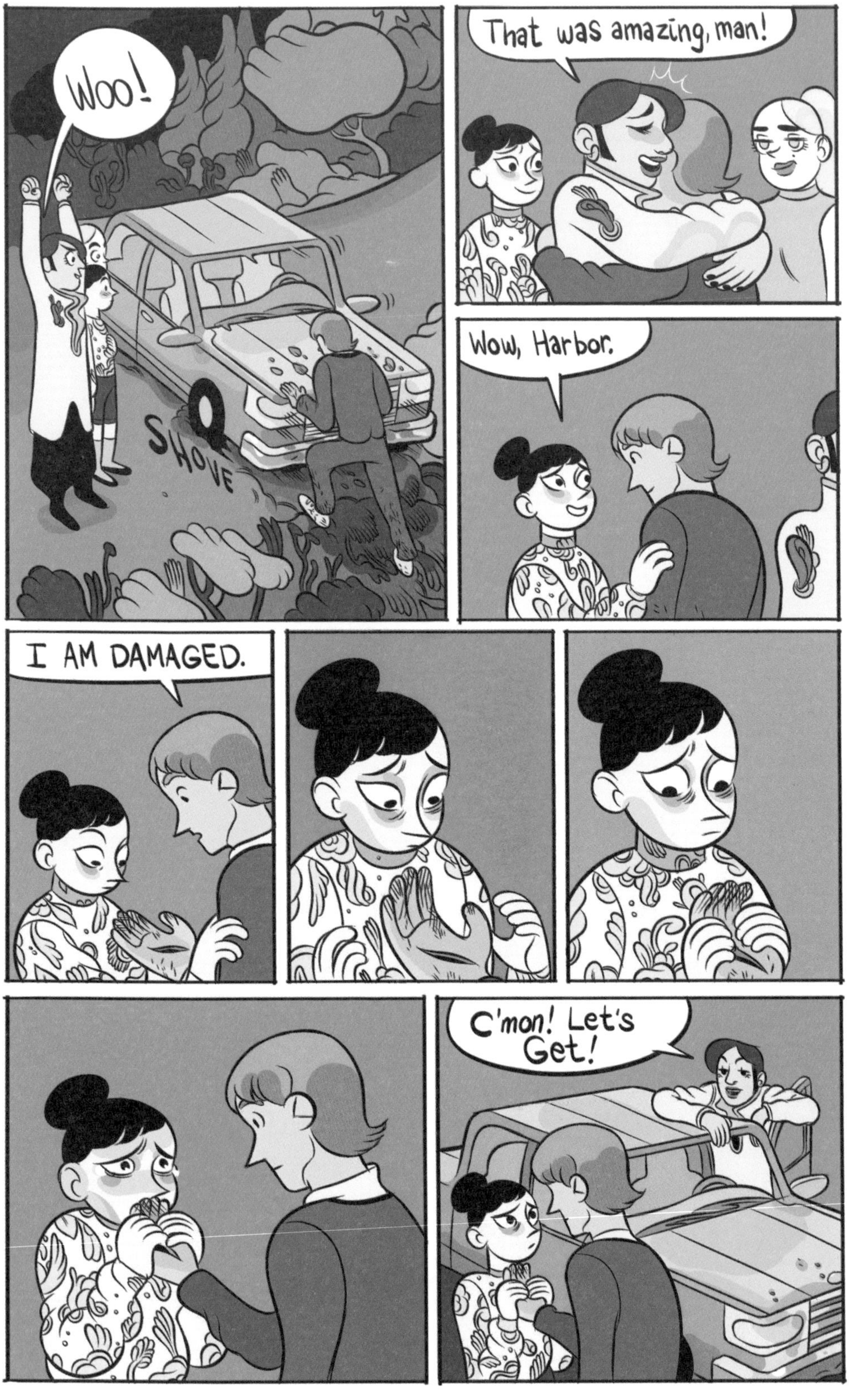
Woo!
SHOVE
That was amazing, man!
Wow, Harbor.
I AM DAMAGED.
C'mon! Let's Get!

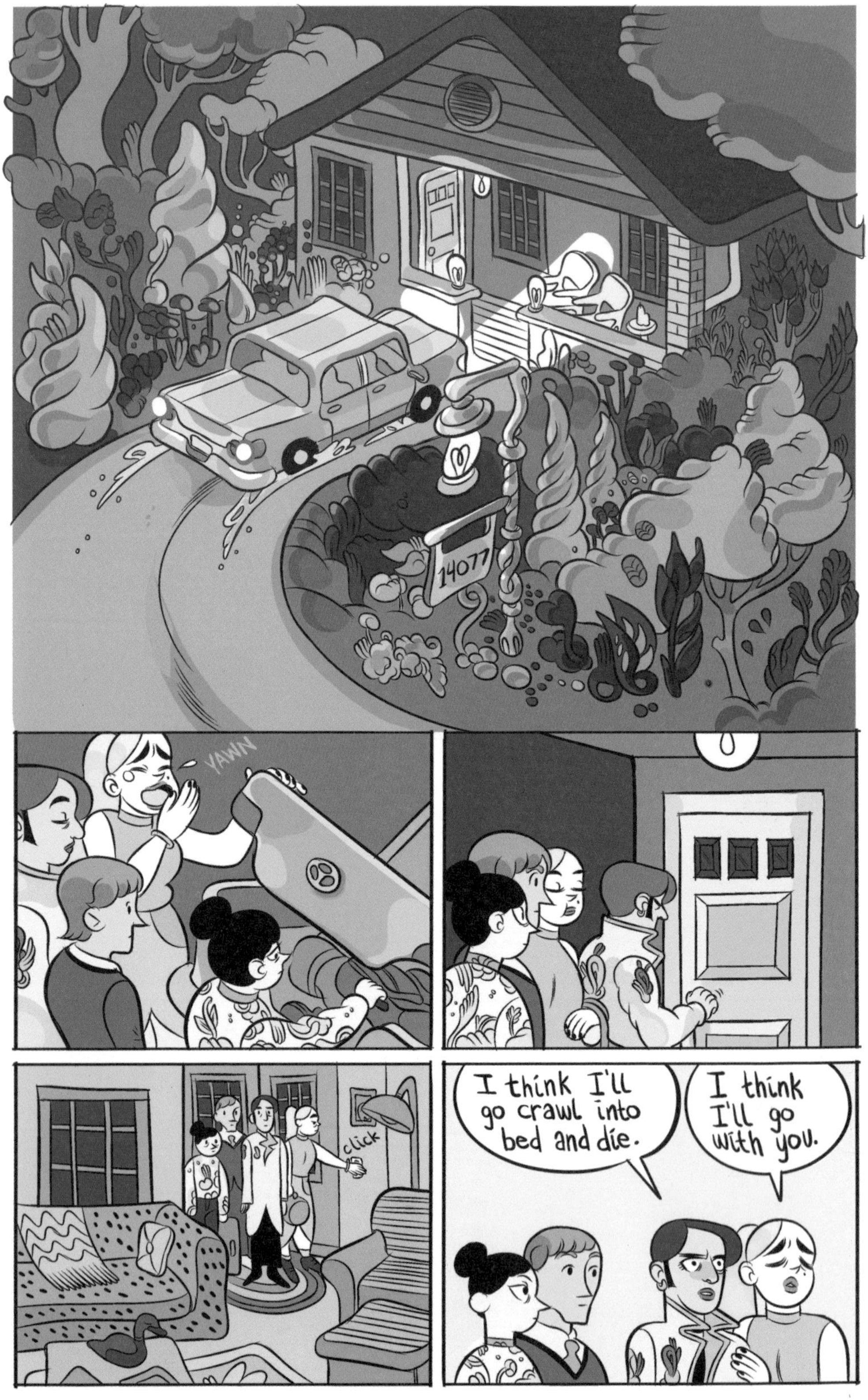
14077
YAWN
click
I think I'll go crawl into bed and die.
I think I'll go with you.

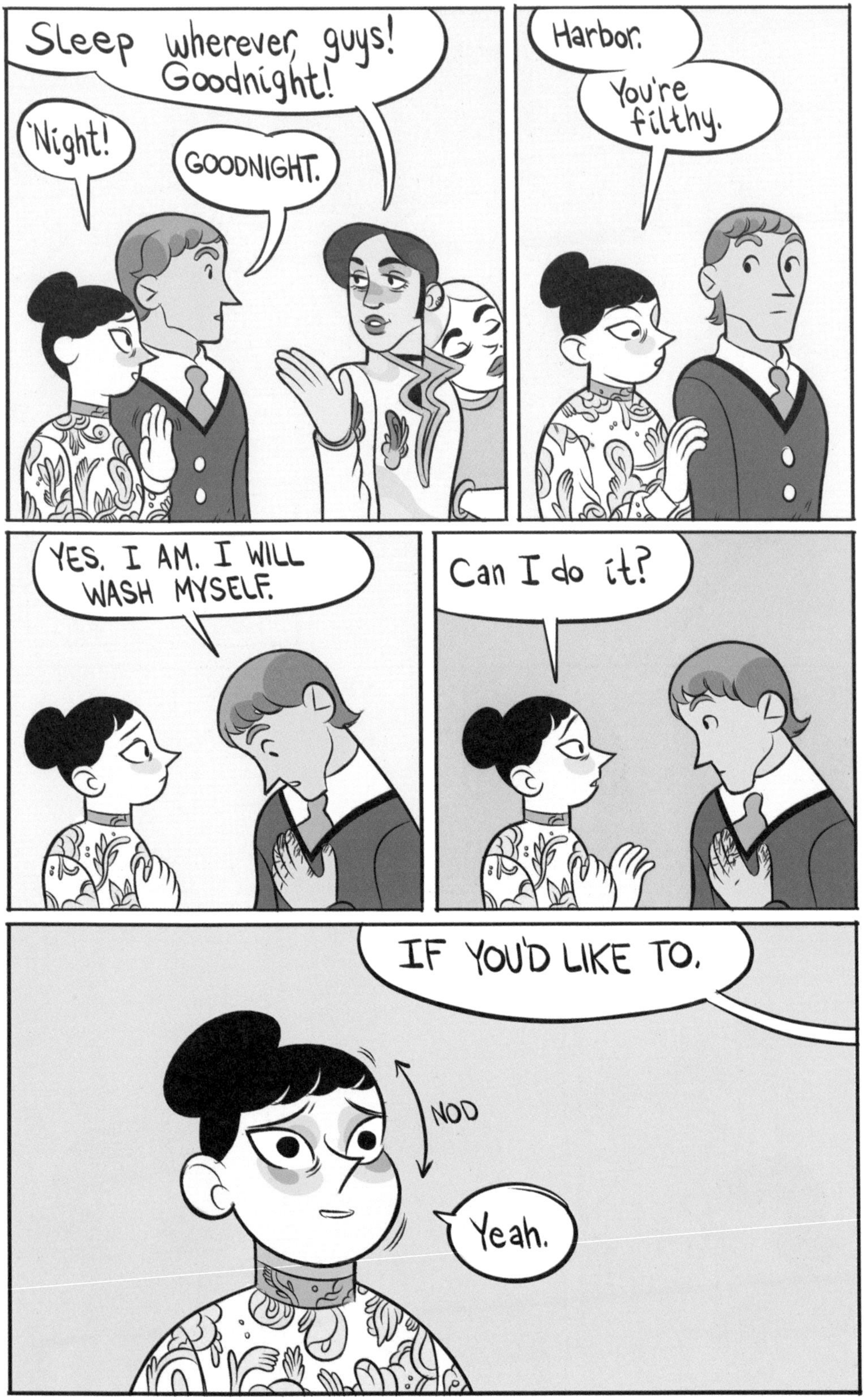

Sleep wherever, guys! Goodnight!
`Night!
GOODNIGHT.
Harbor.
You're filthy.
YES. I AM. I WILL WASH MYSELF.
Can I do it?
IF YOU'D LIKE TO.
NOD
Yeah.

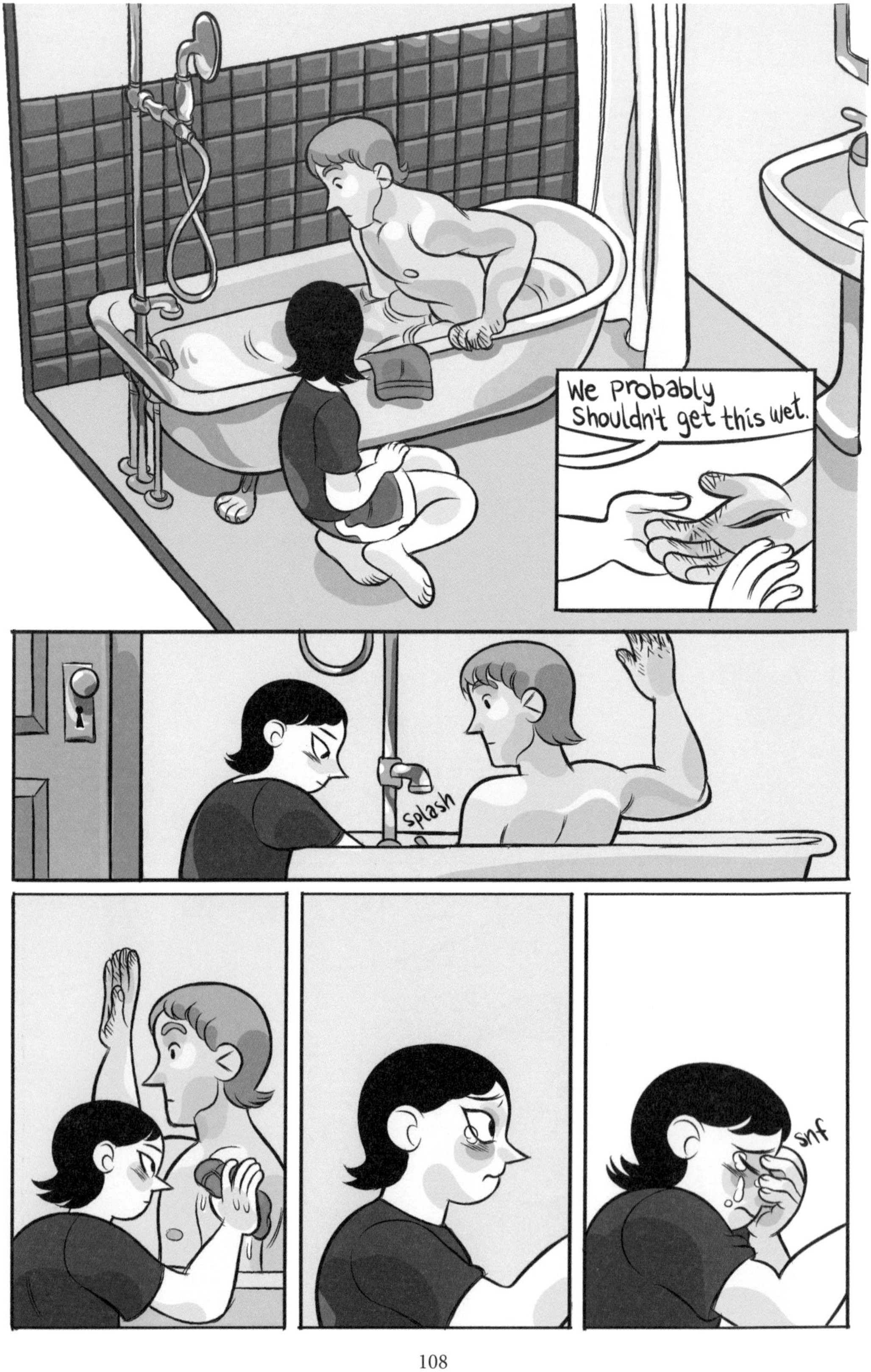

We probably shouldn't get this wet.
splash
snf

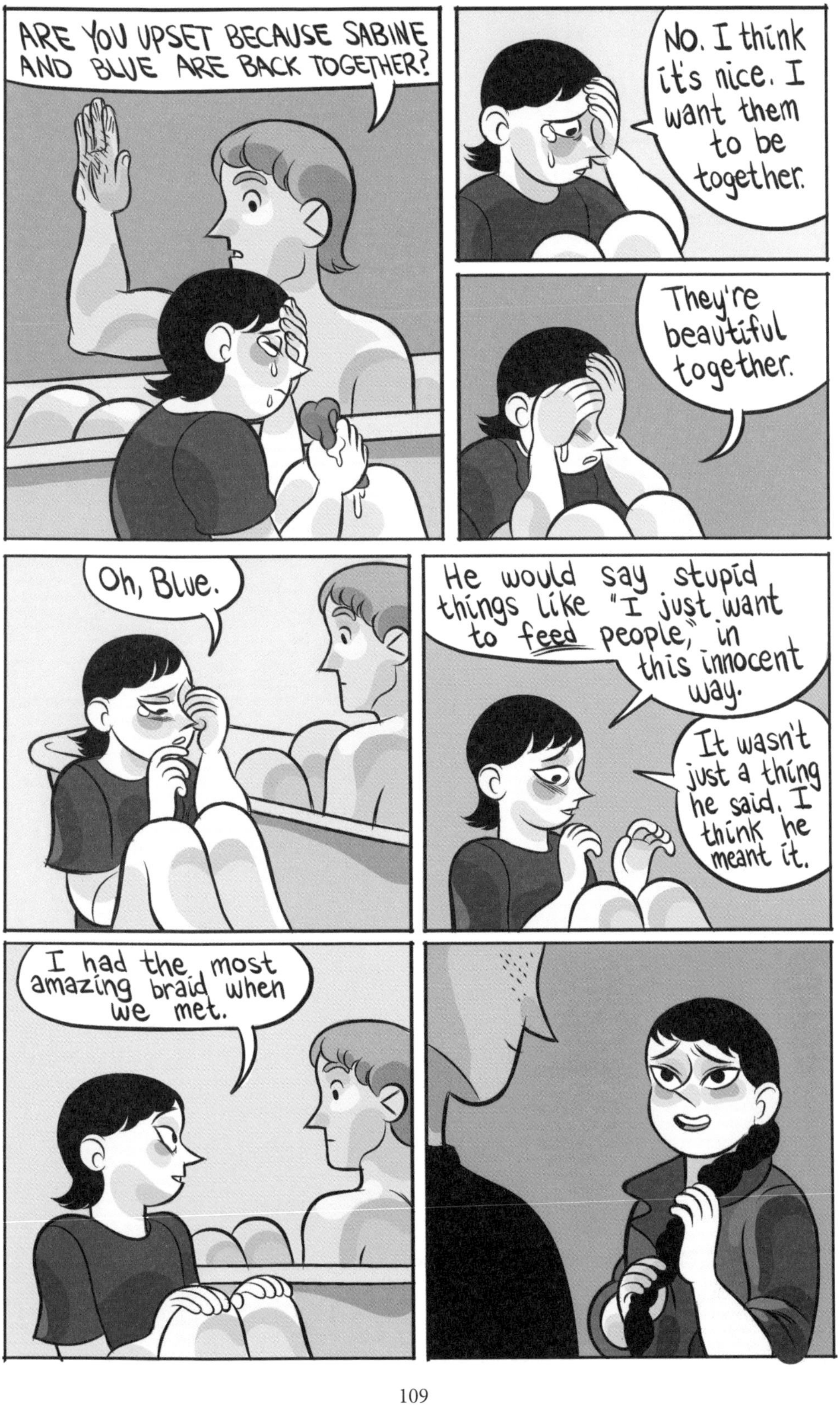
ARE YOU UPSET BECAUSE SABINE AND BLUE ARE BACK TOGETHER?
No. I think it's nice. I want them to be together.
They're beautiful together.
Oh, Blue.
He would say stupid things like "I just want to feed people," in this innocent way.
It wasn't just a thing he said. I think he meant it.
I had the most amazing braid when we met.

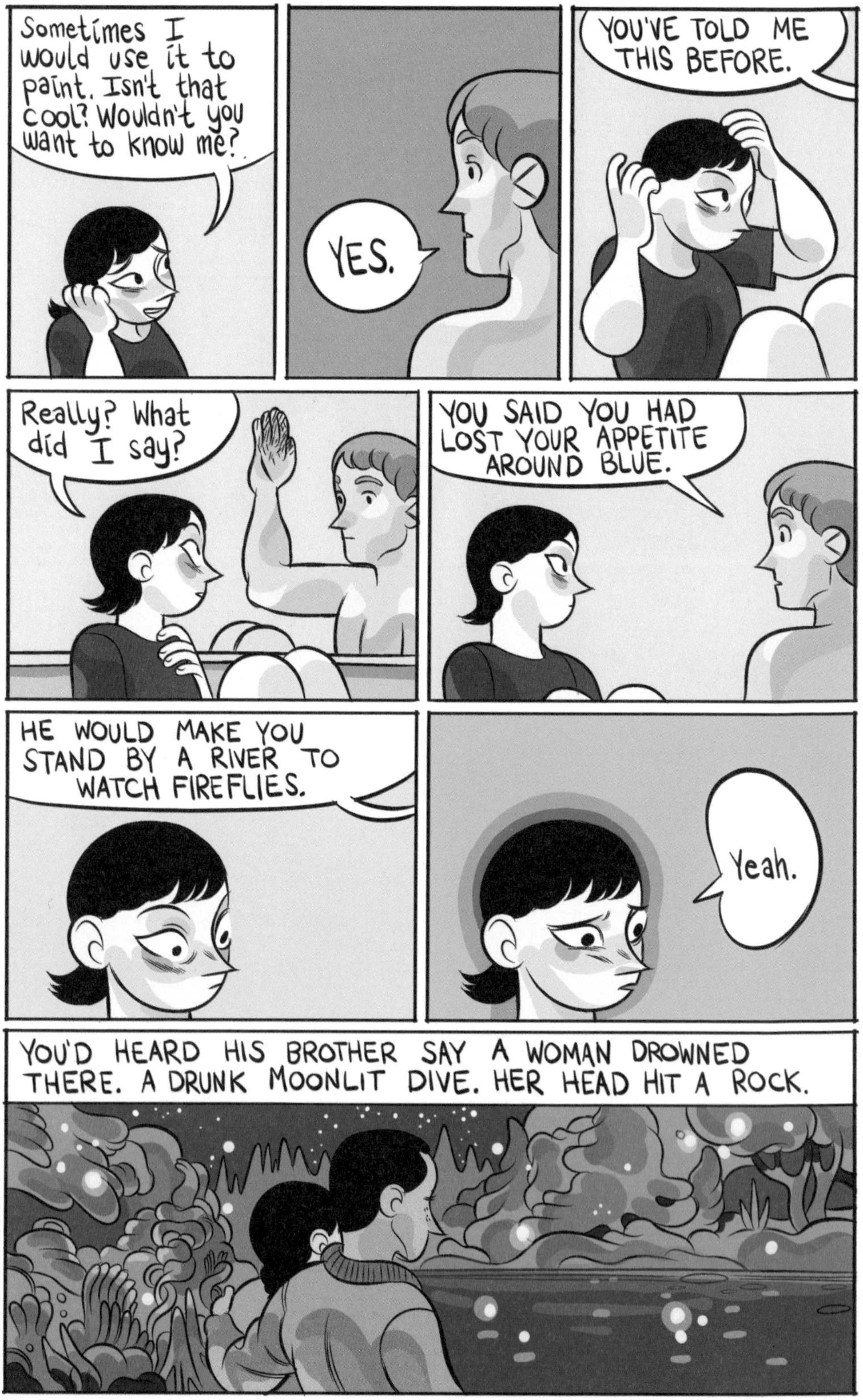
Sometimes I would use it to paint. Isn't that cool? Wouldn't you want to know me?
YES.
YOU'VE TOLD ME THIS BEFORE.
Really? What did I say?
YOU SAID YOU HAD LOST YOUR APPETITE AROUND BLUE.
HE WOULD MAKE YOU STAND BY A RIVER TO WATCH FIREFLIES.
Yeah.
YOU'D HEARD HIS BROTHER SAY A WOMAN DROWNED THERE. A DRUNK MOONLIT DIVE. HER HEAD HIT A ROCK.

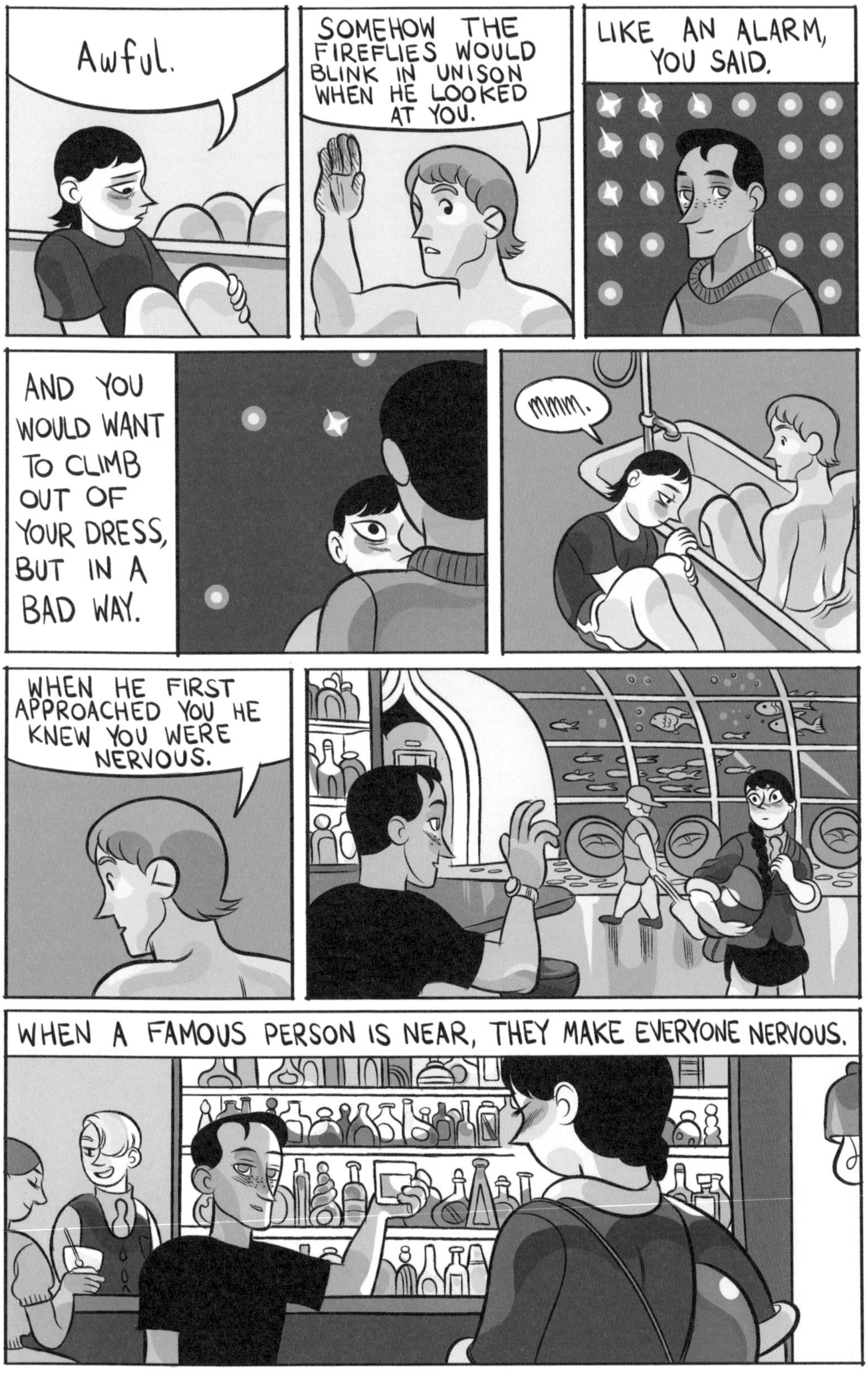
Awful.
SOMEHOW THE FIREFLIES WOULD BLINK IN UNISON WHEN HE LOOKED AT YOU.
LIKE AN ALARM, YOU SAID.
AND YOU WOULD WANT TO CLIMB OUT OF YOUR DRESS, BUT IN A BAD WAY.
mmm.
WHEN HE FIRST APPROACHED YOU HE KNEW YOU WERE NERVOUS.
WHEN A FAMOUS PERSON IS NEAR, THEY MAKE EVERYONE NERVOUS.

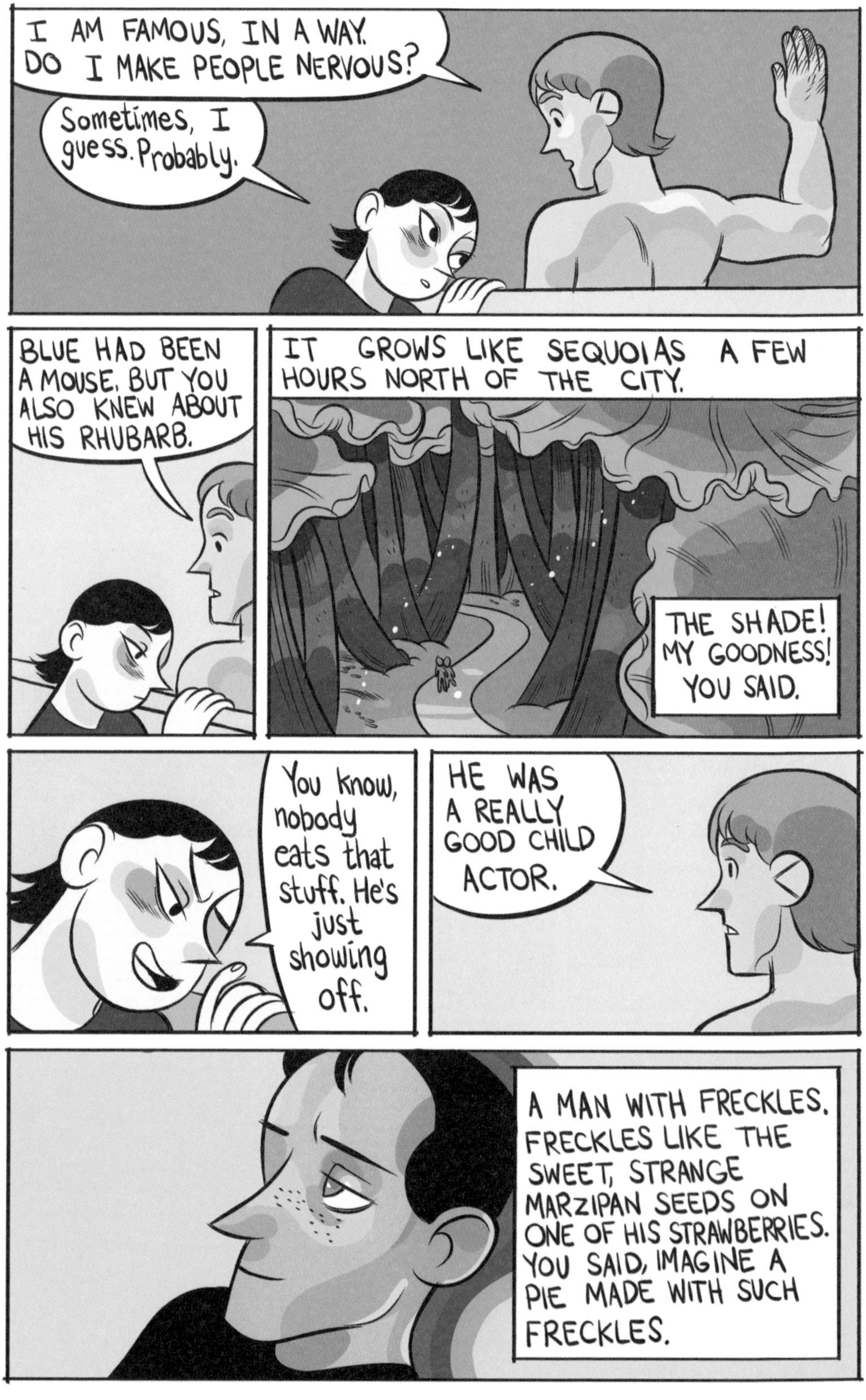
I AM FAMOUS, IN A WAY. DO I MAKE PEOPLE NERVOUS?
Sometimes, I guess. Probably.
BLUE HAD BEEN A MOUSE. BUT YOU ALSO KNEW ABOUT HIS RHUBARB.
IT GROWS LIKE SEQUOIAS A FEW HOURS NORTH OF THE CITY.
THE SHADE! MY GOODNESS! YOU SAID.
You know, nobody eats that stuff. He's just showing off.
HE WAS A REALLY GOOD CHILD ACTOR.
A MAN WITH FRECKLES. FRECKLES LIKE THE SWEET, STRANGE MARZIPAN SEEDS ON ONE OF HIS STRAWBERRIES. YOU SAID, IMAGINE A PIE MADE WITH SUCH FRECKLES.

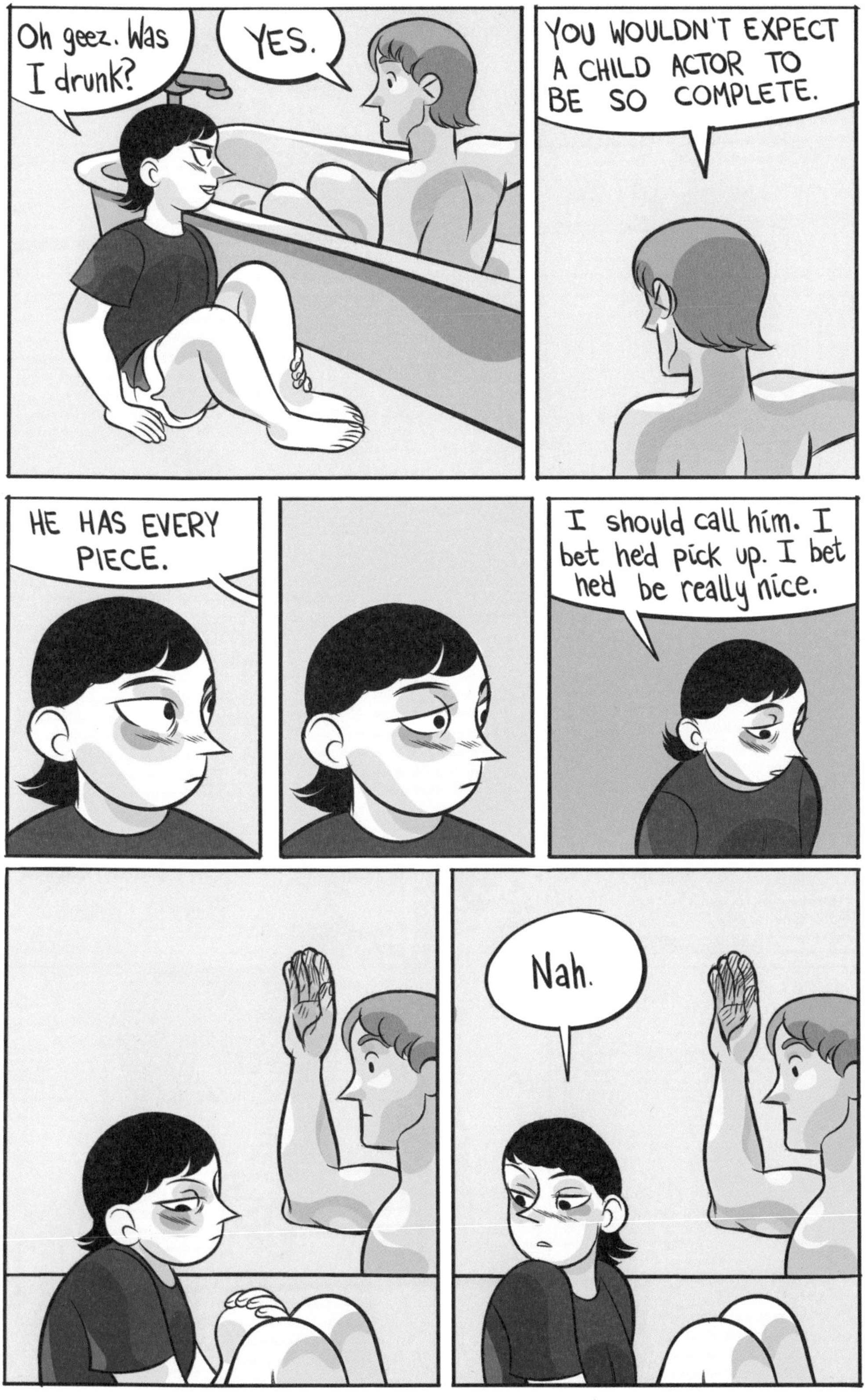
Oh geez. Was I drunk?
YES.
YOU WOULDN'T EXPECT A CHILD ACTOR TO BE SO COMPLETE.
HE HAS EVERY PIECE.
I should call him. I bet he'd pick up. I bet he'd be really nice.
Nah.

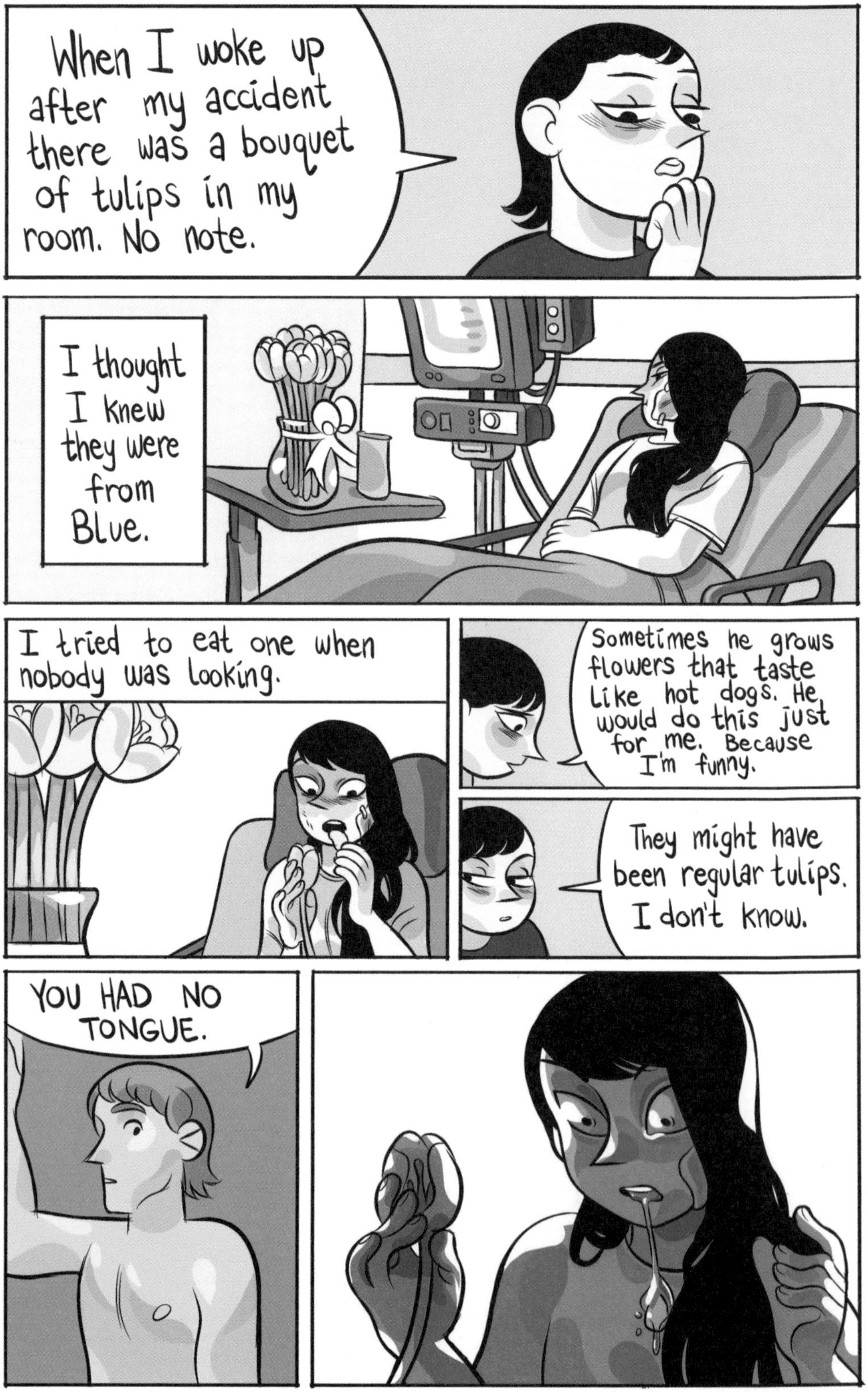
When I woke up after my accident there was a bouquet of tulips in my room. No note.
I thought I knew they were from Blue.
I tried to eat one when nobody was looking.
Sometimes he grows flowers that taste like hot dogs. He would do this just for me. Because I'm funny.
They might have been regular tulips. I don't know.
YOU HAD NO TONGUE.

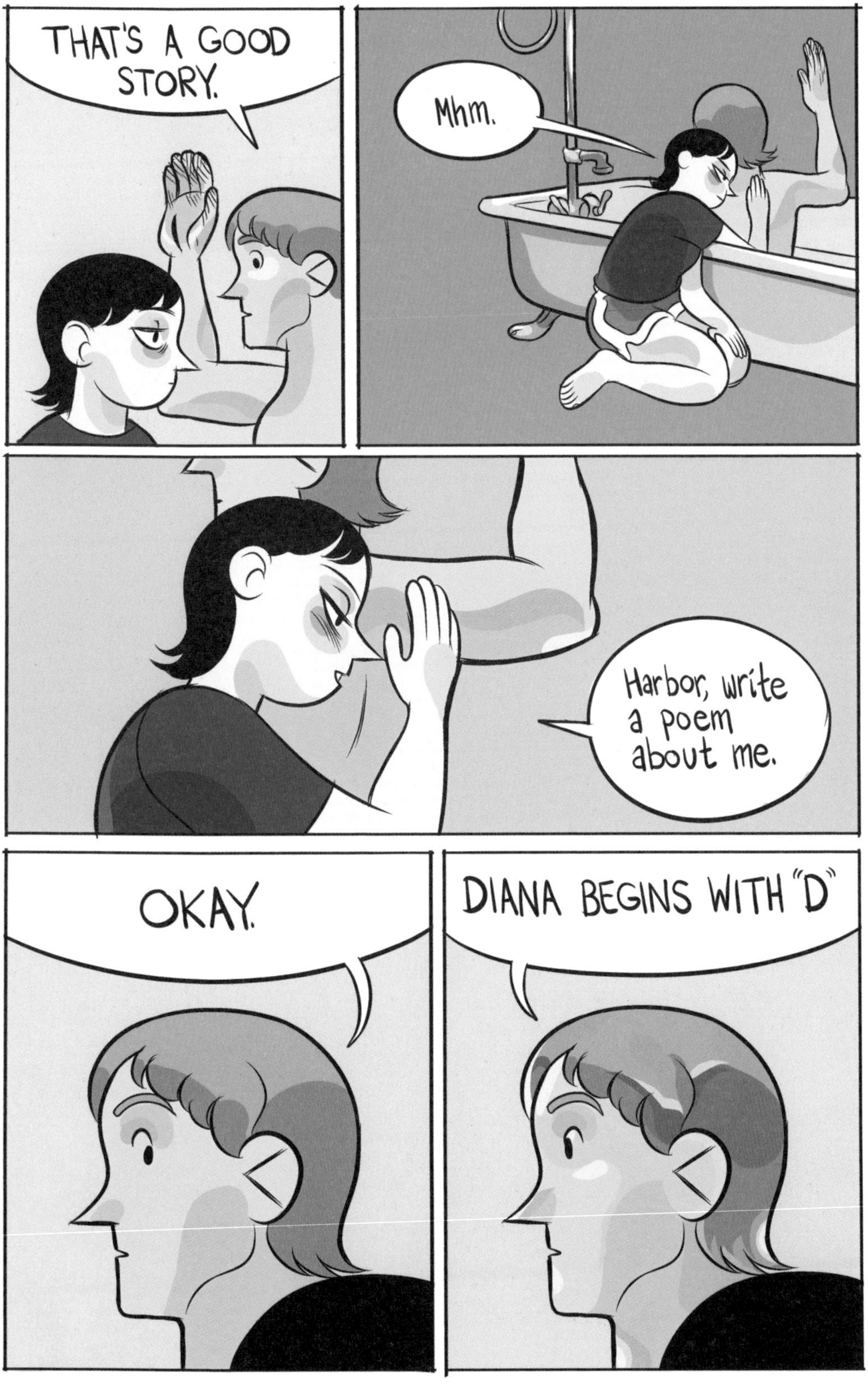
THAT'S A GOOD STORY.
Mhm.
Harbor, write a poem about me.
OKAY.
DIANA BEGINS WITH "D"

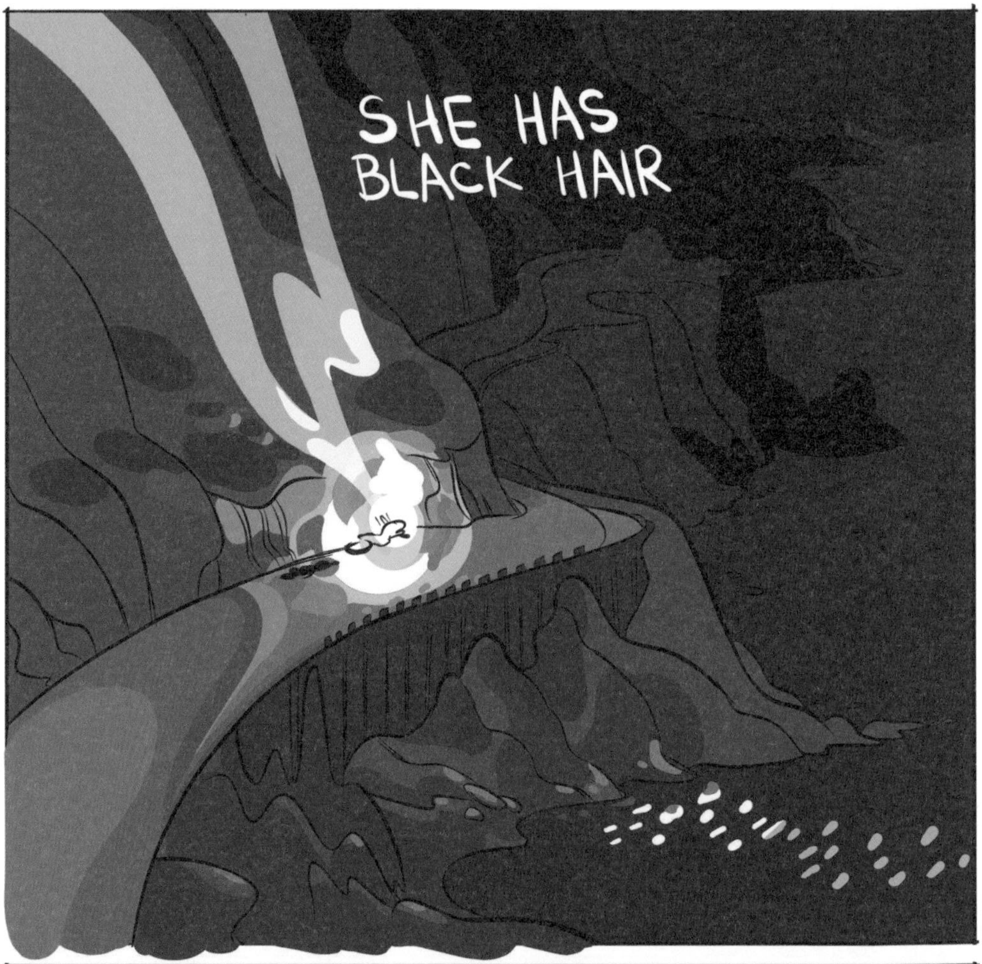
SHE HAS
BLACK HAIR

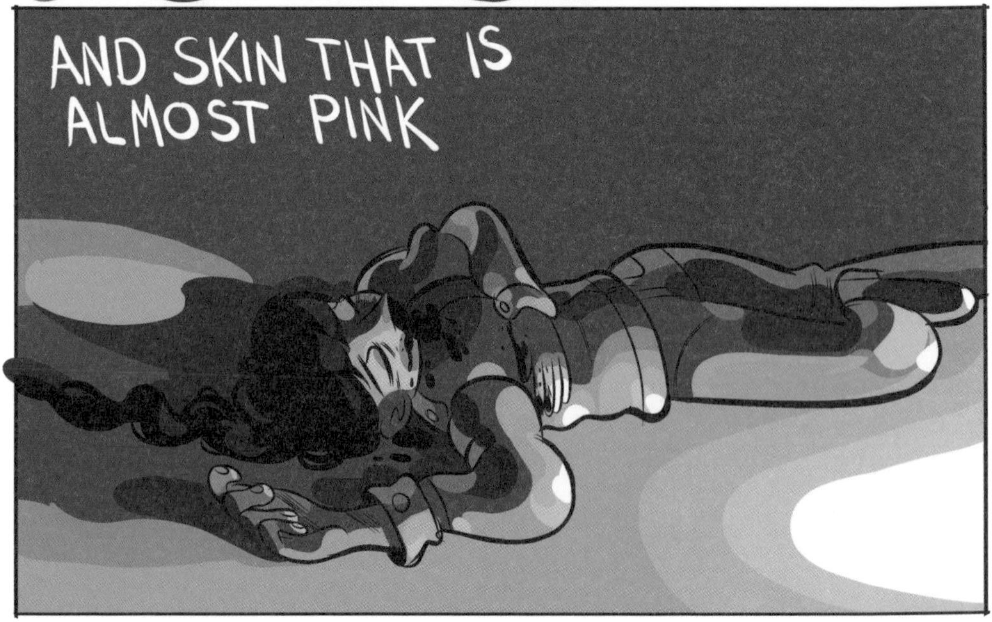
AND SKIN THAT IS
ALMOST PINK

I WILL BE
WITH HER UNTIL SHE
DOESN'T WANT ME
ANYMORE.

2016

THE BIG BURNING HOUSE

THE CONSTELLATION
~~HARVEY~~

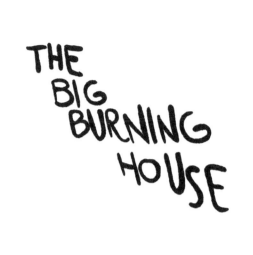

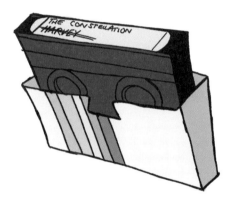

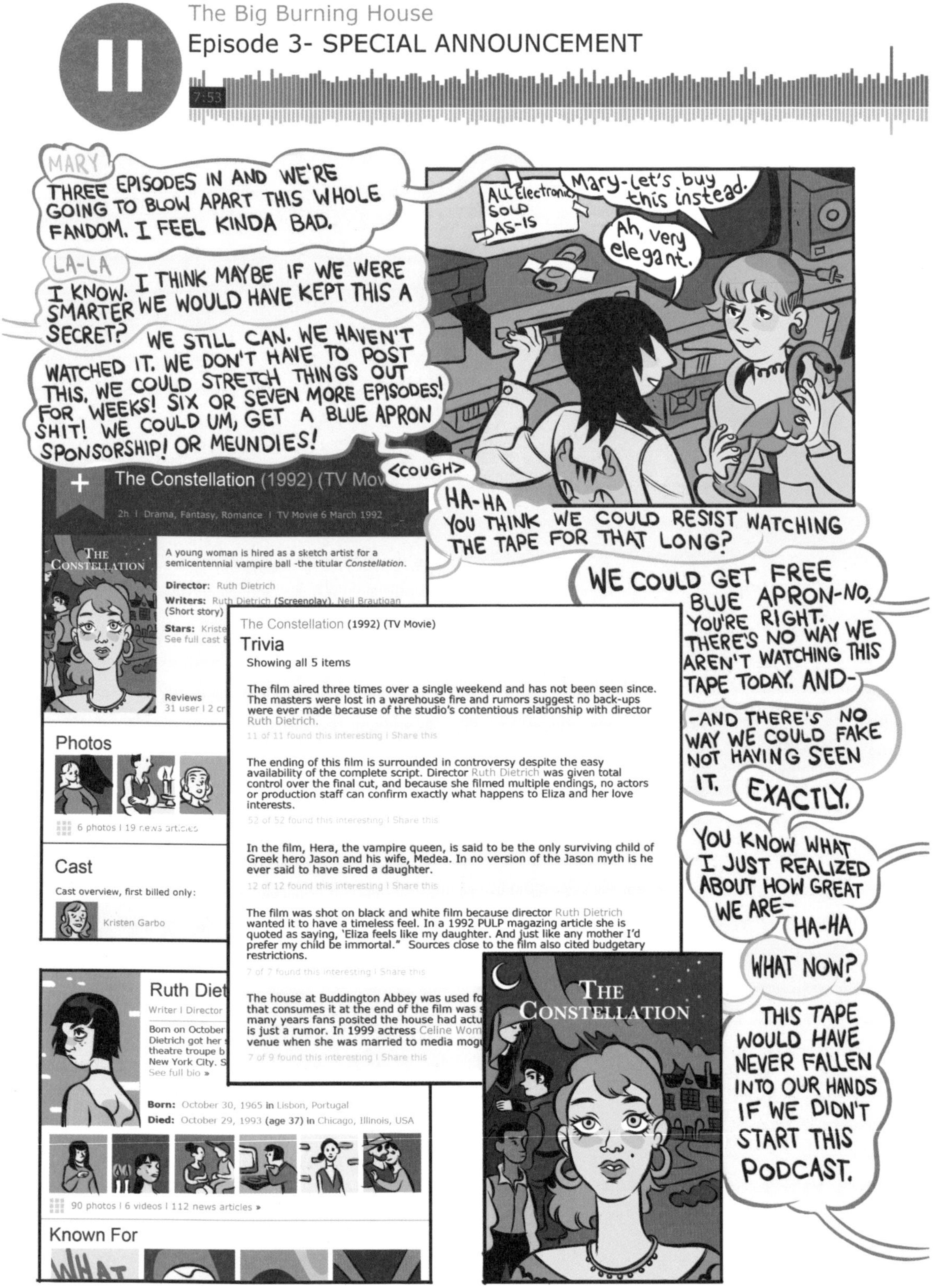
The Big Burning House
Episode 3- SPECIAL ANNOUNCEMENT
7:53
MARY
THREE EPISODES IN AND WE'RE GOING TO BLOW APART THIS WHOLE FANDOM. I FEEL KINDA BAD.
LA-LA
I KNOW. I THINK MAYBE IF WE WERE SMARTER WE WOULD HAVE KEPT THIS A SECRET?
WE STILL CAN. WE HAVEN'T WATCHED IT. WE DON'T HAVE TO POST THIS. WE COULD STRETCH THINGS OUT FOR WEEKS! SIX OR SEVEN MORE EPISODES! SHIT! WE COULD UM, GET A BLUE APRON SPONSORSHIP! OR MEUNDIES!
ALL Electronics SOLD AS-IS
Mary-Let's buy this instead.
Ah, very elegant.
<COUGH>
HA-HA
YOU THINK WE COULD RESIST WATCHING THE TAPE FOR THAT LONG?
WE COULD GET FREE BLUE APRON-NO, YOU'RE RIGHT. THERE'S NO WAY WE AREN'T WATCHING THIS TAPE TODAY. AND-
-AND THERE'S NO WAY WE COULD FAKE NOT HAVING SEEN IT.
EXACTLY.
YOU KNOW WHAT I JUST REALIZED ABOUT HOW GREAT WE ARE-
HA-HA
WHAT NOW?
THIS TAPE WOULD HAVE NEVER FALLEN INTO OUR HANDS IF WE DIDN'T START THIS PODCAST.
The Constellation (1992) (TV Mov
2h I Drama, Fantasy, Romance I TV Movie 6 March 1992
THE CONSTELLATION
A young woman is hired as a sketch artist for a semicentennial vampire ball -the titular *Constellation*.
Director: Ruth Dietrich
Writers: Ruth Dietrich (Screenplay), Neil Brautigan (Short story)
Stars: Kriste
See full cast
Reviews
31 user I 2 cr
Photos
6 photos I 19 news articles
Cast
Cast overview, first billed only:
Kristen Garbo
The Constellation (1992) (TV Movie)
Trivia
Showing all 5 items
The film aired three times over a single weekend and has not been seen since. The masters were lost in a warehouse fire and rumors suggest no back-ups were ever made because of the studio's contentious relationship with director Ruth Dietrich.
11 of 11 found this interesting I Share this
The ending of this film is surrounded in controversy despite the easy availability of the complete script. Director Ruth Dietrich was given total control over the final cut, and because she filmed multiple endings, no actors or production staff can confirm exactly what happens to Eliza and her love interests.
52 of 52 found this interesting I Share this
In the film, Hera, the vampire queen, is said to be the only surviving child of Greek hero Jason and his wife, Medea. In no version of the Jason myth is he ever said to have sired a daughter.
12 of 12 found this interesting I Share this
The film was shot on black and white film because director Ruth Dietrich wanted it to have a timeless feel. In a 1992 PULP magazing article she is quoted as saying, 'Eliza feels like my daughter. And just like any mother I'd prefer my child be immortal." Sources close to the film also cited budgetary restrictions.
7 of 7 found this interesting I Share this
The house at Buddington Abbey was used fo
that consumes it at the end of the film was
many years fans posited the house had actu
is just a rumor. In 1999 actress Celine Wom
venue when she was married to media mogu
7 of 9 found this interesting I Share this
Ruth Diet
Writer I Director
Born on October
Dietrich got her
theatre troupe b
New York City. S
See full bio »
Born: October 30, 1965 in Lisbon, Portugal
Died: October 29, 1993 (age 37) in Chicago, Illinois, USA
90 photos I 6 videos I 112 news articles »
Known For
WHAT
THE CONSTELLATION

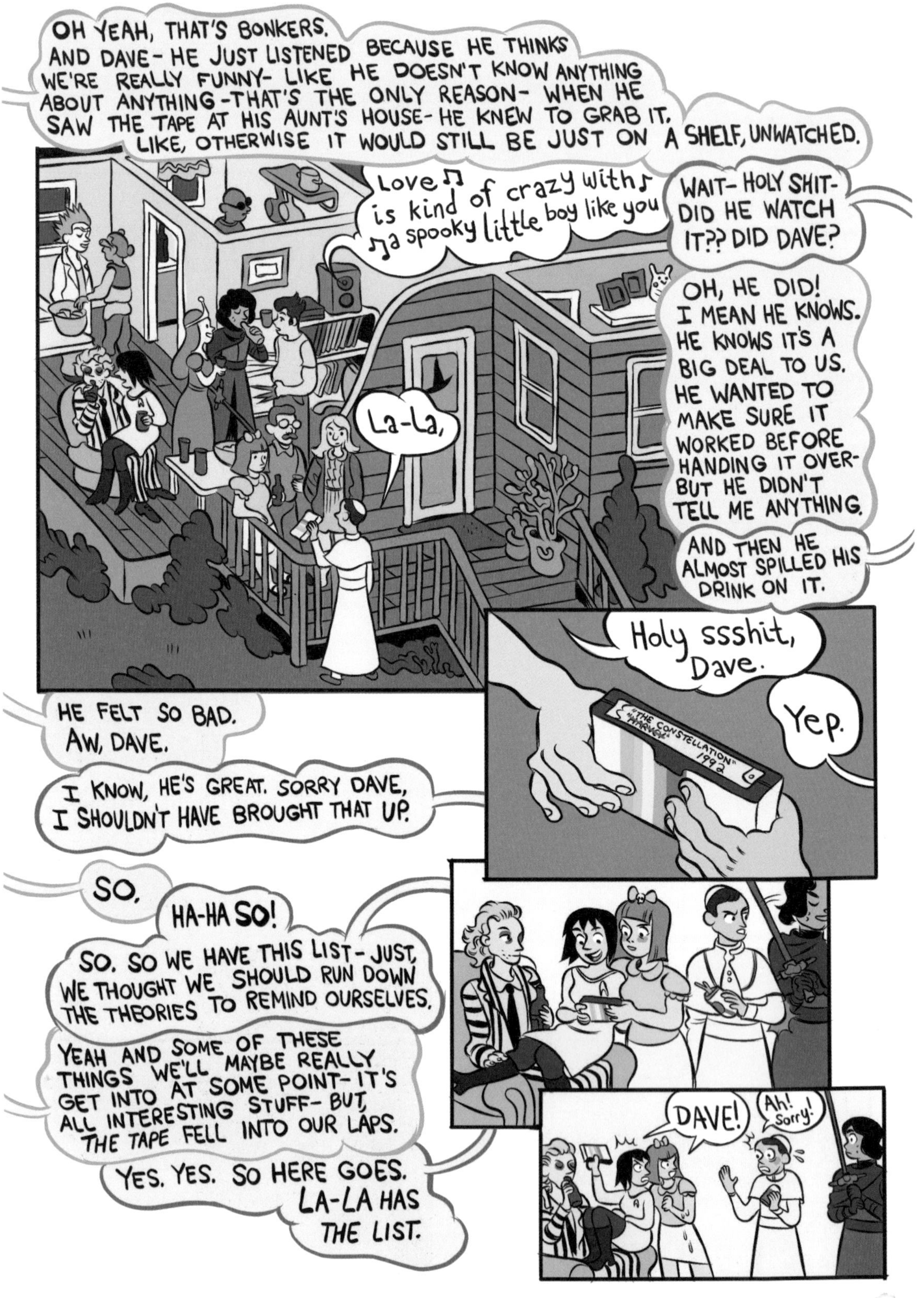

OH YEAH, THAT'S BONKERS. AND DAVE- HE JUST LISTENED BECAUSE HE THINKS WE'RE REALLY FUNNY- LIKE HE DOESN'T KNOW ANYTHING ABOUT ANYTHING -THAT'S THE ONLY REASON- WHEN HE SAW THE TAPE AT HIS AUNT'S HOUSE- HE KNEW TO GRAB IT. LIKE, OTHERWISE IT WOULD STILL BE JUST ON A SHELF, UNWATCHED.
Love ♫ is kind of crazy with ♪ ♫ a spooky little boy like you
WAIT- HOLY SHIT- DID HE WATCH IT?? DID DAVE?
OH, HE DID! I MEAN HE KNOWS. HE KNOWS IT'S A BIG DEAL TO US. HE WANTED TO MAKE SURE IT WORKED BEFORE HANDING IT OVER- BUT HE DIDN'T TELL ME ANYTHING.
La-La,
AND THEN HE ALMOST SPILLED HIS DRINK ON IT.
Holy ssshit, Dave.
"THE CONSTELLATION" 1992
Yep.
HE FELT SO BAD. AW, DAVE.
I KNOW, HE'S GREAT. SORRY DAVE, I SHOULDN'T HAVE BROUGHT THAT UP.
SO,
HA-HA SO!
SO. SO WE HAVE THIS LIST- JUST, WE THOUGHT WE SHOULD RUN DOWN THE THEORIES TO REMIND OURSELVES.
YEAH AND SOME OF THESE THINGS WE'LL MAYBE REALLY GET INTO AT SOME POINT- IT'S ALL INTERESTING STUFF- BUT, THE TAPE FELL INTO OUR LAPS.
DAVE!
Ah! Sorry!
YES. YES. SO HERE GOES. LA-LA HAS THE LIST.

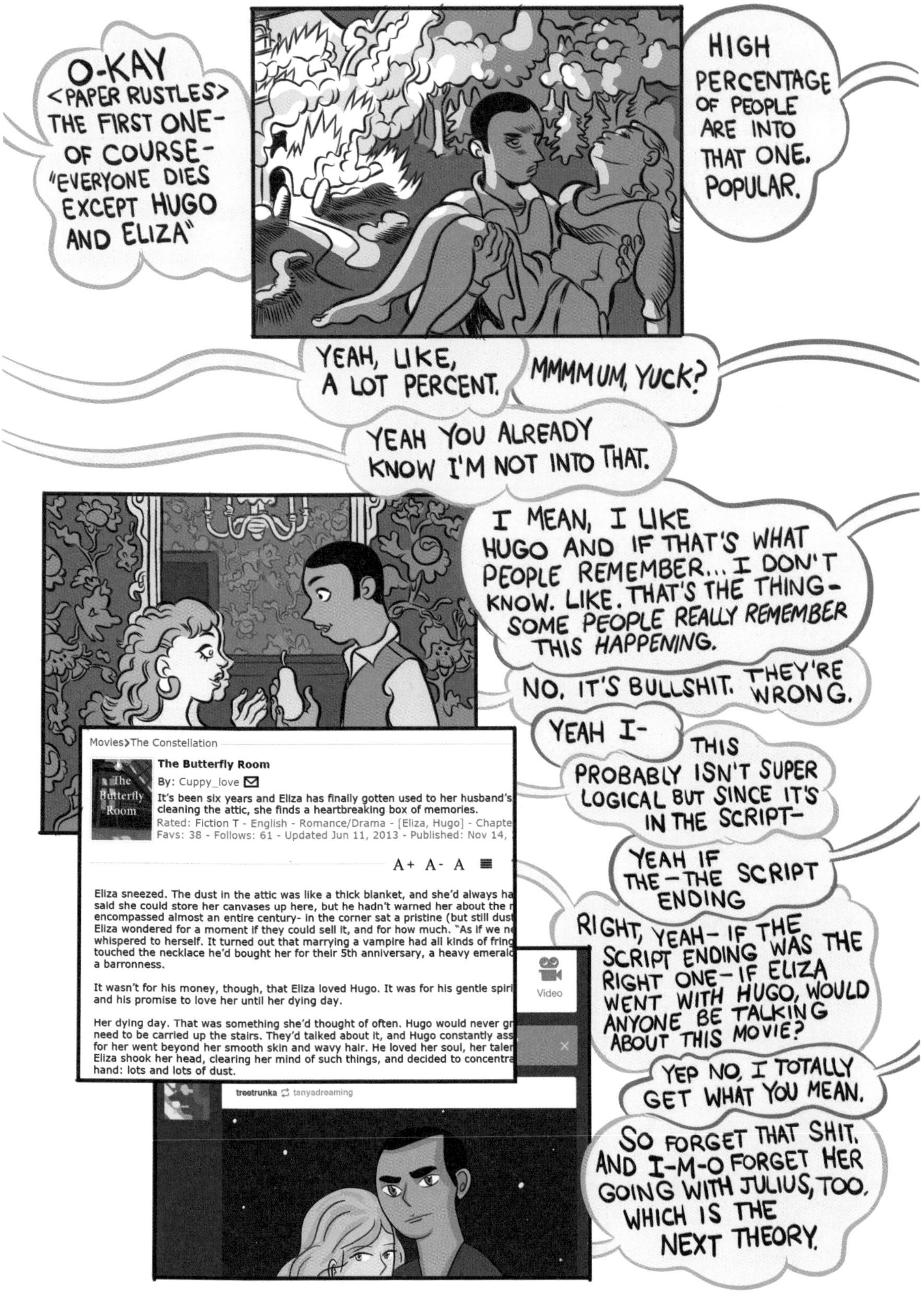
O-KAY <PAPER RUSTLES> THE FIRST ONE- OF COURSE- "EVERYONE DIES EXCEPT HUGO AND ELIZA"
HIGH PERCENTAGE OF PEOPLE ARE INTO THAT ONE. POPULAR.
YEAH, LIKE, A LOT PERCENT.
MMMMUM, YUCK?
YEAH YOU ALREADY KNOW I'M NOT INTO THAT.
I MEAN, I LIKE HUGO AND IF THAT'S WHAT PEOPLE REMEMBER... I DON'T KNOW. LIKE. THAT'S THE THING- SOME PEOPLE REALLY REMEMBER THIS HAPPENING.
NO. IT'S BULLSHIT. THEY'RE WRONG.
YEAH I-
THIS PROBABLY ISN'T SUPER LOGICAL BUT SINCE IT'S IN THE SCRIPT-
YEAH IF THE-THE SCRIPT ENDING
RIGHT, YEAH- IF THE SCRIPT ENDING WAS THE RIGHT ONE- IF ELIZA WENT WITH HUGO, WOULD ANYONE BE TALKING ABOUT THIS MOVIE?
YEP NO, I TOTALLY GET WHAT YOU MEAN.
SO FORGET THAT SHIT. AND I-M-O FORGET HER GOING WITH JULIUS, TOO. WHICH IS THE NEXT THEORY.
Movies›The Constellation
The Butterfly Room
By: Cuppy_love
It's been six years and Eliza has finally gotten used to her husband's
cleaning the attic, she finds a heartbreaking box of memories.
Rated: Fiction T - English - Romance/Drama - [Eliza, Hugo] - Chapte
Favs: 38 - Follows: 61 - Updated Jun 11, 2013 - Published: Nov 14,
A+ A- A
Eliza sneezed. The dust in the attic was like a thick blanket, and she'd always ha
said she could store her canvases up here, but he hadn't warned her about the
encompassed almost an entire century- in the corner sat a pristine (but still dus
Eliza wondered for a moment if they could sell it, and for how much. "As if we n
whispered to herself. It turned out that marrying a vampire had all kinds of frin
touched the necklace he'd bought her for their 5th anniversary, a heavy emeral
a barronness.
It wasn't for his money, though, that Eliza loved Hugo. It was for his gentle spir
and his promise to love her until her dying day.
Her dying day. That was something she'd thought of often. Hugo would never g
need to be carried up the stairs. They'd talked about it, and Hugo constantly as
for her went beyond her smooth skin and wavy hair. He loved her soul, her tale
Eliza shook her head, clearing her mind of such things, and decided to concentr
hand: lots and lots of dust.
Video
treetrunka tanyadreaming

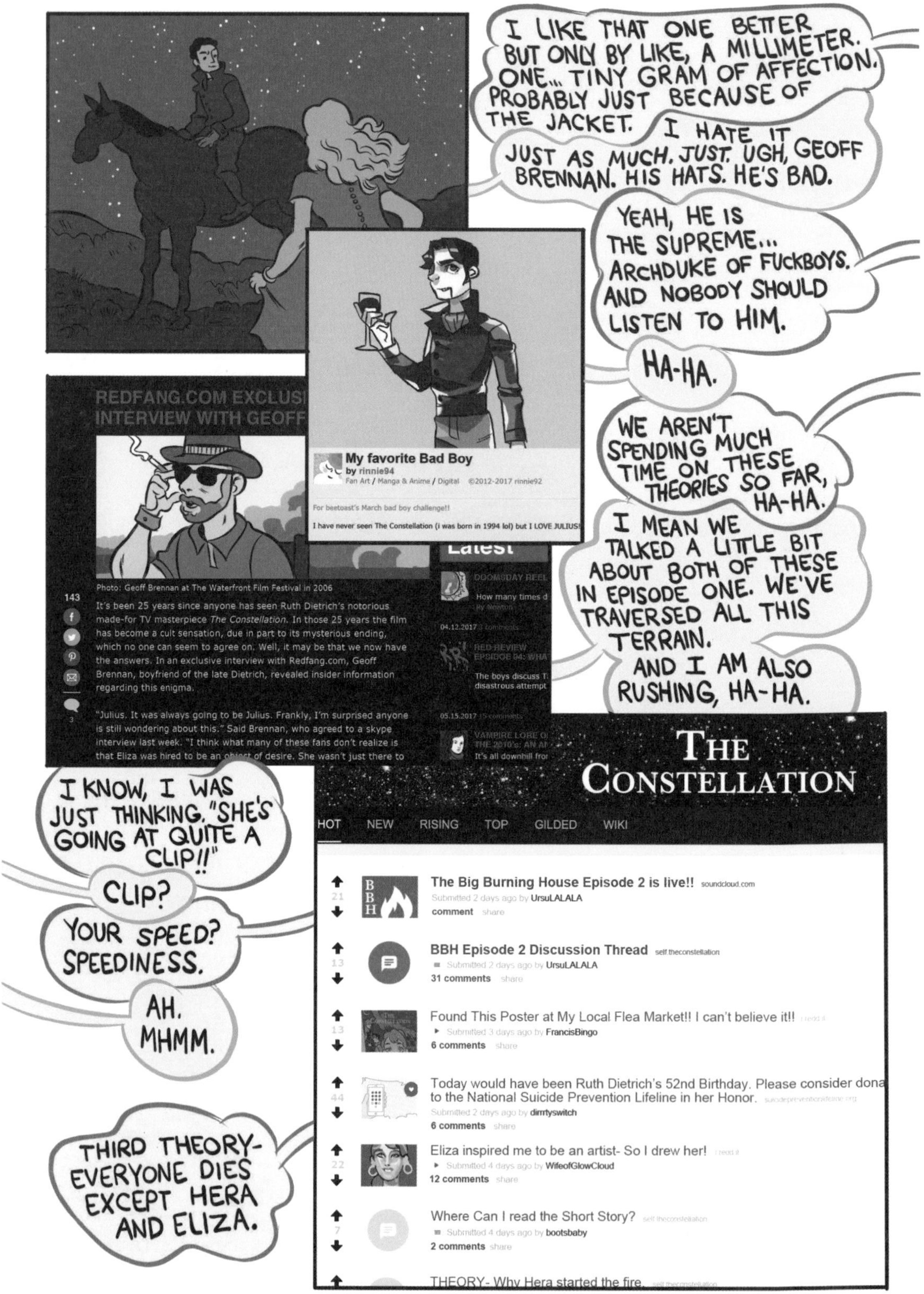
I LIKE THAT ONE BETTER BUT ONLY BY LIKE, A MILLIMETER. ONE... TINY GRAM OF AFFECTION. PROBABLY JUST BECAUSE OF THE JACKET.
I HATE IT JUST AS MUCH. JUST. UGH, GEOFF BRENNAN. HIS HATS. HE'S BAD.
YEAH, HE IS THE SUPREME... ARCHDUKE OF FUCKBOYS. AND NOBODY SHOULD LISTEN TO HIM.
HA-HA.
WE AREN'T SPENDING MUCH TIME ON THESE THEORIES SO FAR, HA-HA.
I MEAN WE TALKED A LITTLE BIT ABOUT BOTH OF THESE IN EPISODE ONE. WE'VE TRAVERSED ALL THIS TERRAIN.
AND I AM ALSO RUSHING, HA-HA.
My favorite Bad Boy
by rinnie94
Fan Art / Manga & Anime / Digital ©2012-2017 rinnie92
For beetoast's March bad boy challenge!!
I have never seen The Constellation (i was born in 1994 lol) but I LOVE JULIUS!
REDFANG.COM EXCLUSI
INTERVIEW WITH GEOFF
Photo: Geoff Brennan at The Waterfront Film Festival in 2006
143
It's been 25 years since anyone has seen Ruth Dietrich's notorious made-for TV masterpiece *The Constellation*. In those 25 years the film has become a cult sensation, due in part to its mysterious ending, which no one can seem to agree on. Well, it may be that we now have the answers. In an exclusive interview with Redfang.com, Geoff Brennan, boyfriend of the late Dietrich, revealed insider information regarding this enigma.
"Julius. It was always going to be Julius. Frankly, I'm surprised anyone is still wondering about this." Said Brennan, who agreed to a skype interview last week. "I think what many of these fans don't realize is that Eliza was hired to be an object of desire. She wasn't just there to
Latest
How many times d
04.12.2017
The boys discuss T disastrous attempt
05.15.2017
It's all downhill fror
THE CONSTELLATION
HOT NEW RISING TOP GILDED WIKI
21 The Big Burning House Episode 2 is live!! soundcloud.com
Submitted 2 days ago by UrsuLALALA
comment share
13 BBH Episode 2 Discussion Thread
Submitted 2 days ago by UrsuLALALA
31 comments share
13 Found This Poster at My Local Flea Market!! I can't believe it!!
Submitted 3 days ago by FrancisBingo
6 comments share
44 Today would have been Ruth Dietrich's 52nd Birthday. Please consider dona to the National Suicide Prevention Lifeline in her Honor.
Submitted 2 days ago by dirrtyswitch
6 comments share
22 Eliza inspired me to be an artist- So I drew her!
Submitted 4 days ago by WifeofGlowCloud
12 comments share
7 Where Can I read the Short Story?
Submitted 4 days ago by bootsbaby
2 comments share
THEORY- Why Hera started the fire.
I KNOW, I WAS JUST THINKING. "SHE'S GOING AT QUITE A CLIP!!"
CLIP?
YOUR SPEED? SPEEDINESS.
AH. MHMM.
THIRD THEORY- EVERYONE DIES EXCEPT HERA AND ELIZA.

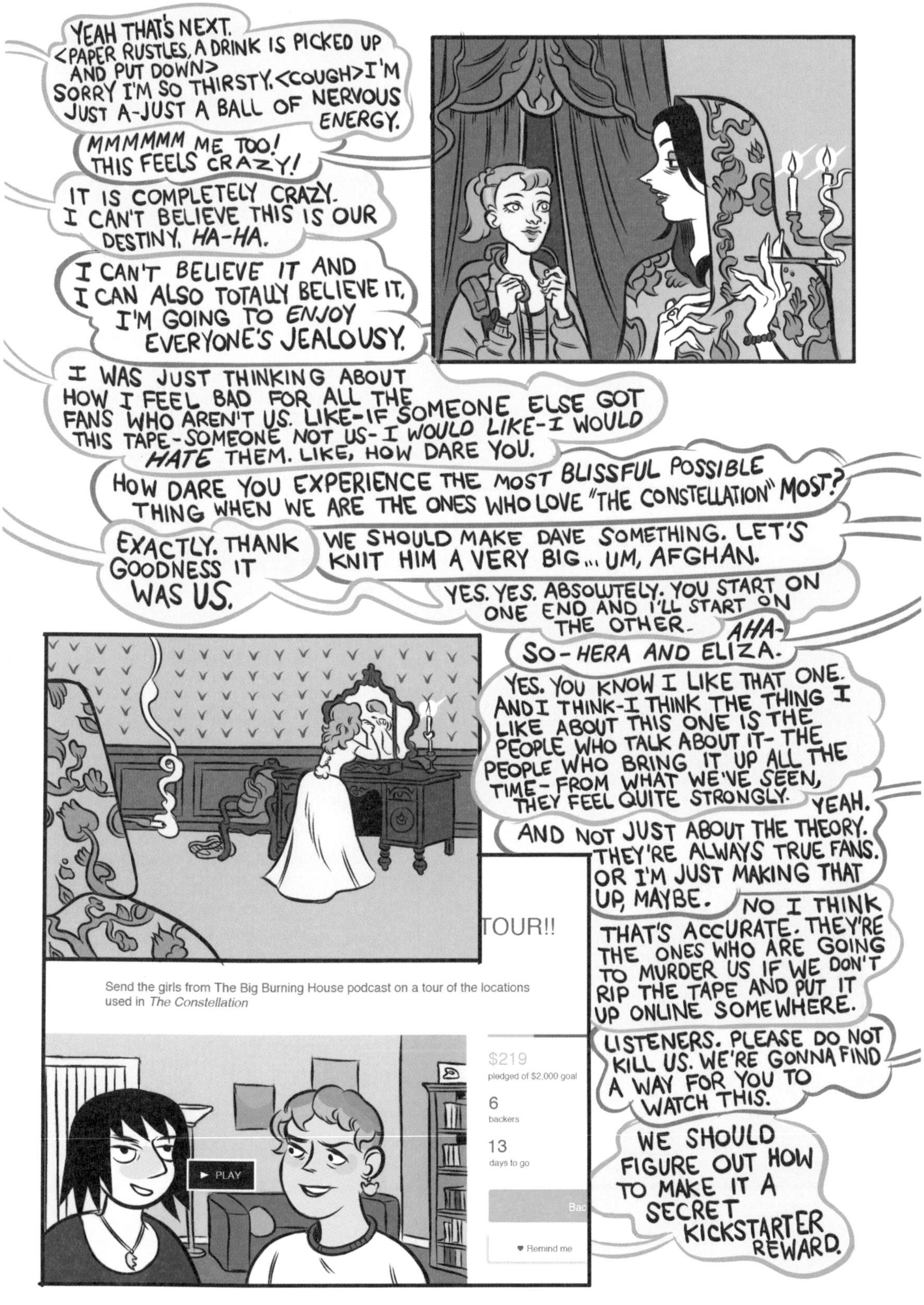

YEAH THAT'S NEXT. <PAPER RUSTLES, A DRINK IS PICKED UP AND PUT DOWN> SORRY I'M SO THIRSTY. <COUGH> I'M JUST A-JUST A BALL OF NERVOUS ENERGY.
MMMMMM ME TOO! THIS FEELS CRAZY!
IT IS COMPLETELY CRAZY. I CAN'T BELIEVE THIS IS OUR DESTINY, HA-HA.
I CAN'T BELIEVE IT AND I CAN ALSO TOTALLY BELIEVE IT. I'M GOING TO ENJOY EVERYONE'S JEALOUSY.
I WAS JUST THINKING ABOUT HOW I FEEL BAD FOR ALL THE FANS WHO AREN'T US. LIKE-IF SOMEONE ELSE GOT THIS TAPE-SOMEONE NOT US-I WOULD LIKE-I WOULD HATE THEM. LIKE, HOW DARE YOU.
HOW DARE YOU EXPERIENCE THE MOST BLISSFUL POSSIBLE THING WHEN WE ARE THE ONES WHO LOVE "THE CONSTELLATION" MOST?
EXACTLY. THANK GOODNESS IT WAS US.
WE SHOULD MAKE DAVE SOMETHING. LET'S KNIT HIM A VERY BIG... UM, AFGHAN.
YES. YES. ABSOLUTELY. YOU START ON ONE END AND I'LL START ON THE OTHER. AHA-
SO-HERA AND ELIZA.
YES. YOU KNOW I LIKE THAT ONE. AND I THINK-I THINK THE THING I LIKE ABOUT THIS ONE IS THE PEOPLE WHO TALK ABOUT IT-THE PEOPLE WHO BRING IT UP ALL THE TIME-FROM WHAT WE'VE SEEN, THEY FEEL QUITE STRONGLY.
YEAH.
AND NOT JUST ABOUT THE THEORY. THEY'RE ALWAYS TRUE FANS. OR I'M JUST MAKING THAT UP, MAYBE.
NO I THINK THAT'S ACCURATE. THEY'RE THE ONES WHO ARE GOING TO MURDER US IF WE DON'T RIP THE TAPE AND PUT IT UP ONLINE SOMEWHERE.
LISTENERS. PLEASE DO NOT KILL US. WE'RE GONNA FIND A WAY FOR YOU TO WATCH THIS.
WE SHOULD FIGURE OUT HOW TO MAKE IT A SECRET KICKSTARTER REWARD.
TOUR!!
Send the girls from The Big Burning House podcast on a tour of the locations used in The Constellation
► PLAY
$219
pledged of $2,000 goal
6
backers
13
days to go
♥ Remind me

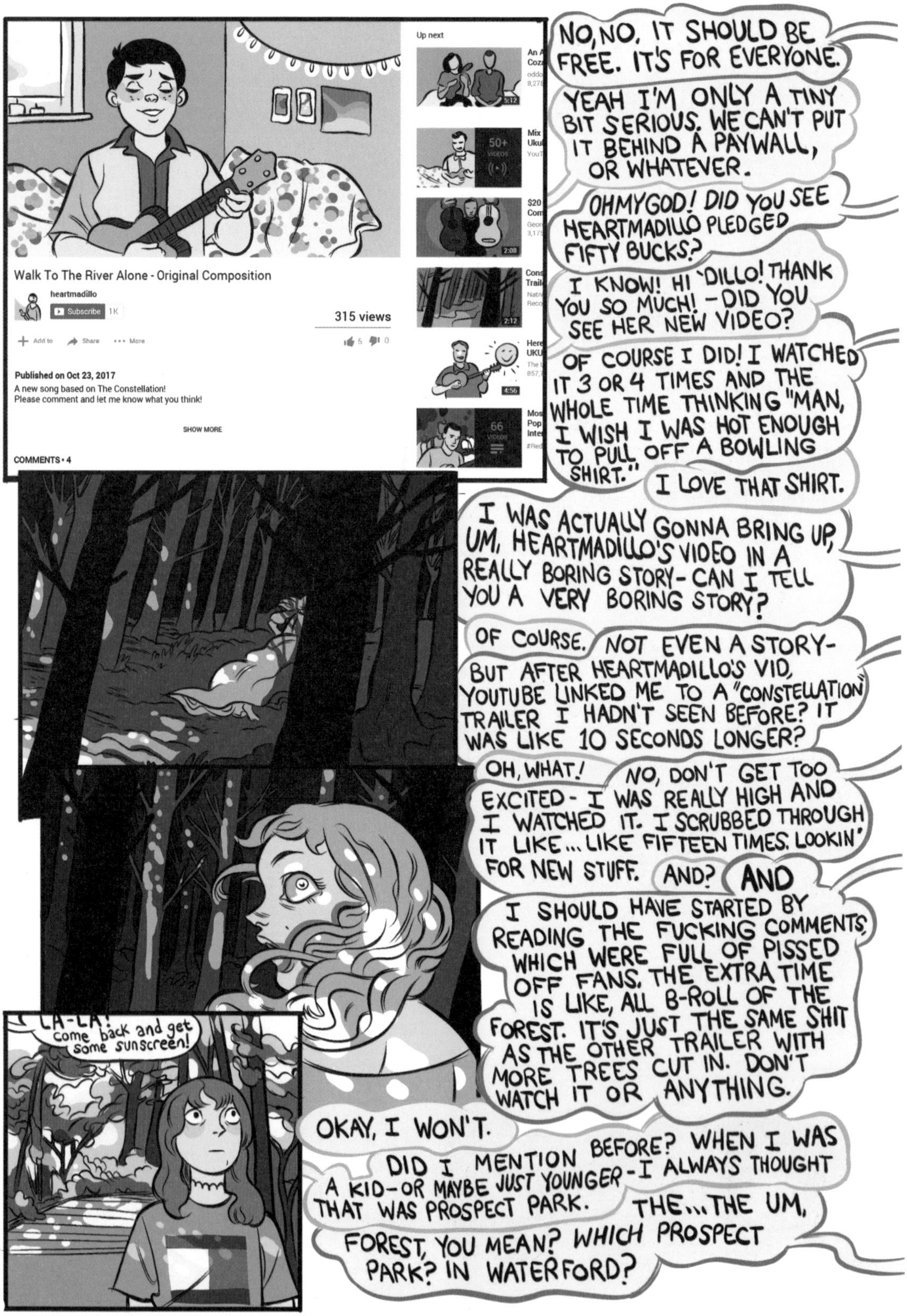
Up next
Walk To The River Alone - Original Composition
heartmadillo
Subscribe 1K
315 views
Add to
Share
More
Published on Oct 23, 2017
A new song based on The Constellation!
Please comment and let me know what you think!
SHOW MORE
COMMENTS • 4
NO, NO. IT SHOULD BE FREE. IT'S FOR EVERYONE.
YEAH I'M ONLY A TINY BIT SERIOUS. WE CAN'T PUT IT BEHIND A PAYWALL, OR WHATEVER.
OHMYGOD! DID YOU SEE HEARTMADILLO PLEDGED FIFTY BUCKS?
I KNOW! HI 'DILLO! THANK YOU SO MUCH! –DID YOU SEE HER NEW VIDEO?
OF COURSE I DID! I WATCHED IT 3 OR 4 TIMES AND THE WHOLE TIME THINKING "MAN, I WISH I WAS HOT ENOUGH TO PULL OFF A BOWLING SHIRT."
I LOVE THAT SHIRT.
I WAS ACTUALLY GONNA BRING UP, UM, HEARTMADILLO'S VIDEO IN A REALLY BORING STORY– CAN I TELL YOU A VERY BORING STORY?
OF COURSE.
NOT EVEN A STORY– BUT AFTER HEARTMADILLO'S VID, YOUTUBE LINKED ME TO A "CONSTELLATION" TRAILER I HADN'T SEEN BEFORE? IT WAS LIKE 10 SECONDS LONGER?
OH, WHAT!
NO, DON'T GET TOO EXCITED– I WAS REALLY HIGH AND I WATCHED IT. I SCRUBBED THROUGH IT LIKE... LIKE FIFTEEN TIMES. LOOKIN' FOR NEW STUFF.
AND?
AND I SHOULD HAVE STARTED BY READING THE FUCKING COMMENTS, WHICH WERE FULL OF PISSED OFF FANS. THE EXTRA TIME IS LIKE, ALL B-ROLL OF THE FOREST. IT'S JUST THE SAME SHIT AS THE OTHER TRAILER WITH MORE TREES CUT IN. DON'T WATCH IT OR ANYTHING.
LA-LA! come back and get some sunscreen!
OKAY, I WON'T.
DID I MENTION BEFORE? WHEN I WAS A KID– OR MAYBE JUST YOUNGER– I ALWAYS THOUGHT THAT WAS PROSPECT PARK.
THE... THE UM, FOREST, YOU MEAN? WHICH PROSPECT PARK? IN WATERFORD?

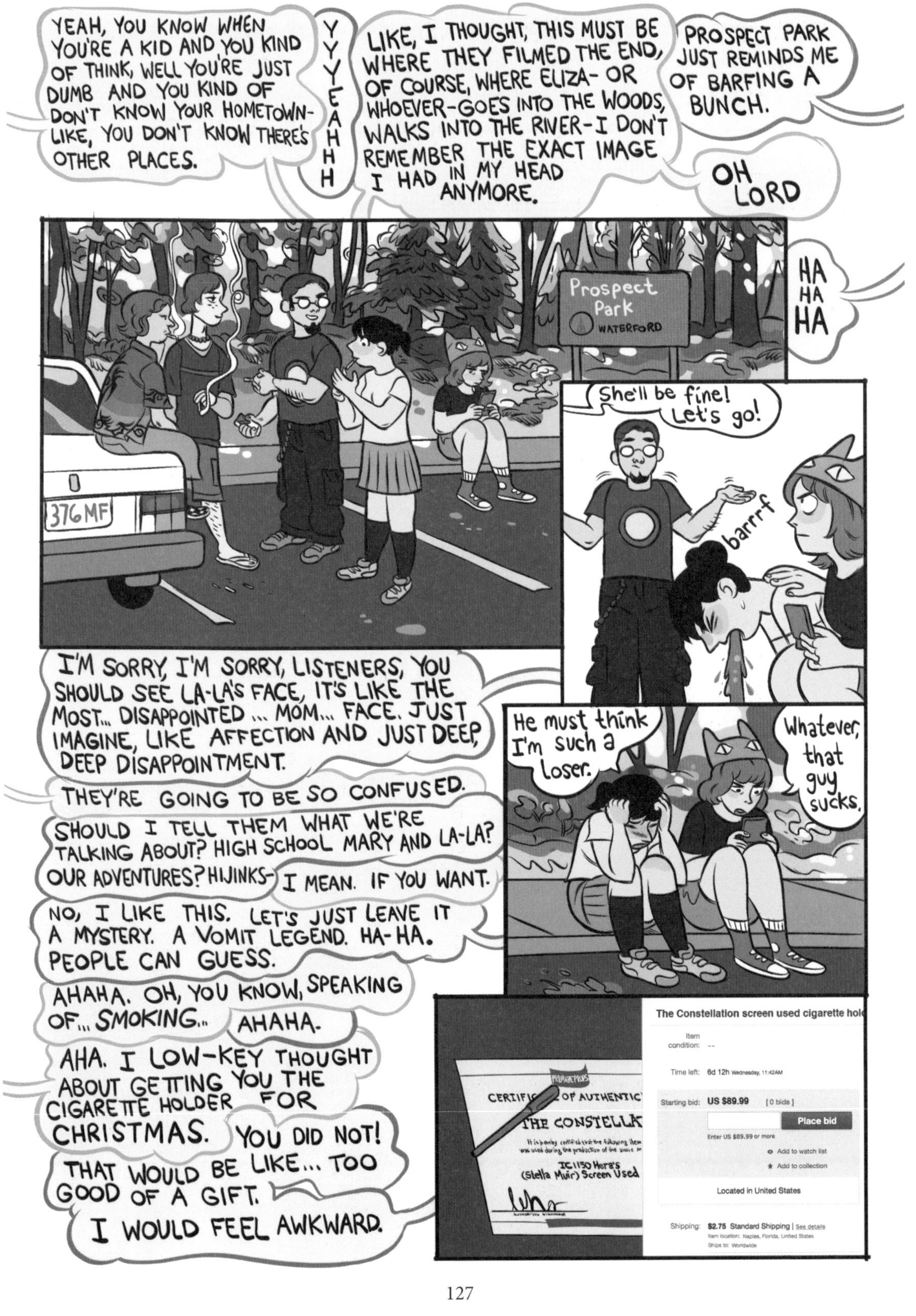

YEAH, YOU KNOW WHEN YOU'RE A KID AND YOU KIND OF THINK, WELL YOU'RE JUST DUMB AND YOU KIND OF DON'T KNOW YOUR HOMETOWN- LIKE, YOU DON'T KNOW THERE'S OTHER PLACES.
YYYEAHHH
LIKE, I THOUGHT, THIS MUST BE WHERE THEY FILMED THE END, OF COURSE, WHERE ELIZA- OR WHOEVER-GOES INTO THE WOODS, WALKS INTO THE RIVER-I DON'T REMEMBER THE EXACT IMAGE I HAD IN MY HEAD ANYMORE.
PROSPECT PARK JUST REMINDS ME OF BARFING A BUNCH.
OH LORD
HA HA HA
Prospect Park
WATERFORD
376MF
She'll be fine! Let's go!
barrrf
I'M SORRY, I'M SORRY, LISTENERS, YOU SHOULD SEE LA-LA'S FACE, IT'S LIKE THE MOST... DISAPPOINTED ... MOM... FACE. JUST IMAGINE, LIKE AFFECTION AND JUST DEEP, DEEP DISAPPOINTMENT.
He must think I'm such a loser.
Whatever, that guy sucks.
THEY'RE GOING TO BE SO CONFUSED.
SHOULD I TELL THEM WHAT WE'RE TALKING ABOUT? HIGH SCHOOL MARY AND LA-LA? OUR ADVENTURES? HIJINKS-
I MEAN. IF YOU WANT.
NO, I LIKE THIS. LET'S JUST LEAVE IT A MYSTERY. A VOMIT LEGEND. HA-HA. PEOPLE CAN GUESS.
AHAHA. OH, YOU KNOW, SPEAKING OF... SMOKING...
AHAHA.
AHA. I LOW-KEY THOUGHT ABOUT GETTING YOU THE CIGARETTE HOLDER FOR CHRISTMAS.
YOU DID NOT!
THAT WOULD BE LIKE... TOO GOOD OF A GIFT.
I WOULD FEEL AWKWARD.
CERTIFI OF AUTHENTIC
THE CONSTELLA
IC1150 Hera's (Stella Muir) Screen Used
The Constellation screen used cigarette hol
Item condition: --
Time left: 6d 12h Wednesday, 11:42AM
Starting bid: US $89.99 [0 bids]
Place bid
Enter US $89.99 or more
Add to watch list
Add to collection
Located in United States
Shipping: $2.75 Standard Shipping | See details
Item location: Naples, Florida, United States
Ships to: Worldwide

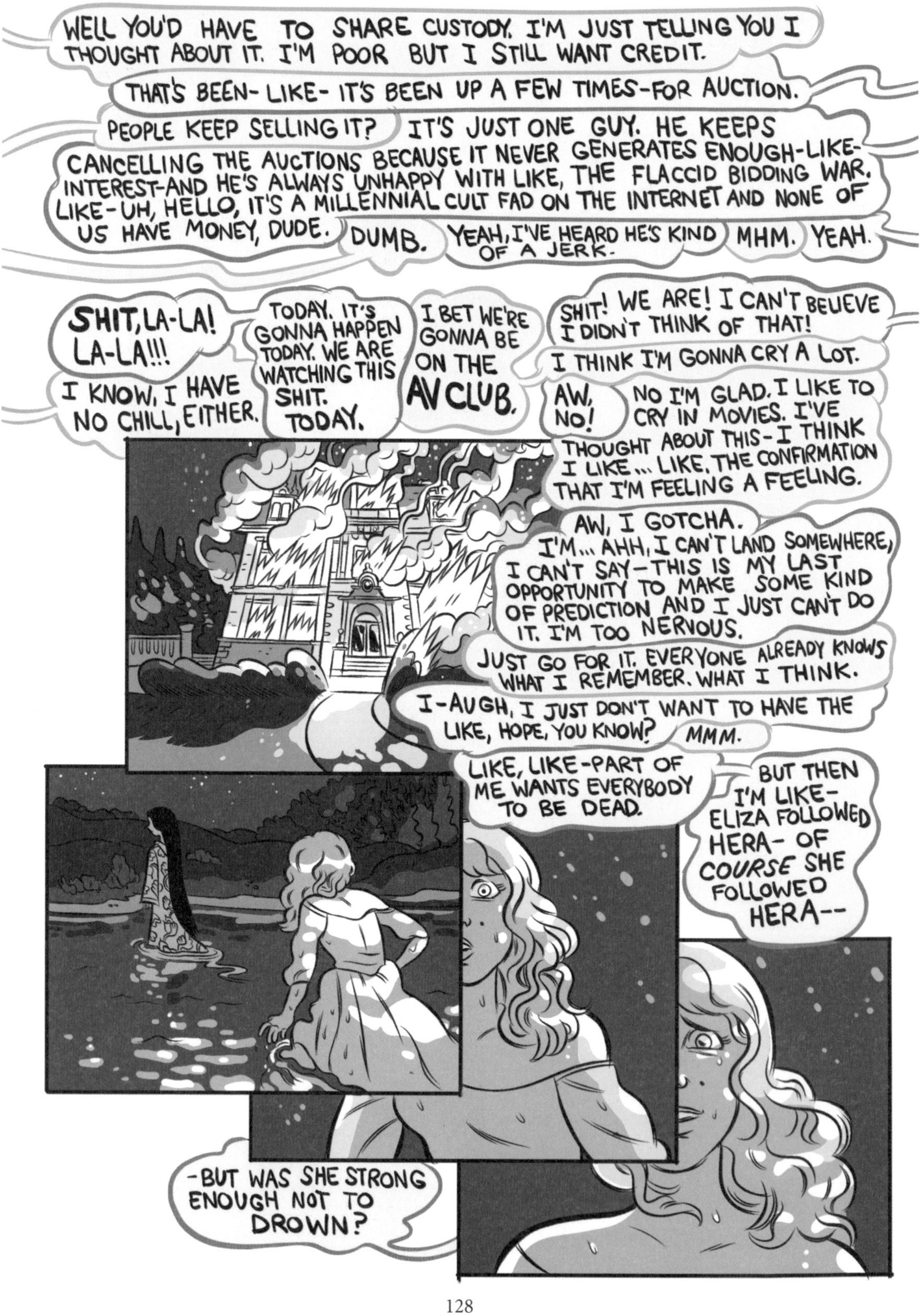

WELL YOU'D HAVE TO SHARE CUSTODY. I'M JUST TELLING YOU I THOUGHT ABOUT IT. I'M POOR BUT I STILL WANT CREDIT.
THAT'S BEEN- LIKE- IT'S BEEN UP A FEW TIMES-FOR AUCTION.
PEOPLE KEEP SELLING IT?
IT'S JUST ONE GUY. HE KEEPS CANCELLING THE AUCTIONS BECAUSE IT NEVER GENERATES ENOUGH-LIKE-INTEREST-AND HE'S ALWAYS UNHAPPY WITH LIKE, THE FLACCID BIDDING WAR. LIKE-UH, HELLO, IT'S A MILLENNIAL CULT FAD ON THE INTERNET AND NONE OF US HAVE MONEY, DUDE.
DUMB.
YEAH, I'VE HEARD HE'S KIND OF A JERK.
MHM.
YEAH.
SHIT, LA-LA! LA-LA!!!
I KNOW, I HAVE NO CHILL, EITHER.
TODAY. IT'S GONNA HAPPEN TODAY. WE ARE WATCHING THIS SHIT. TODAY.
I BET WE'RE GONNA BE ON THE AV CLUB.
SHIT! WE ARE! I CAN'T BELIEVE I DIDN'T THINK OF THAT!
I THINK I'M GONNA CRY A LOT.
AW, NO!
NO I'M GLAD. I LIKE TO CRY IN MOVIES. I'VE THOUGHT ABOUT THIS-I THINK I LIKE... LIKE, THE CONFIRMATION THAT I'M FEELING A FEELING.
AW, I GOTCHA.
I'M... AHH, I CAN'T LAND SOMEWHERE, I CAN'T SAY-THIS IS MY LAST OPPORTUNITY TO MAKE SOME KIND OF PREDICTION AND I JUST CAN'T DO IT. I'M TOO NERVOUS.
JUST GO FOR IT. EVERYONE ALREADY KNOWS WHAT I REMEMBER. WHAT I THINK.
I-AUGH, I JUST DON'T WANT TO HAVE THE LIKE, HOPE, YOU KNOW?
MMM.
LIKE, LIKE-PART OF ME WANTS EVERYBODY TO BE DEAD.
BUT THEN I'M LIKE-ELIZA FOLLOWED HERA- OF COURSE SHE FOLLOWED HERA--
-BUT WAS SHE STRONG ENOUGH NOT TO DROWN?

2017

PLEASE SLEEP OVER

RACE
5K
AROUND THE PATCH

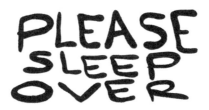

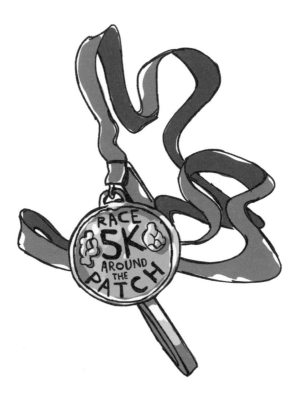

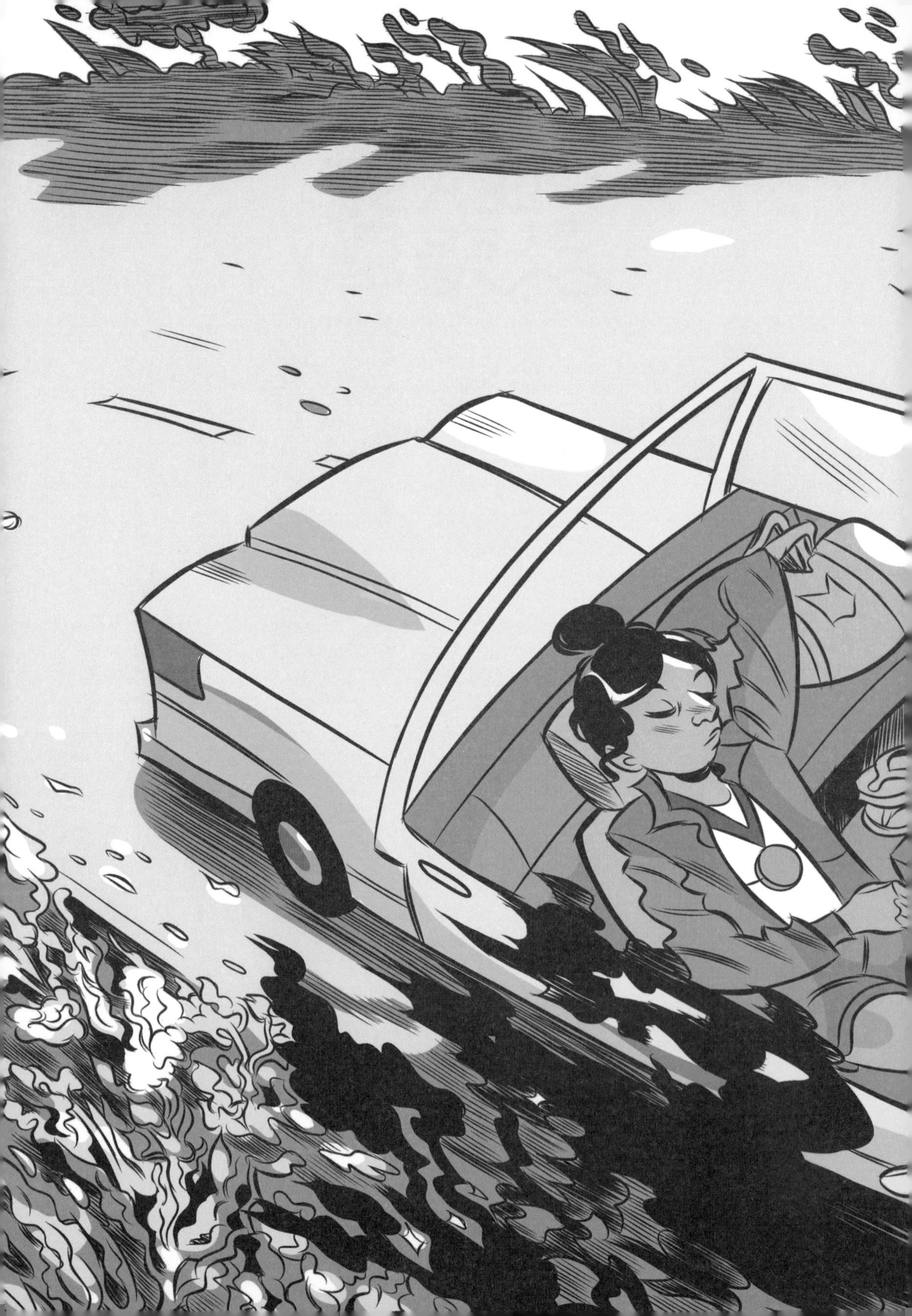

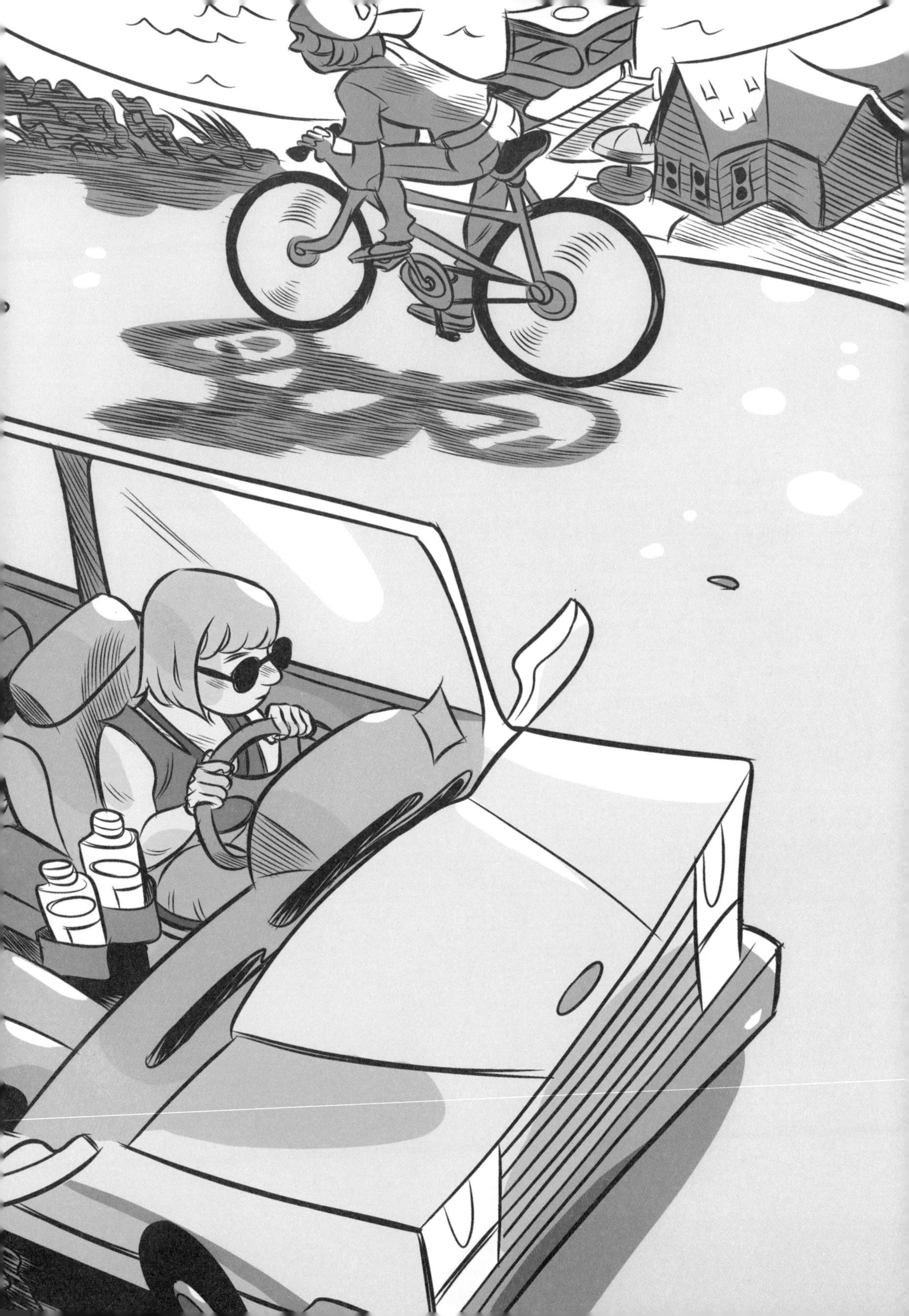

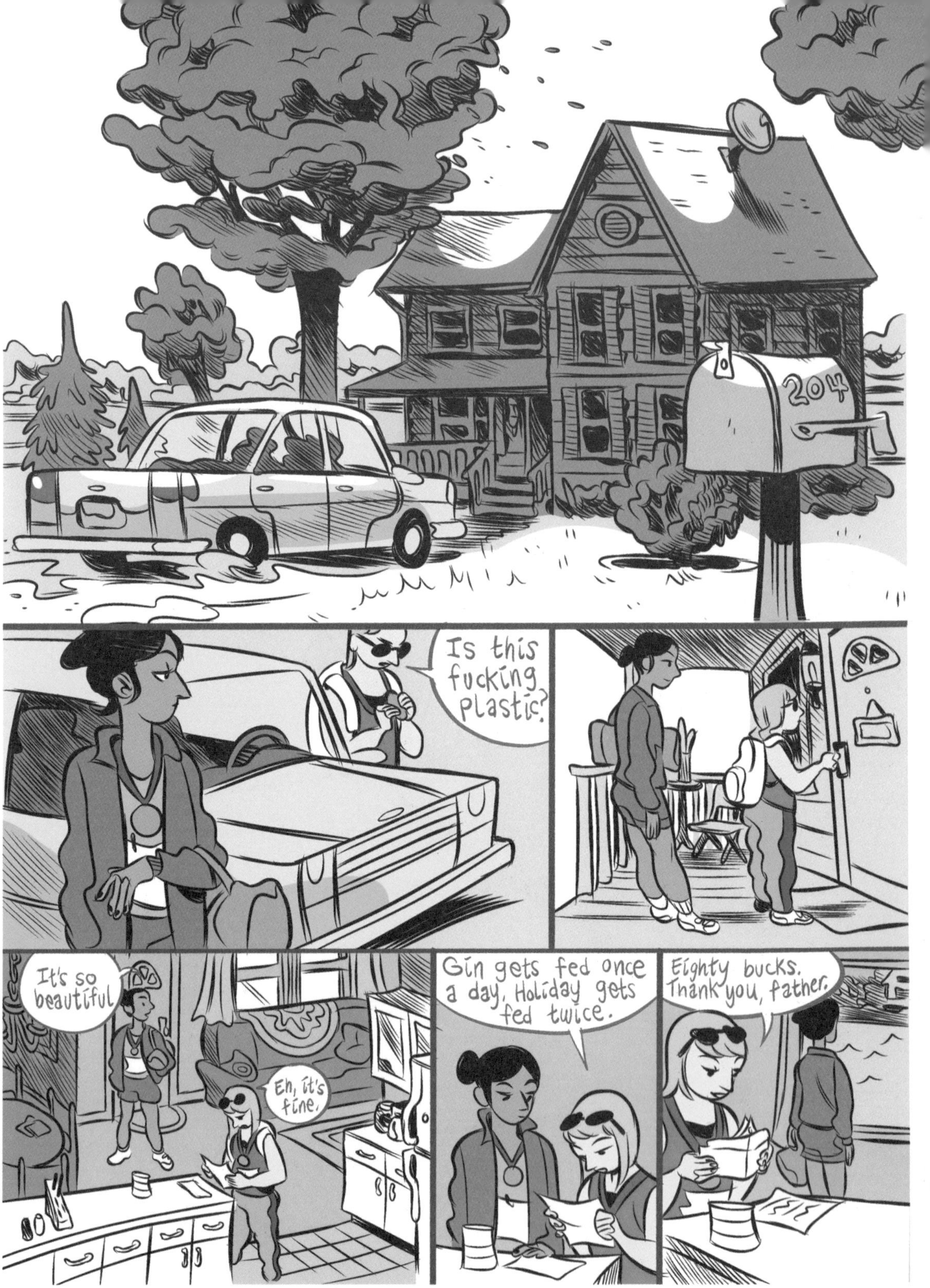
204
Is this fucking plastic?
It's so beautiful
Eh, it's fine.
Gin gets fed once a day, Holiday gets fed twice.
Eighty bucks. Thank you, father.

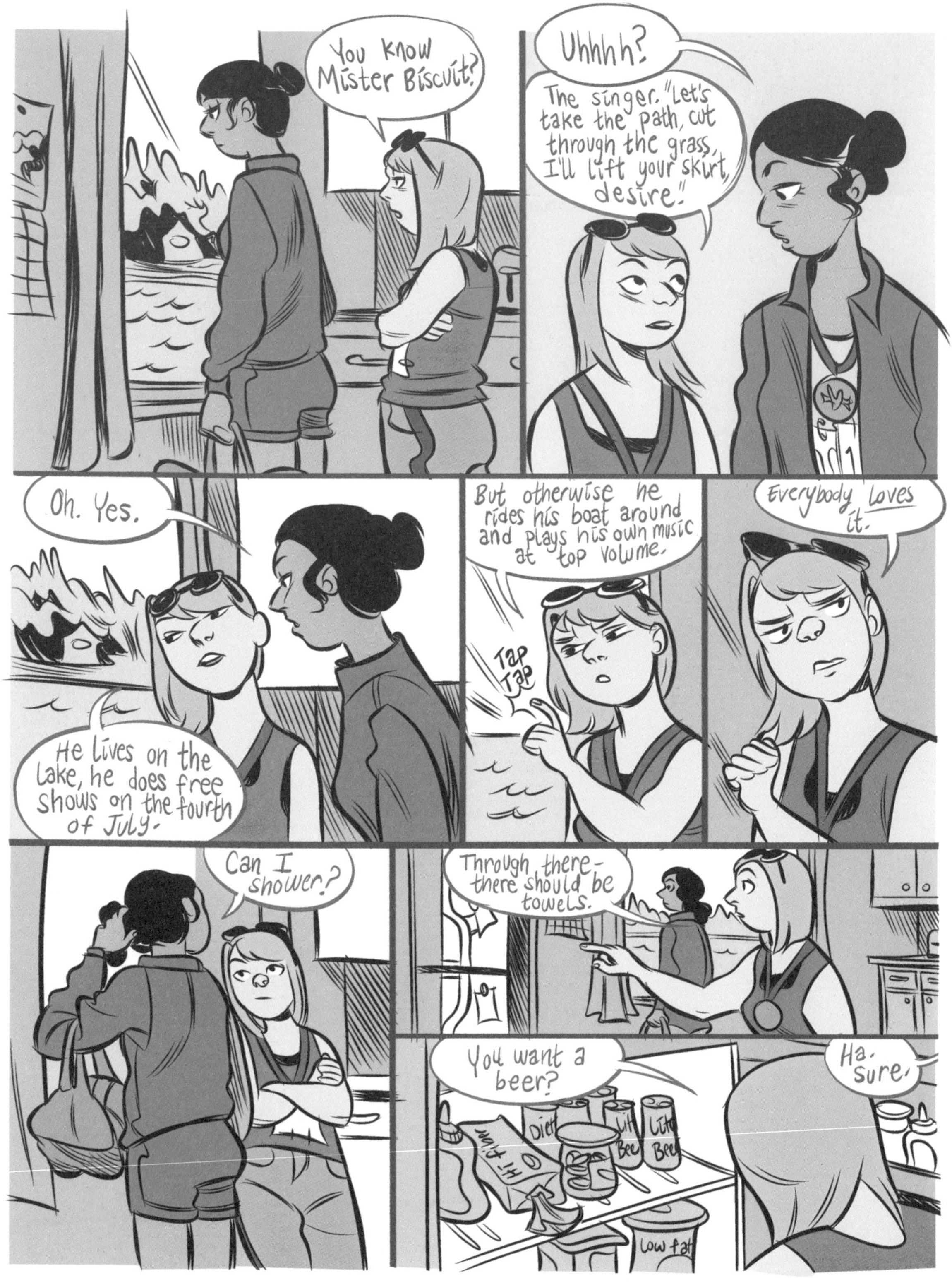
You know Mister Biscuit?
Uhhhh?
The singer. "Let's take the path, cut through the grass, I'll lift your skirt, desire."
Oh. Yes.
He lives on the lake, he does free shows on the fourth of July.
But otherwise he rides his boat around and plays his own music at top volume.
TAP TAP
Everybody loves it.
Can I shower?
Through there- there should be towels.
You want a beer?
Ha. Sure.
Diet
Lite Beer
Lite Beer
Hi Fiber
Low fat

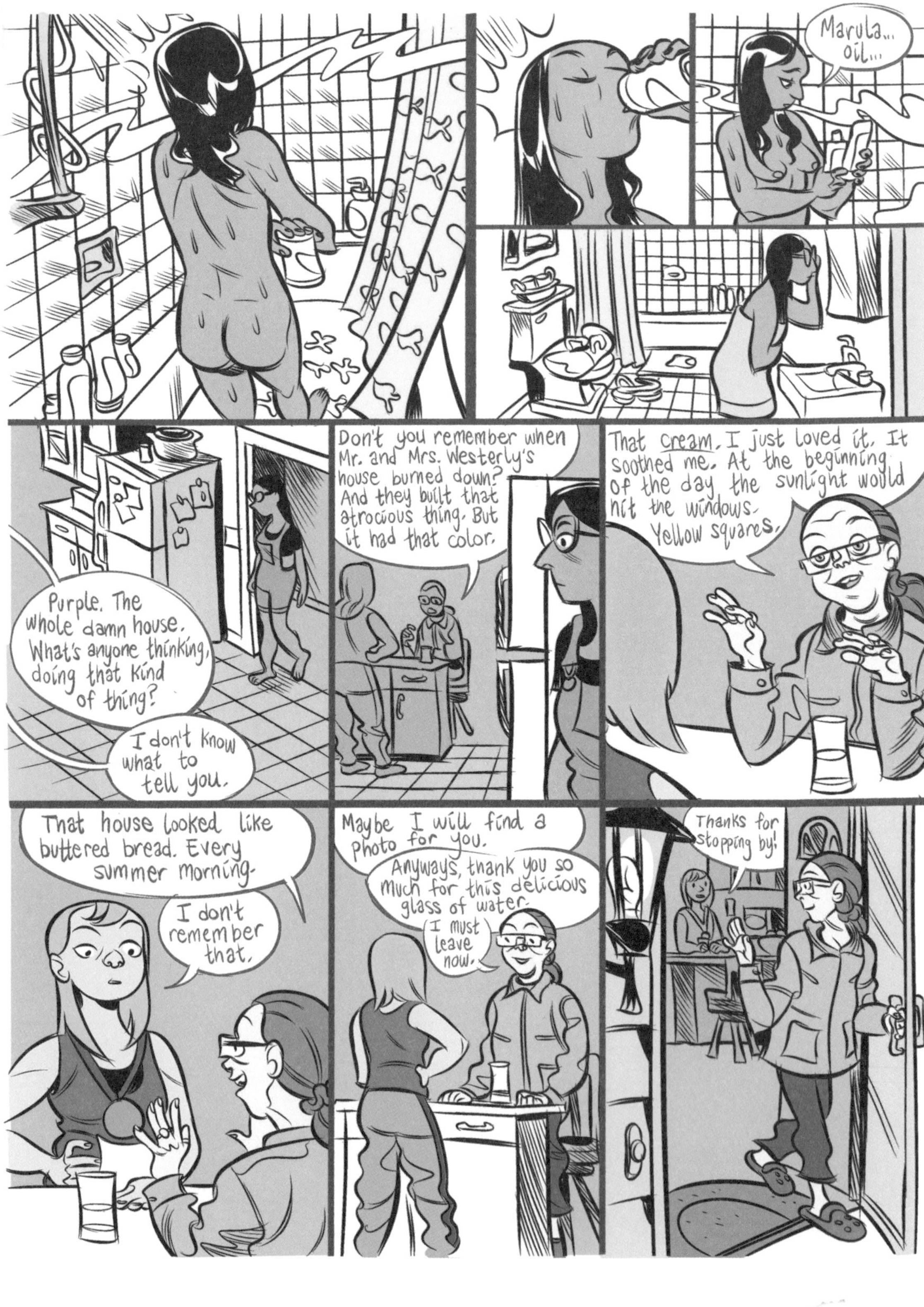
Marula... oil...
Purple. The whole damn house. What's anyone thinking, doing that kind of thing?
I don't know what to tell you.
Don't you remember when Mr. and Mrs. Westerly's house burned down? And they built that atrocious thing. But it had that color.
That cream. I just loved it. It soothed me. At the beginning of the day the sunlight would hit the windows.
Yellow squares.
That house looked like buttered bread. Every summer morning.
I don't remember that.
Maybe I will find a photo for you.
Anyways, thank you so much for this delicious glass of water.
I must leave now.
Thanks for stopping by!

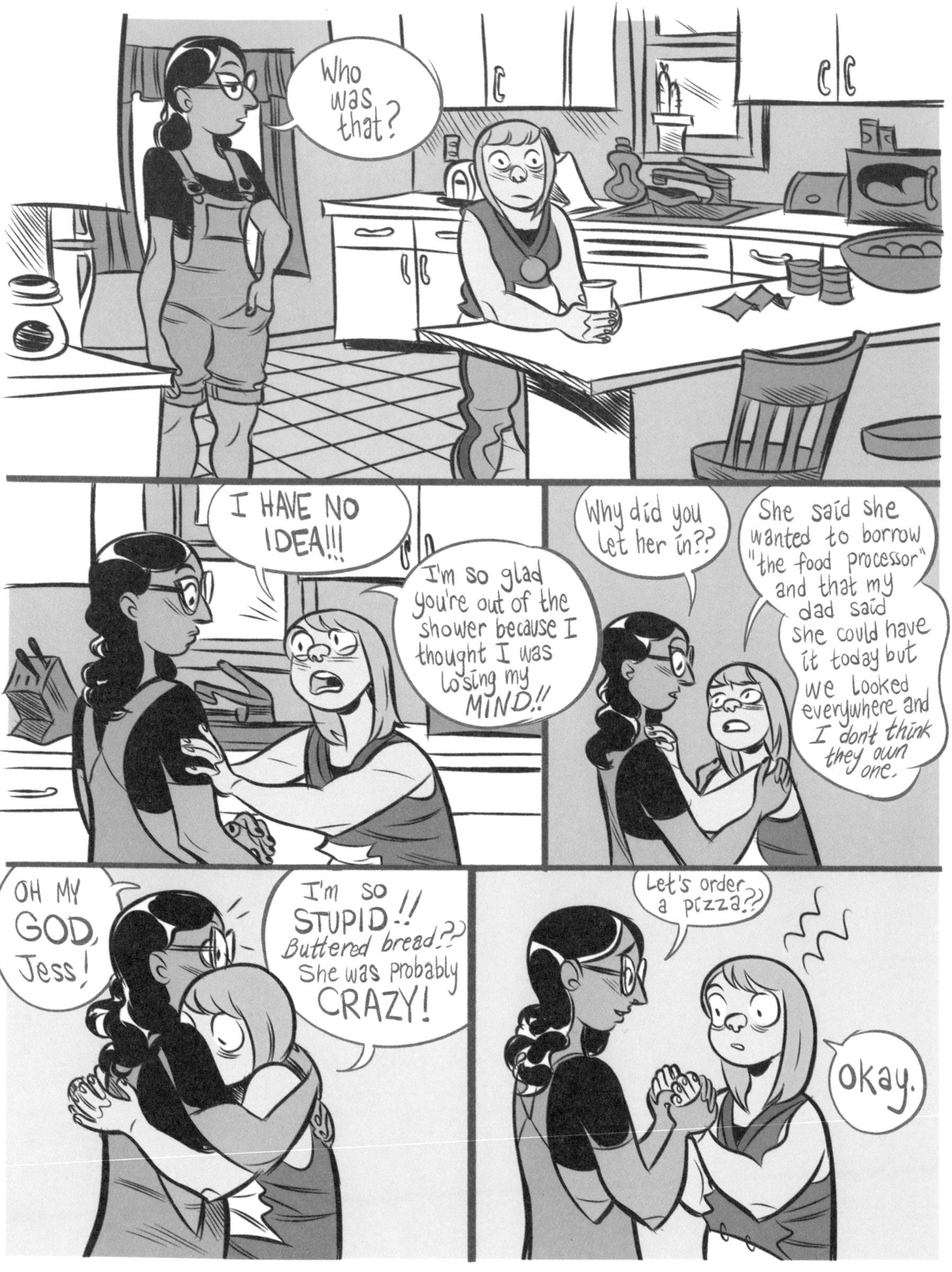
Who was that?
I HAVE NO IDEA!!!
I'm so glad you're out of the shower because I thought I was losing my MIND!!
Why did you let her in??
She said she wanted to borrow "the food processor" and that my dad said she could have it today but we looked everywhere and I don't think they own one.
OH MY GOD, Jess!
I'm so STUPID!! Buttered bread?? She was probably CRAZY!
Let's order a pizza??
Okay.

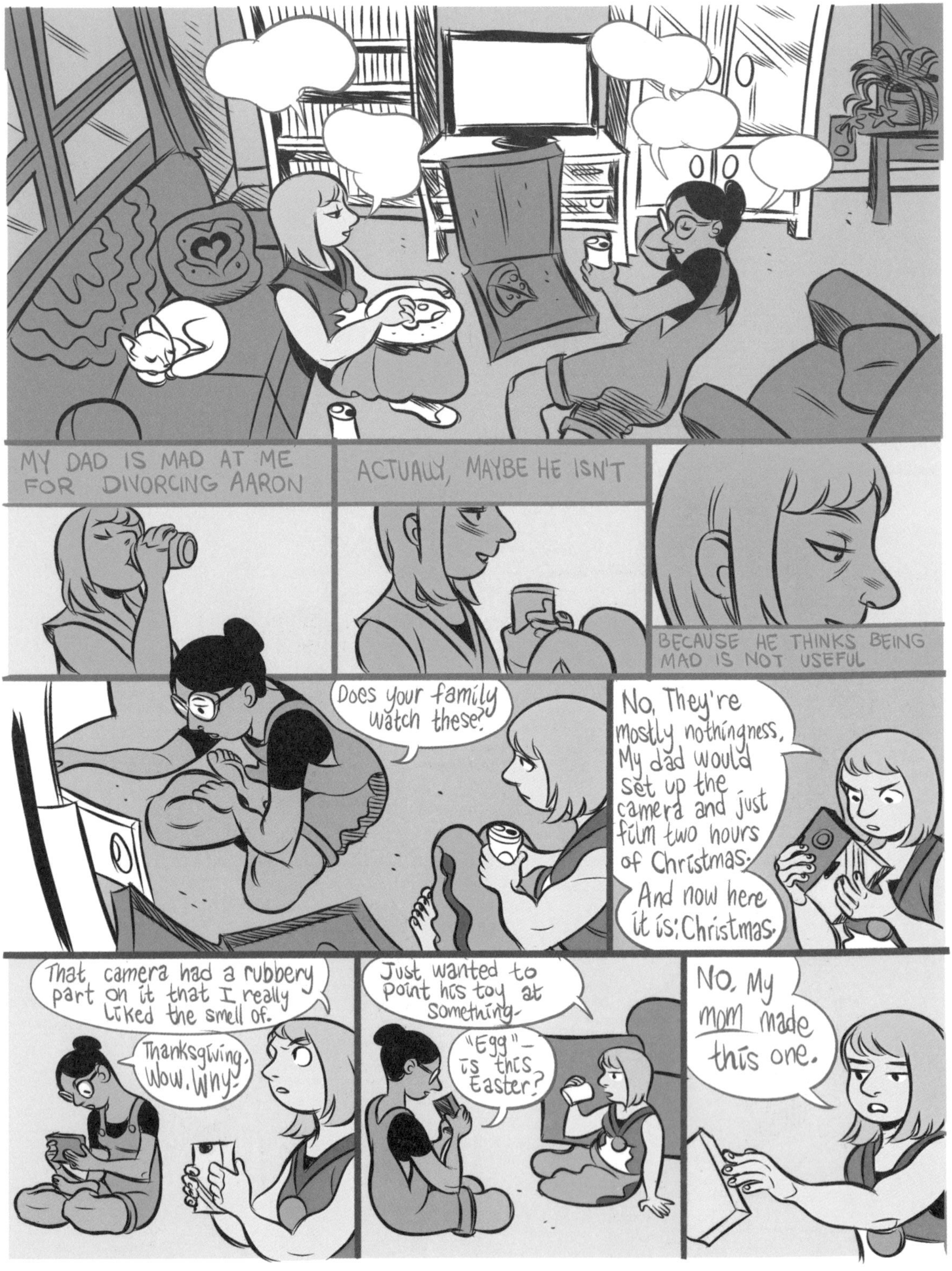

MY DAD IS MAD AT ME FOR DIVORCING AARON
ACTUALLY, MAYBE HE ISN'T
BECAUSE HE THINKS BEING MAD IS NOT USEFUL
Does your family watch these?
No, They're mostly nothingness. My dad would set up the camera and just film two hours of Christmas.
And now here it is: Christmas.
That camera had a rubbery part on it that I really liked the smell of.
Thanksgiving. Wow. Why?
Just wanted to point his toy at something.
"Egg"— is this Easter?
No. My mom made this one.

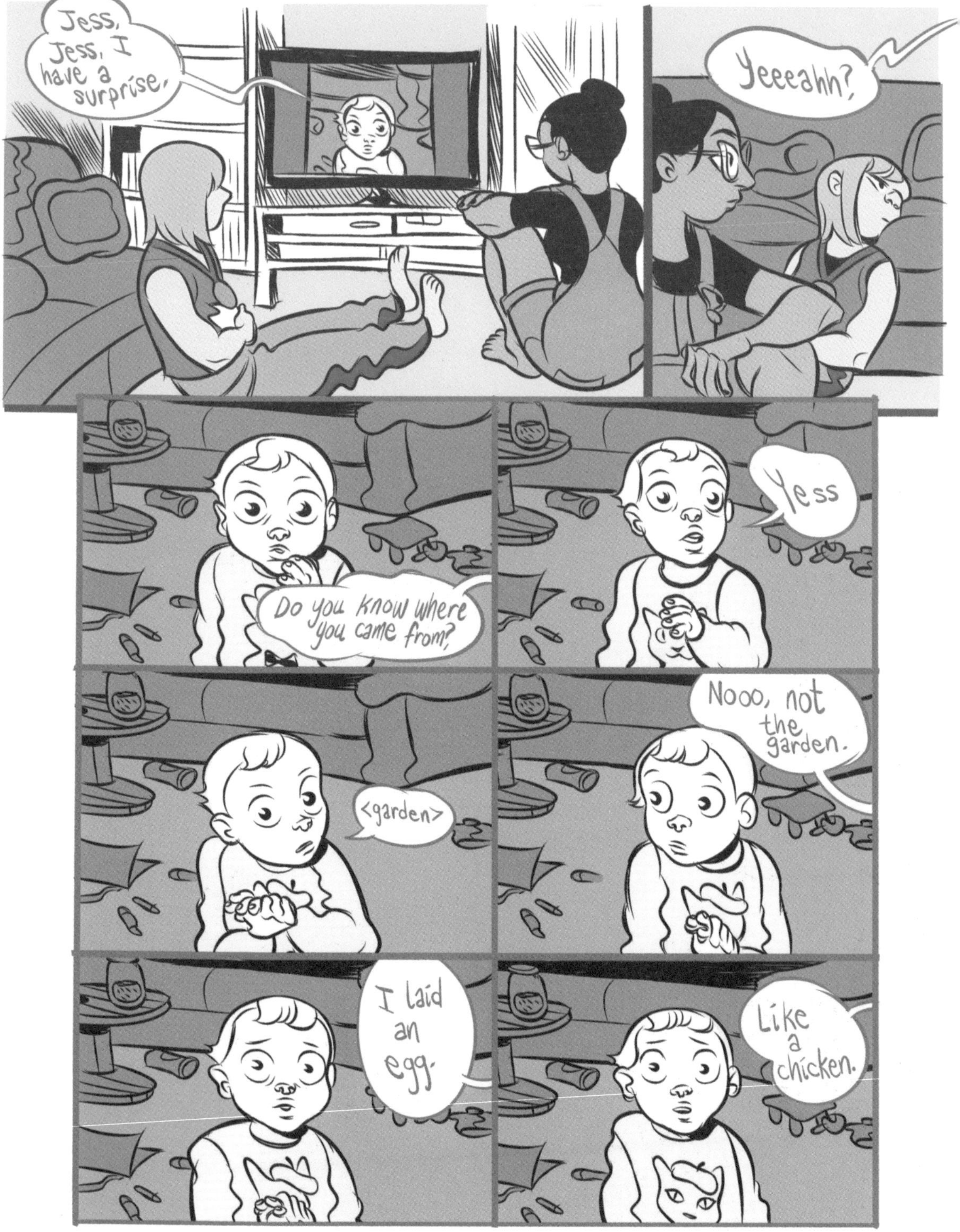
Jess, Jess, I have a surprise,
Yeeeahh?,
Do you know where you came from?,
Yess
<garden>
Nooo, not the garden.
I laid an egg.
Like a chicken.

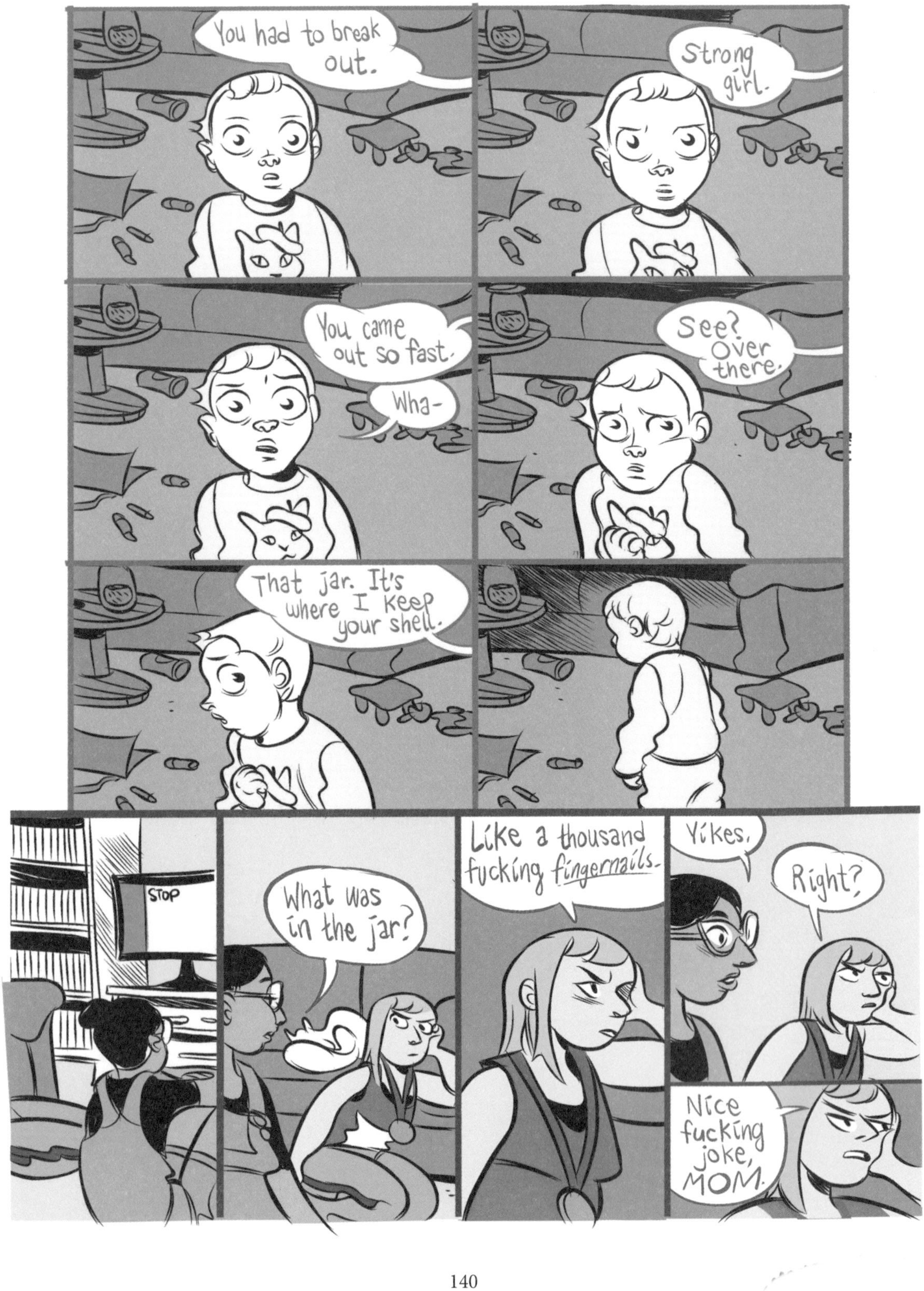
You had to break out.
Strong girl.
You came out so fast.
Wha-
See? Over there.
That jar. It's where I keep your shell.
STOP
What was in the jar?
Like a thousand fucking fingernails.
Yikes.
Right?
Nice fucking joke, MOM.

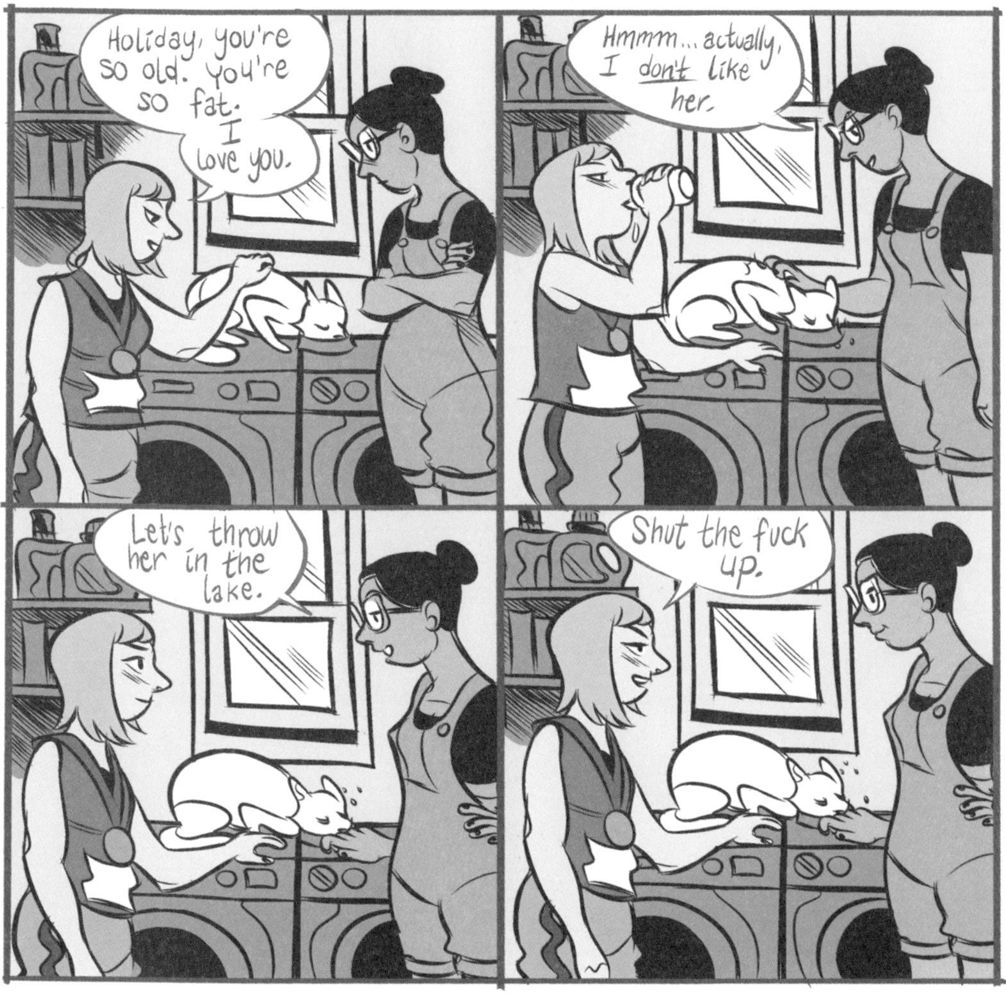

Holiday, you're so old. You're so fat.
I love you.
Hmmm... actually, I don't like her.
Let's throw her in the lake.
Shut the fuck up.

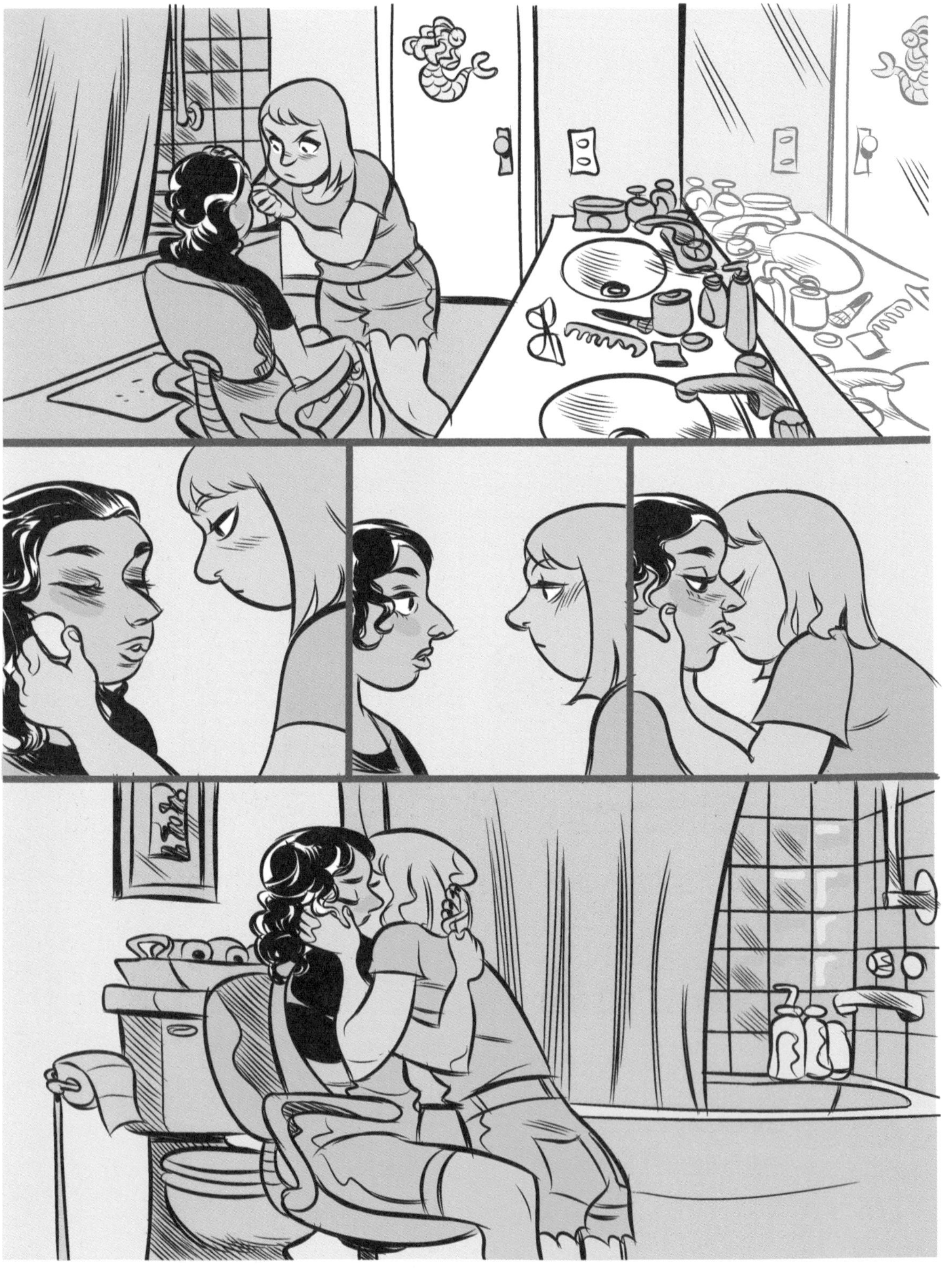

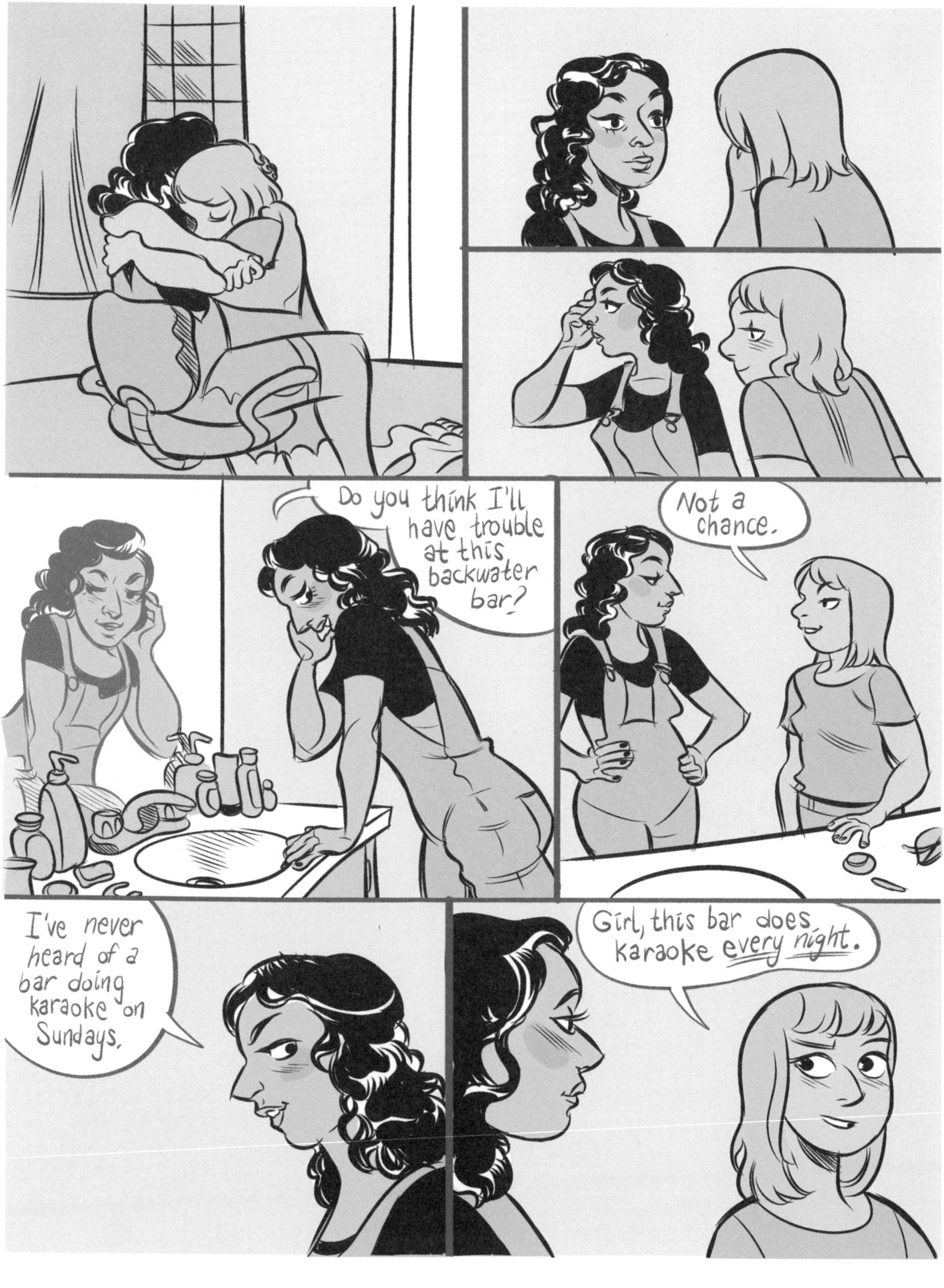
Do you think I'll have trouble at this backwater bar?
Not a chance.
I've never heard of a bar doing karaoke on Sundays.
Girl, this bar does karaoke every night.

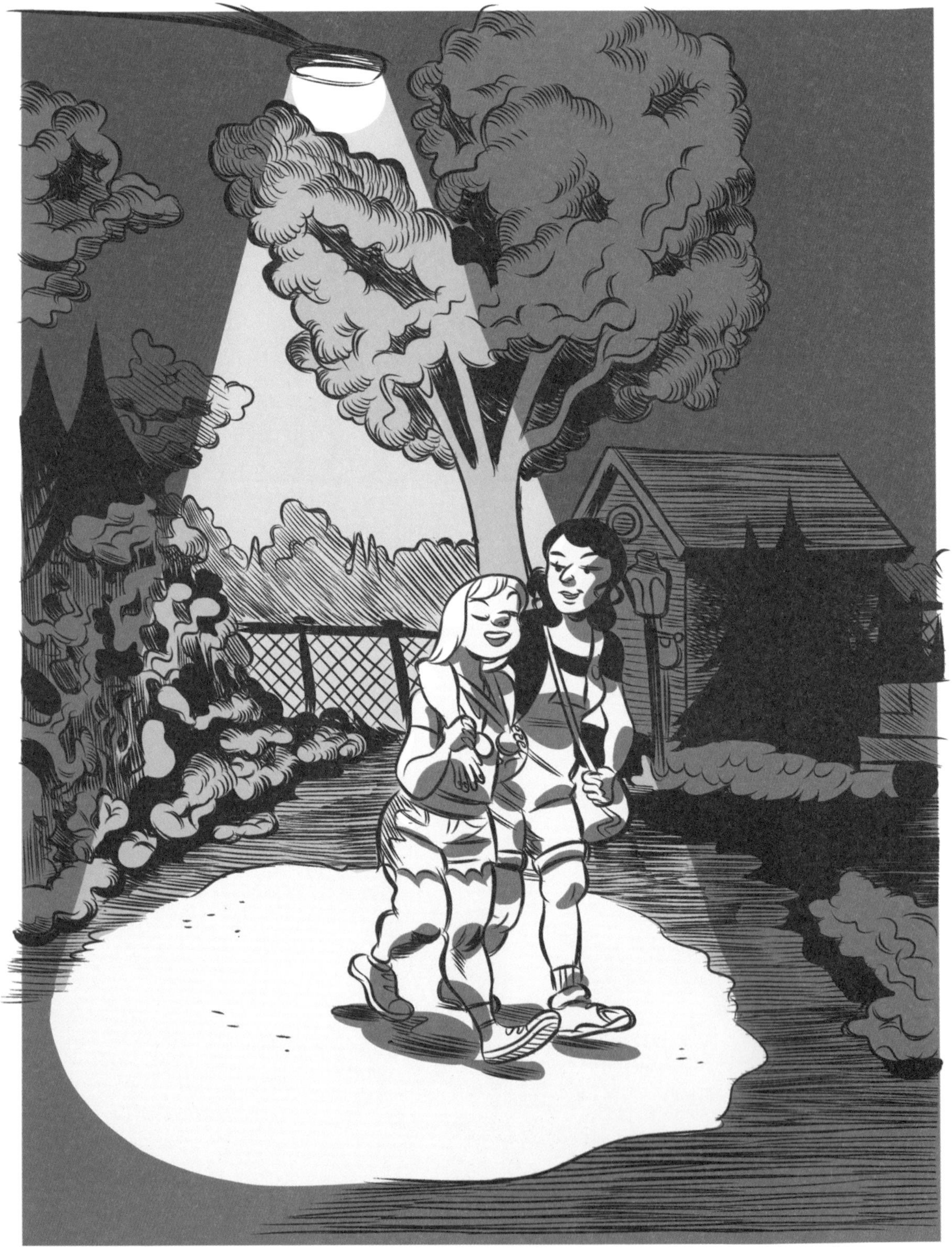

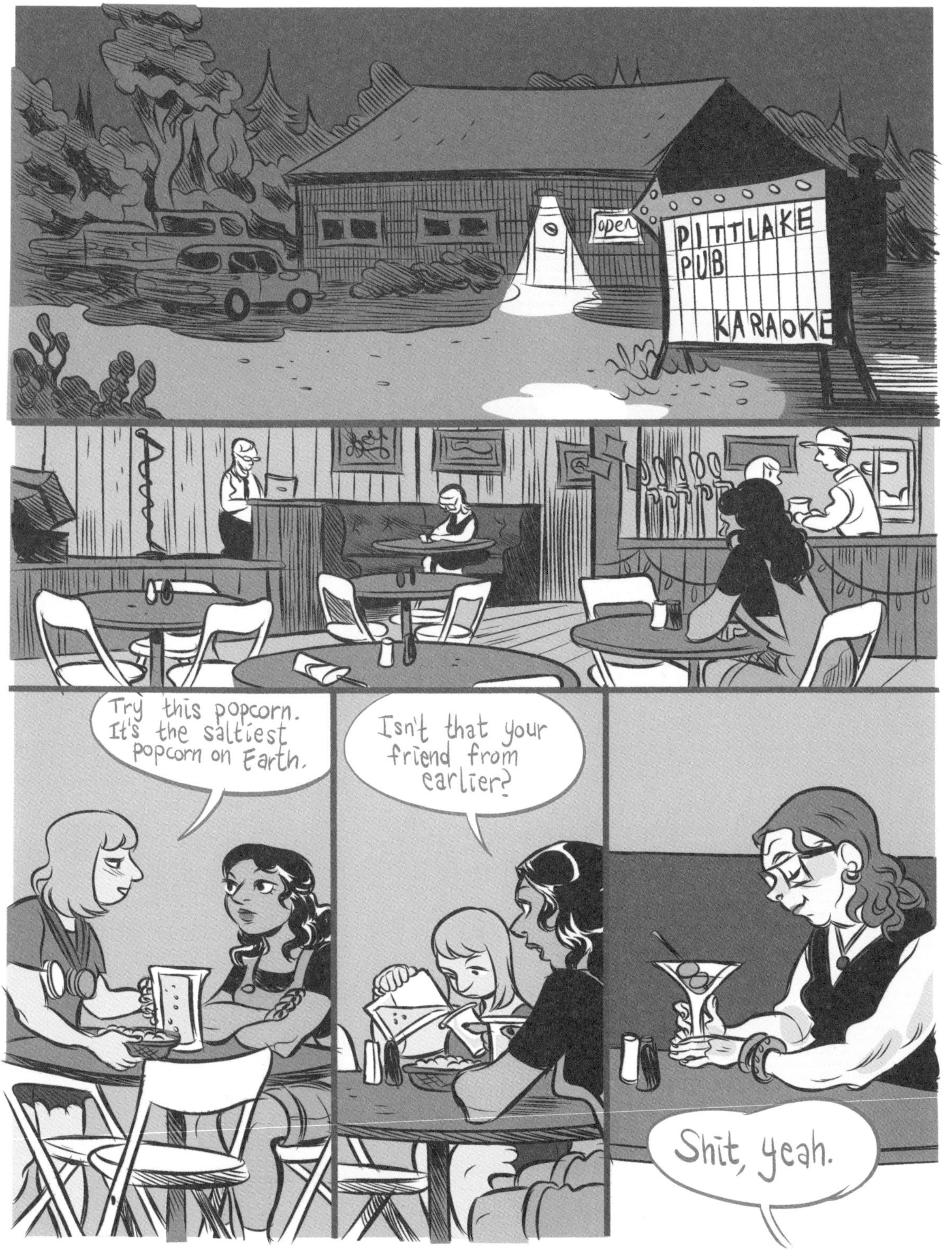
open
PITTLAKE
PUB
KARAOKE
Try this popcorn. It's the saltiest popcorn on Earth.
Isn't that your friend from earlier?
Shit, yeah.

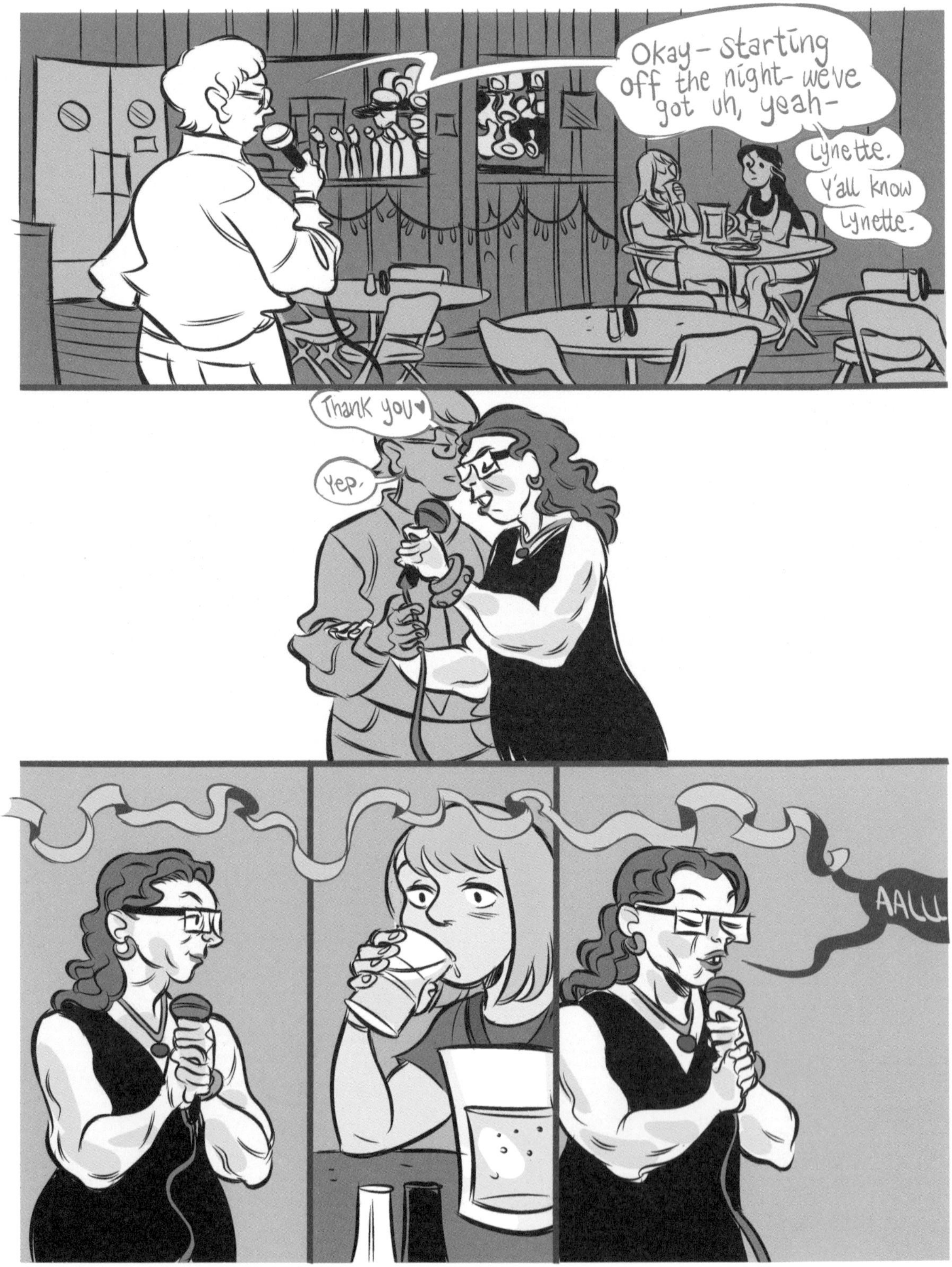
Okay - starting off the night - we've got uh, yeah-
Lynette. Y'all know Lynette.
Thank you♥
Yep.
AALLL

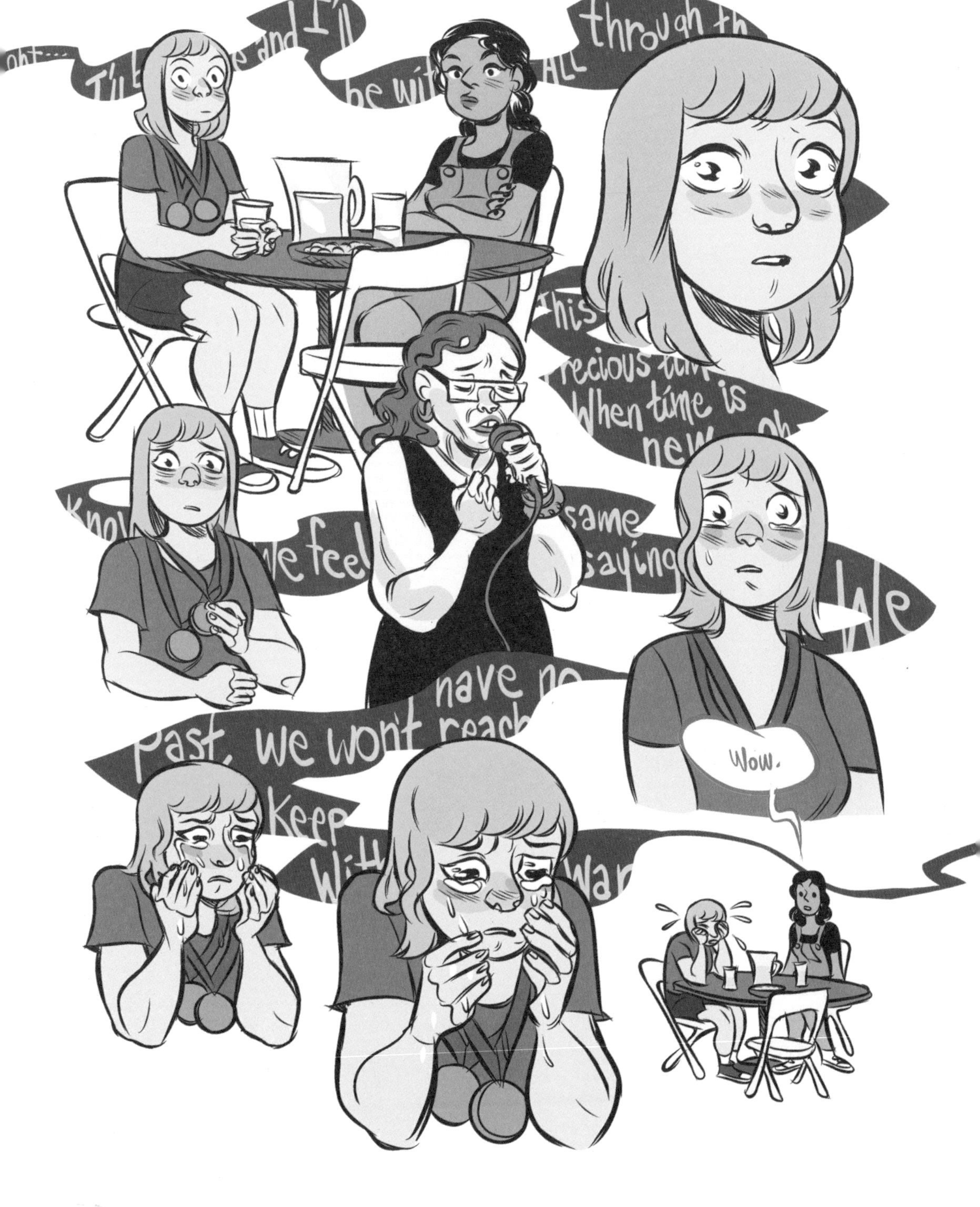

I'll b... e and I'll
be wit... ALL through th...
This
precious tim...
When time is
new... oh
Know... we feel... same... saying
We
have no
past, we won't reach
Keep
With... wa...
Wow.

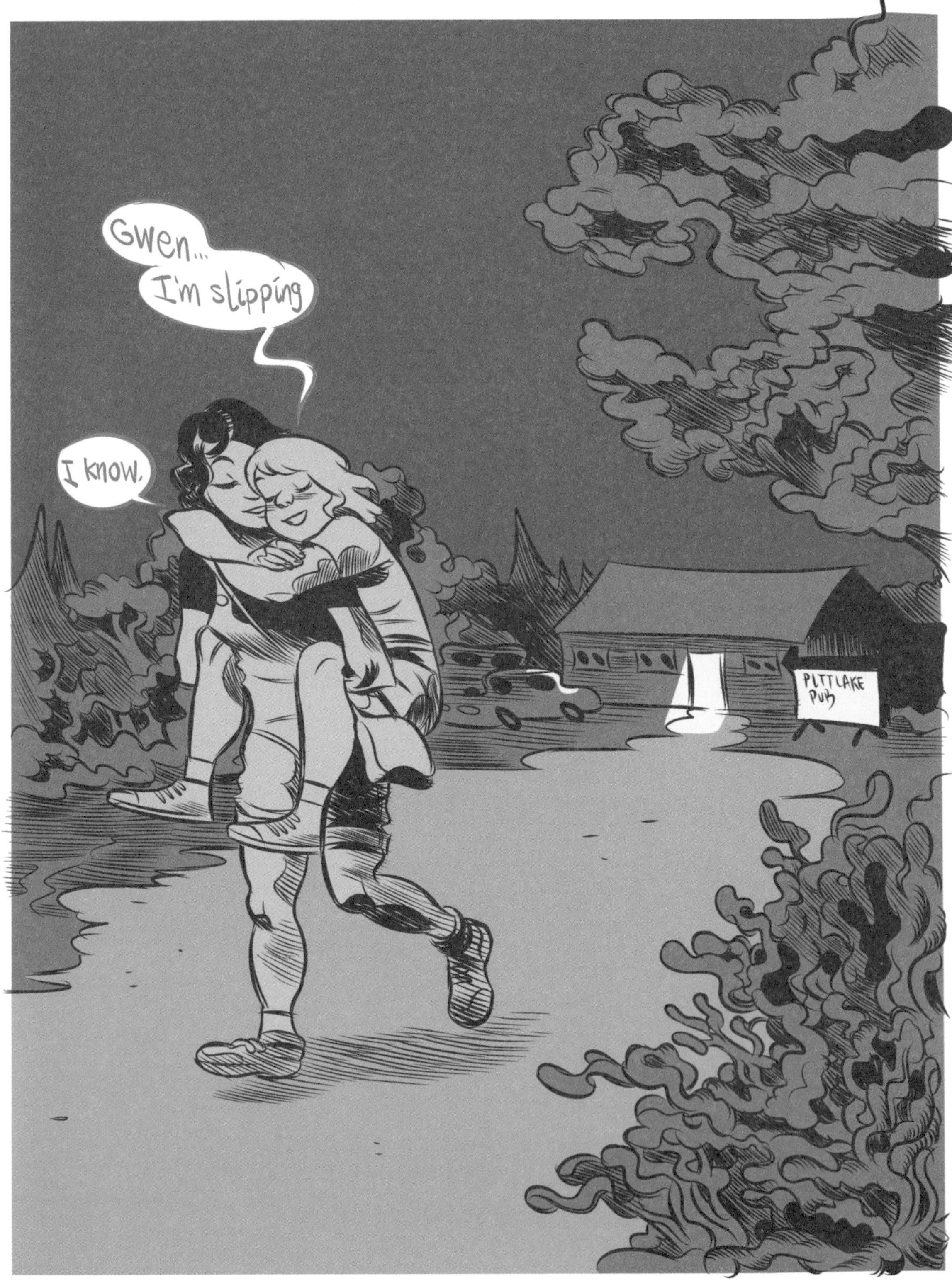
Gwen... I'm slipping
I know.
PITTLAKE PUB

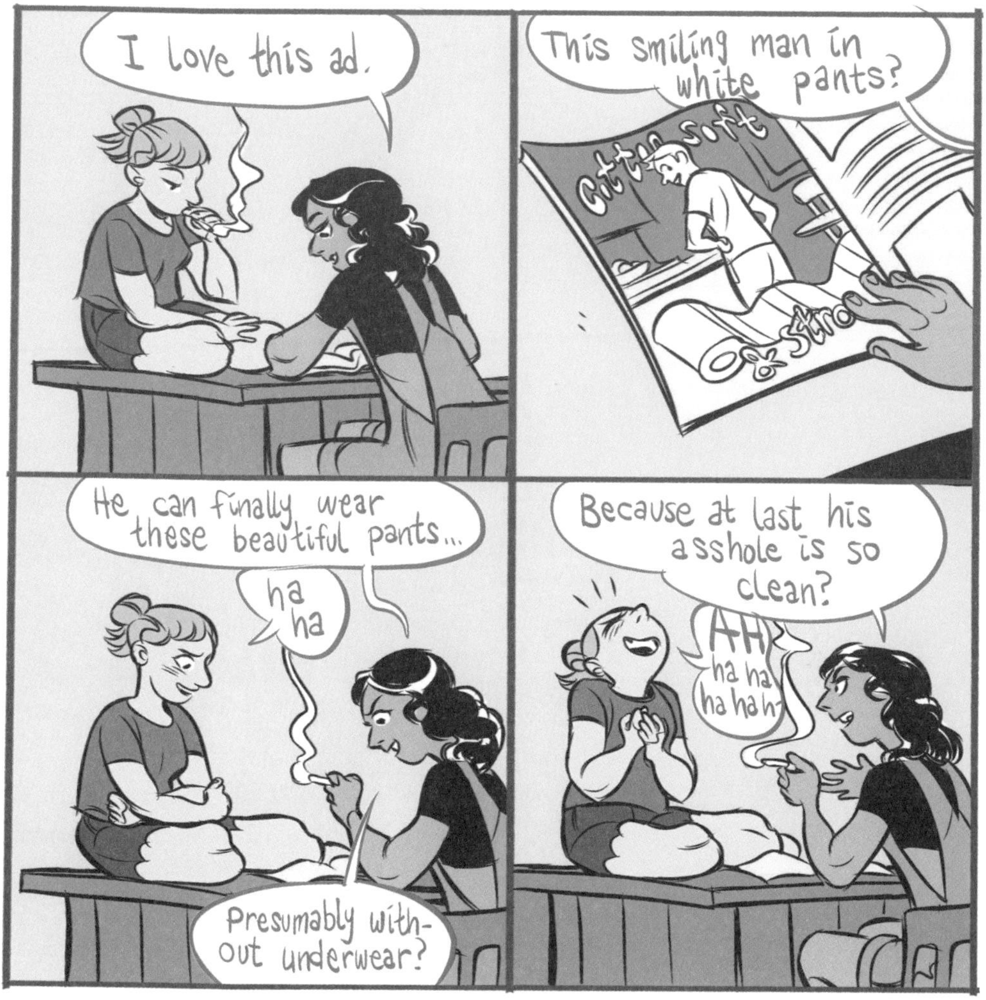
I love this ad.
This smiling man in white pants?
He can finally wear these beautiful pants...
ha ha
Presumably with-out underwear?
Because at last his asshole is so clean?
AH ha ha ha ha h-

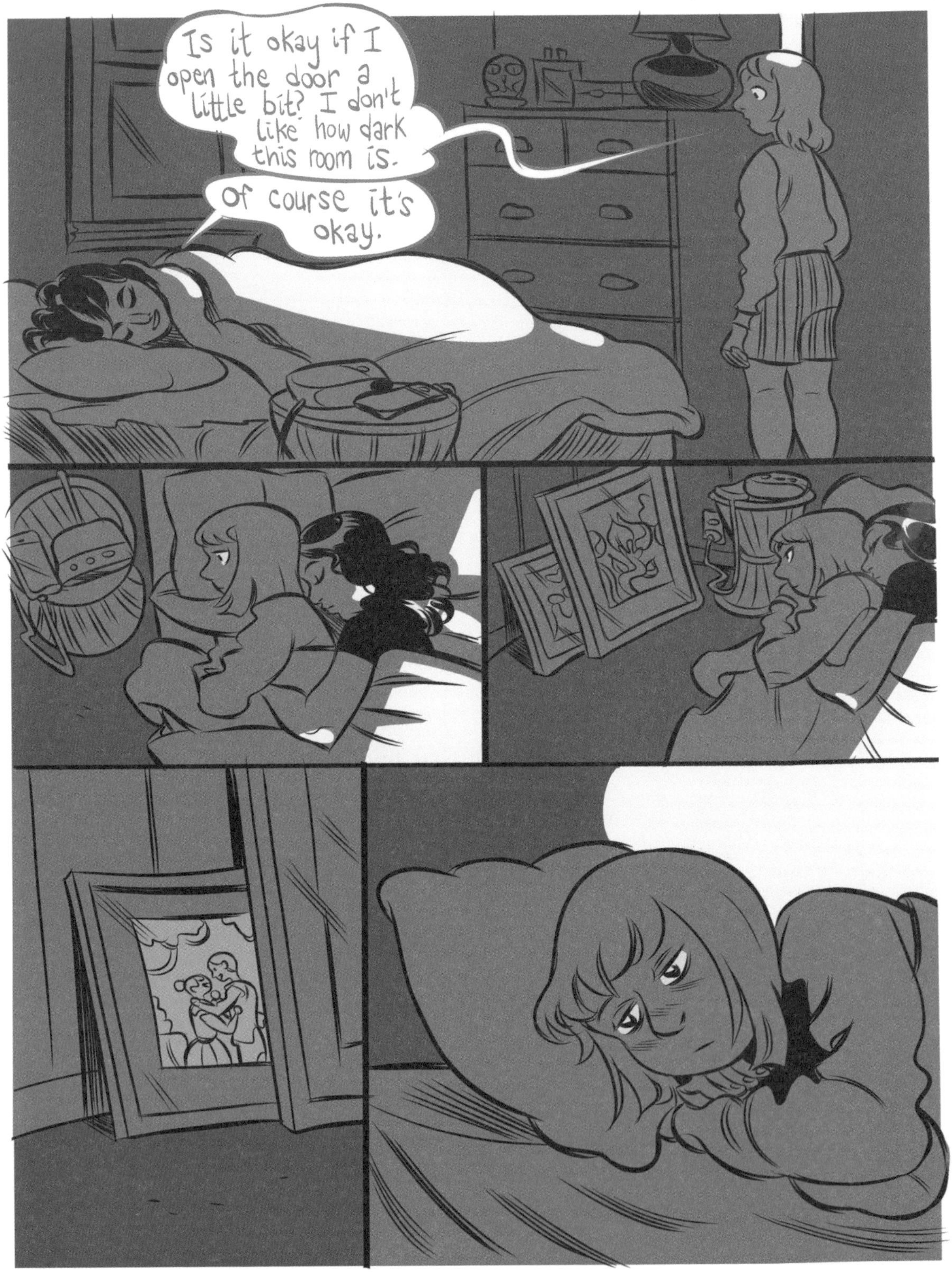
Is it okay if I open the door a little bit? I don't like how dark this room is.
Of course it's okay.

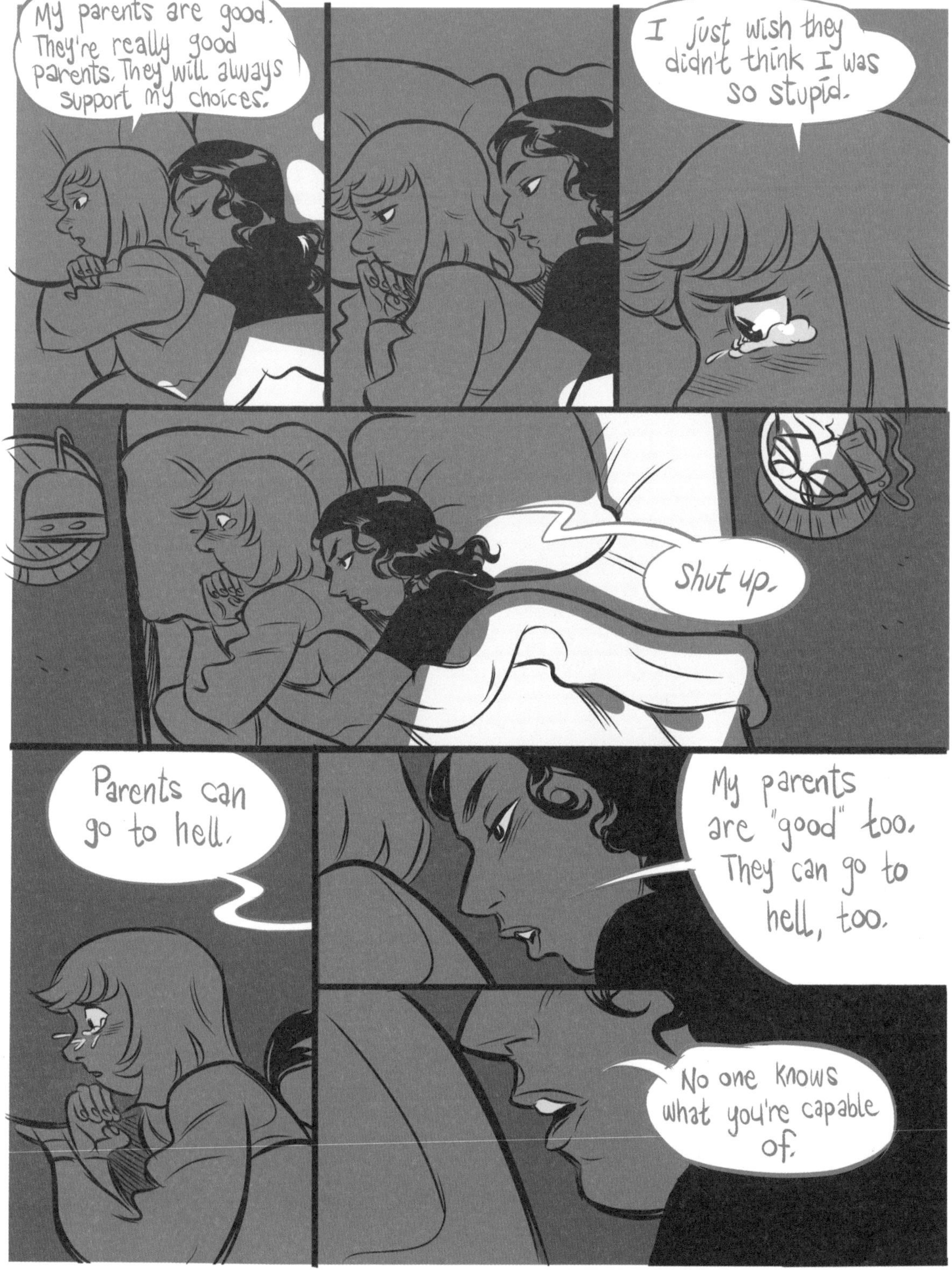
My parents are good. They're really good parents. They will always support my choices.
I just wish they didn't think I was so stupid.
Shut up.
Parents can go to hell.
My parents are "good" too. They can go to hell, too.
No one knows what you're capable of.

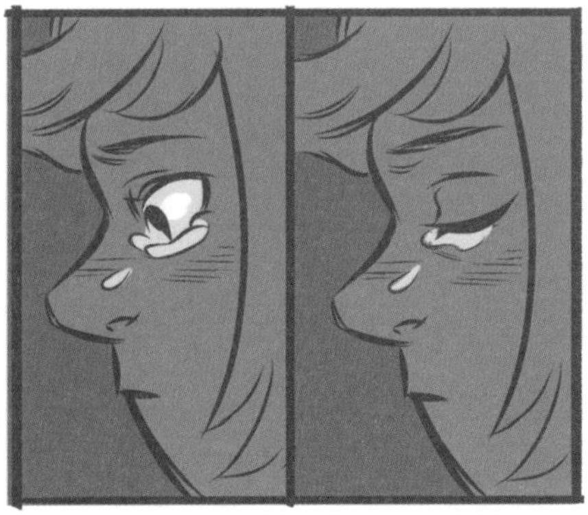

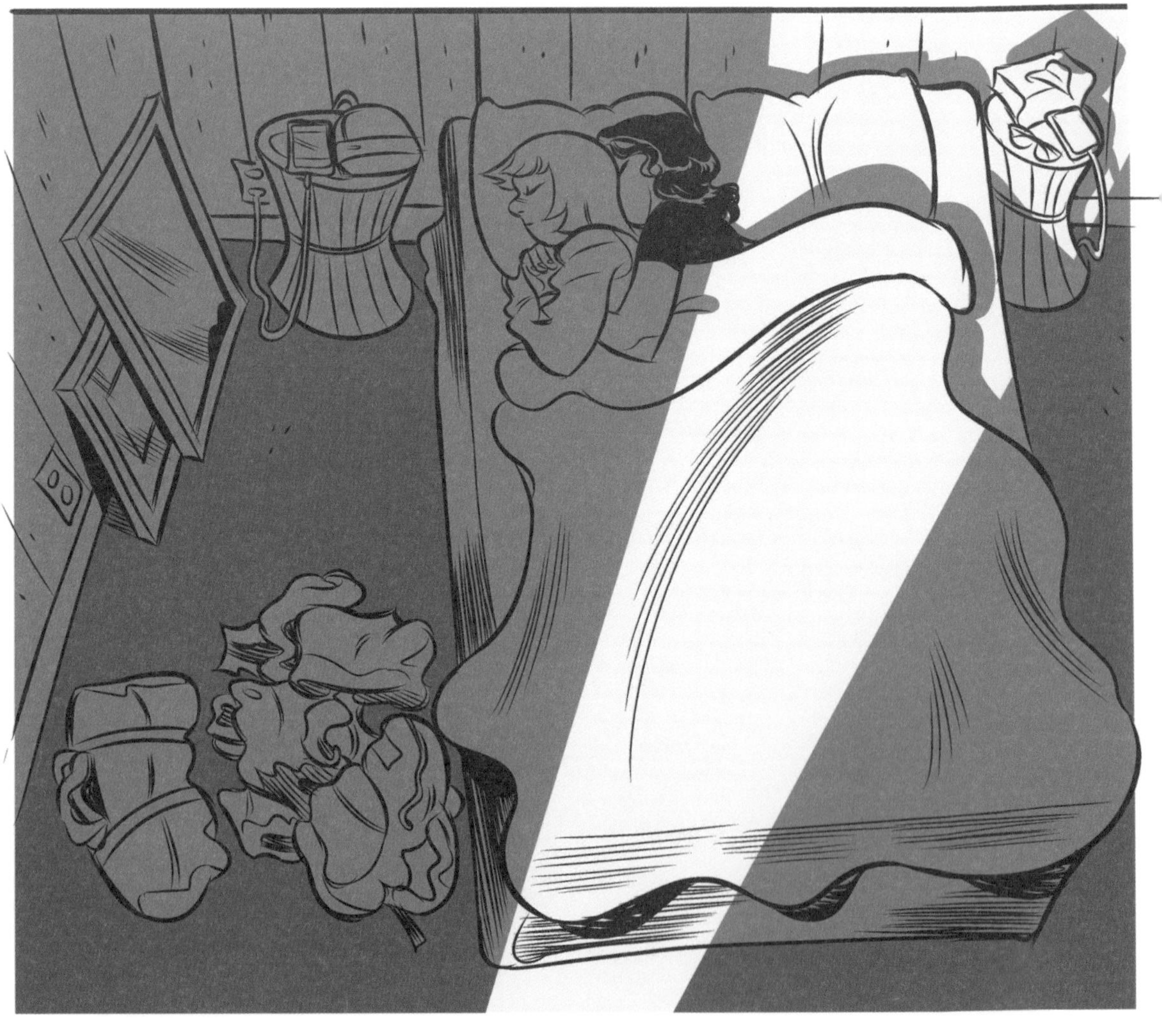

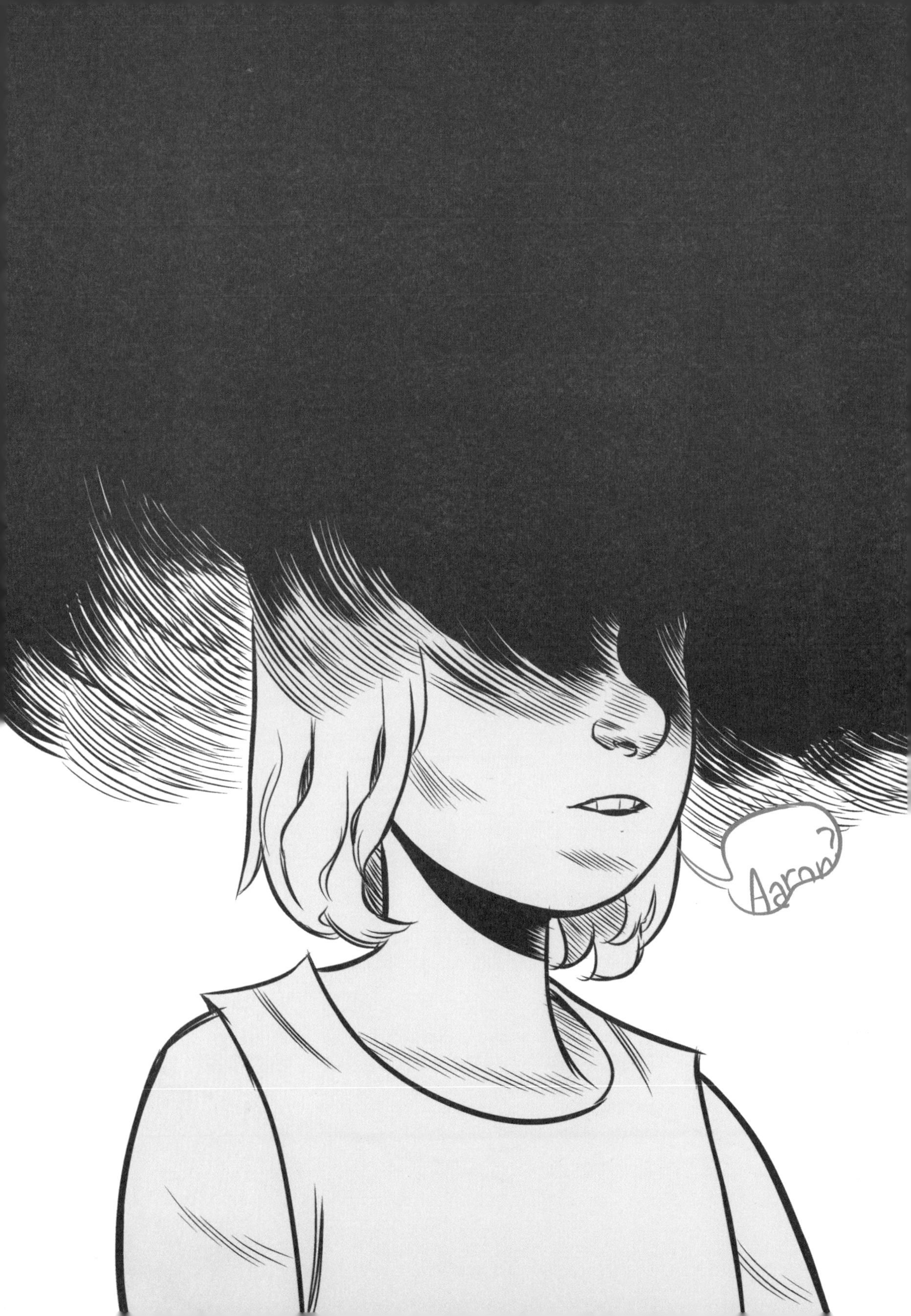
Aaron?

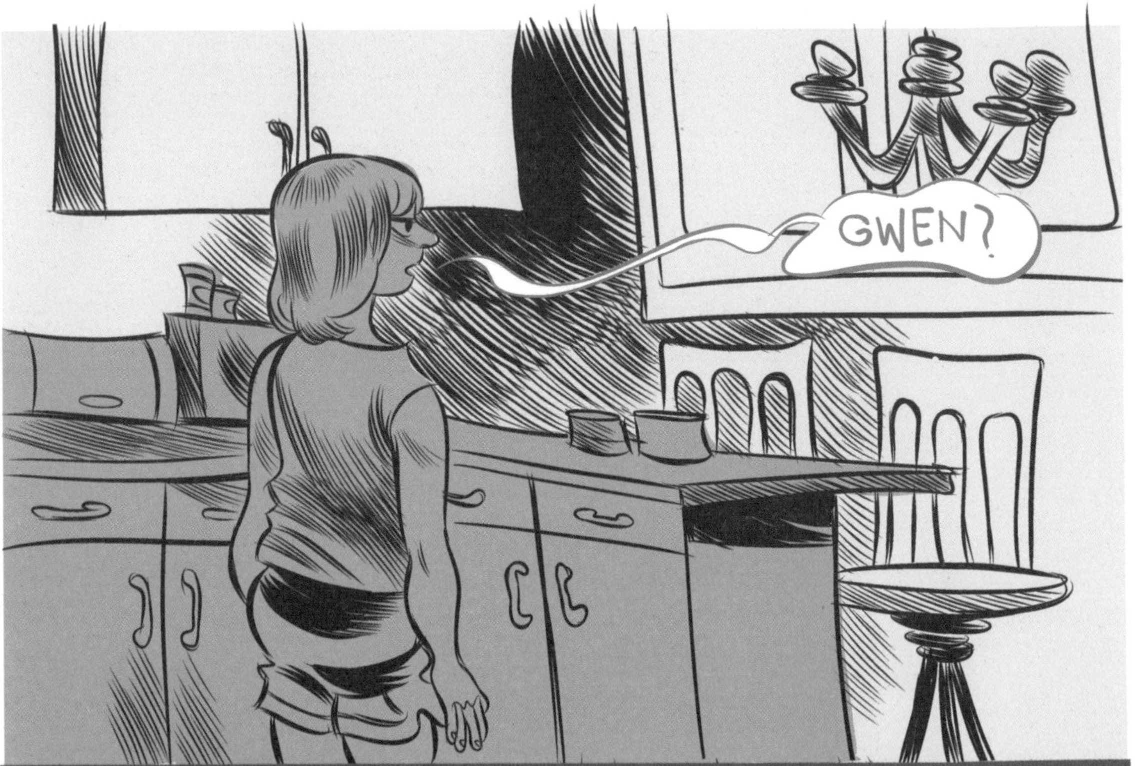
GWEN?

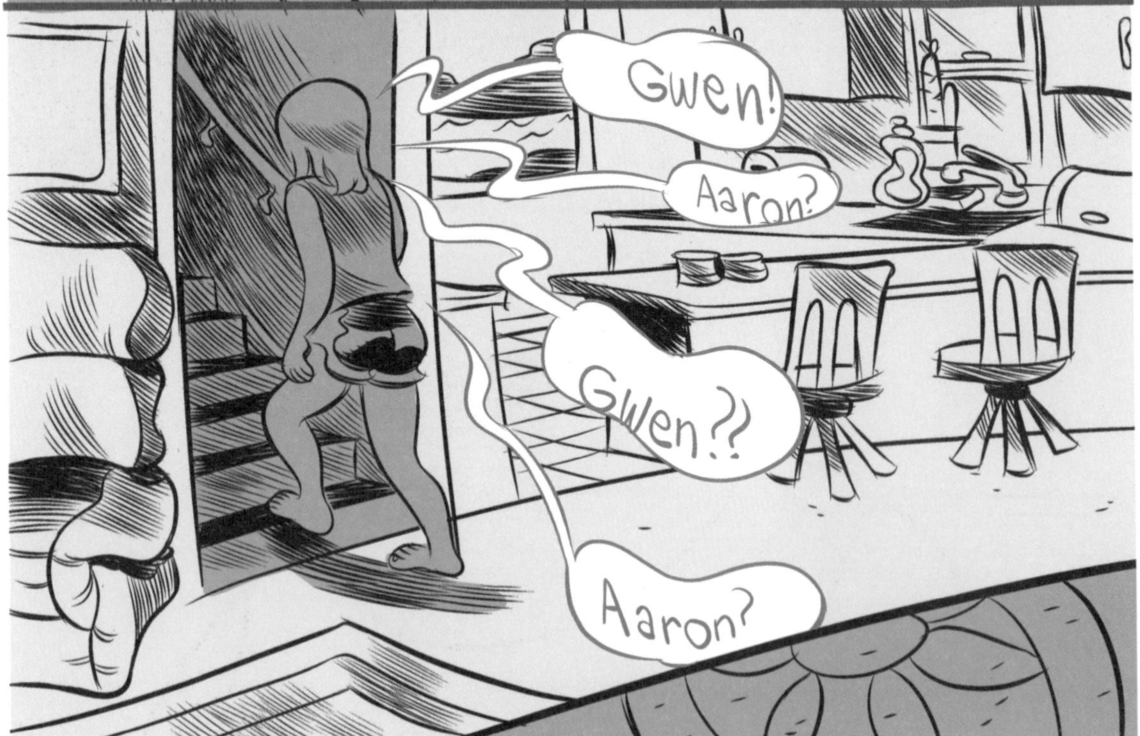
Gwen!
Aaron?
Gwen??
Aaron?

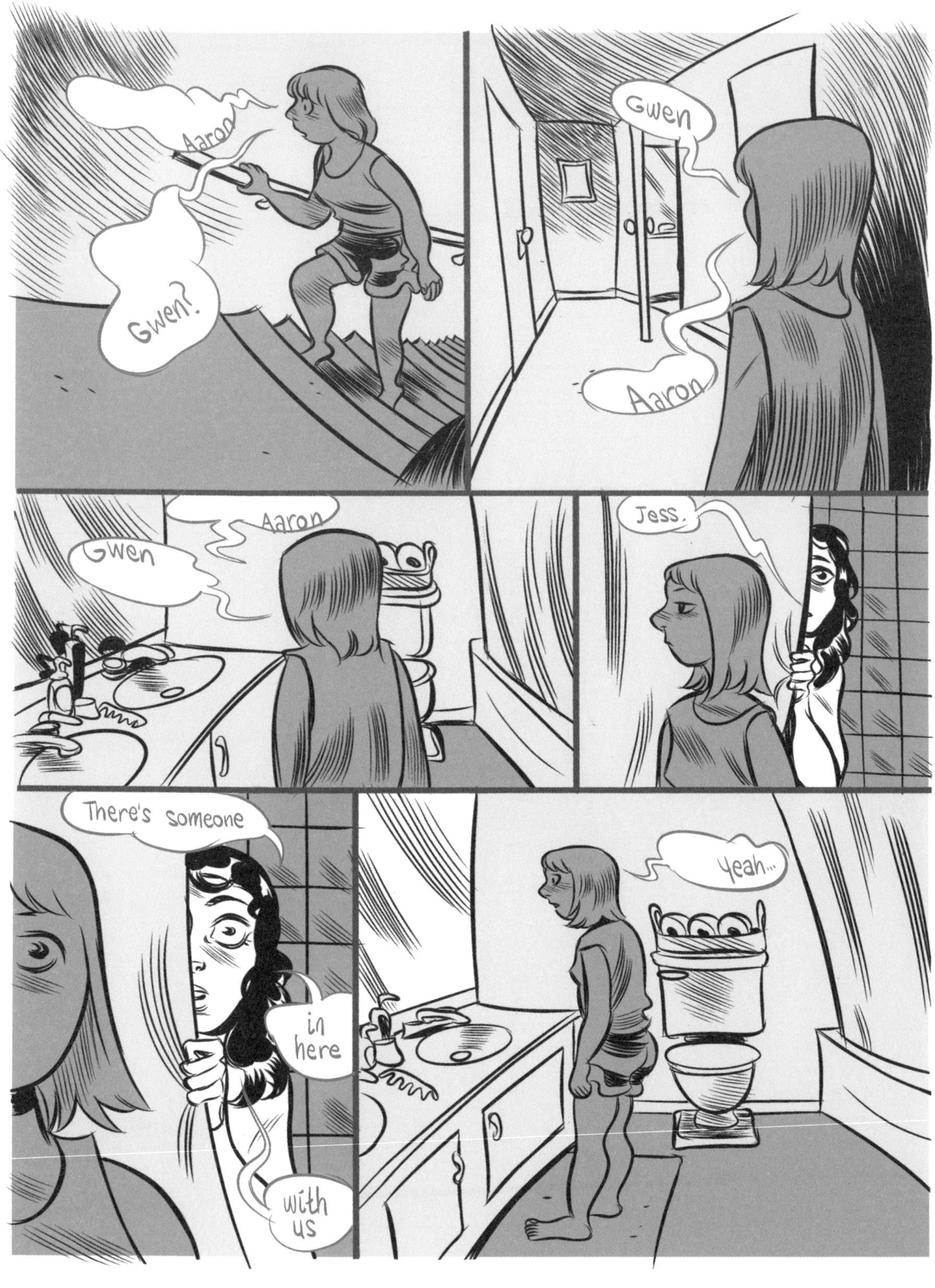
Aaron
Gwen?
Gwen
Aaron
Gwen
Aaron
Jess.
There's someone
in here
with us
Yeah...

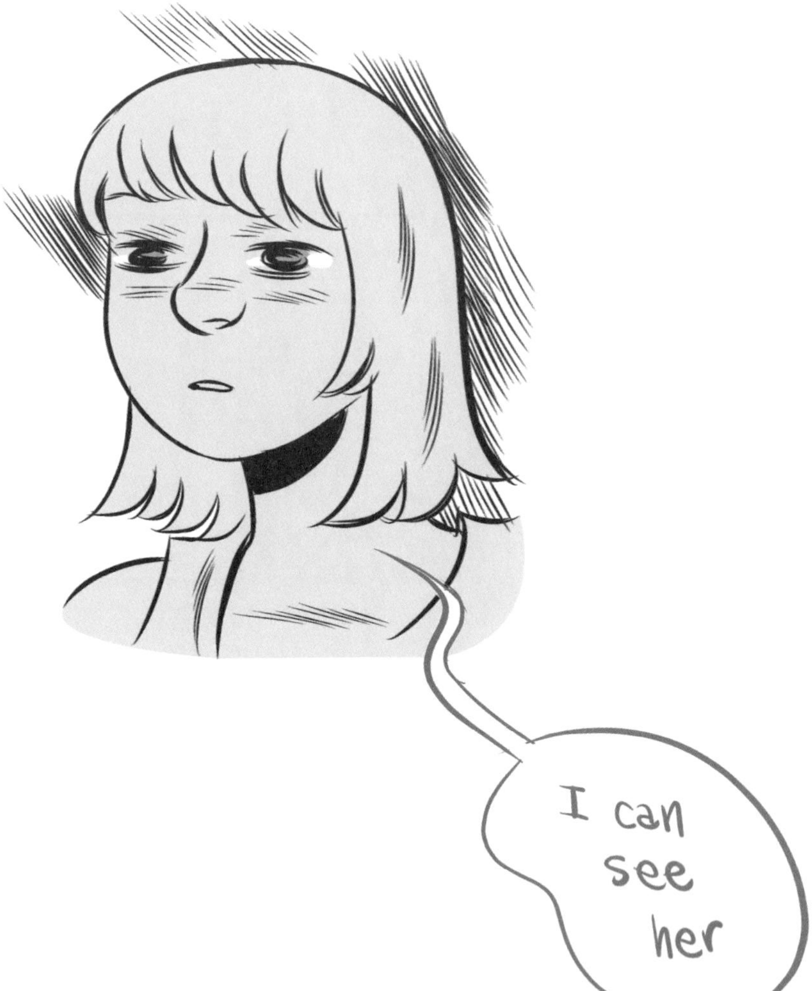
I can see her

2018